P9-DEC-073

On Core Mathematics

Middle School Grade 8

HOUGHTON MIFFLIN HARCOURT

Cover photo: chameleon tail   Gail Shumway/Getty Images

Copyright © by Houghton Mifflin Harcourt Publishing Company

Printed in the U.S.A.

ISBN 978-0-547-61750-3

5 6 7 8 9 10 1413 20 19 18 17 16 15 14 13 12

4500361198   B C D E F G

Table of Contents Grade 8

COMMON CORE

Learning the Common Core State Standards

Has your state adopted the Common Core standards? If so, then students will be learning both mathematical content standards and the mathematical practice standards that underlie them. The supplementary material found in *On Core Mathematics Grade 8* will help students succeed with both.

> Here are some of the special features you'll find in *On Core Mathematics Grade 8.*

INTERACTIVE LESSONS

Students actively participate in every aspect of a lesson. They carry out an activity in an Explore and complete the solution of an Example. This interactivity promotes a deeper understanding of the mathematics.

Name _____ Class _____ Date _____

2-2

COMMON CORE
CC.8.F.5
CC.8.F.3

Graphing Linear Functions

Essential question: *How do you graph a linear function?*

1 EXPLORE Investigating Change

The U.S. Department of Agriculture defines heavy rain as rain that falls at a rate of 1.5 centimeters per hour.

A The table shows the total amount of rain that falls in various amounts of time during a heavy rain. Complete the table.

Time (h)	0	1	2	3	4	5
Total Amount of Rain (cm)	0	1.5	3	4.5	6	7.5

B Plot the ordered pairs from the table on the coordinate plane at the right.

C How much rain falls in 3.5 hours?

5.25 cm

D Plot the point corresponding to 3.5 hours of heavy rain.

E What do you notice about all of the points you plotted?

All of the points lie along a straight line.

Heavy Rainfall

REFLECT

1a. Suppose you continued to plot points for times between ___,
such as 1.2 hours or 4.5 hours. What can you ___
these points?

The points would fill in the gaps along ___

determined by the existing points of t ___

1b. The U.S. Department of Agriculture defines ___
a rate of 4 centimeters per hour. How do you ___
would compare to the graph of heavy rainfall?

The points for excessive rainfall would lie a ___

that is steeper than the line for heavy rainfall.

Unit 2   39   Lesson 2

A **linear function** is a function whose graph is a nonvertical straight line. The function describing heavy rainfall in ① is a linear function because its graph is a set of points that form a straight line.

A **linear equation** is an equation that represents a linear function. The solutions of a linear equation are ordered pairs that form a straight line on the coordinate plane.

2 EXAMPLE Graphing a Linear Equation

Experts recommend that adult dogs have a daily intake of 50 calories per kilogram of the dog's weight plus 100 calories. Write an equation that gives the recommended number of daily calories *y* for a dog that weighs *x* kilograms. Then show that the equation is a linear equation.

Write an equation.

Daily calories equals 50 times weight plus 100.

$$y = 50x + 100$$

Complete the table to find some solutions of the equation.

Weight (kg), x	6	8	10	12	14
Calories, y	400	500	600	700	800

Plot the points, then draw a line through the points to represent all the possible *x*-values and their corresponding *y*-values.

The equation is a linear equation because the graph of the solutions is a straight line.

Recommended Daily Intake

TRY THIS!

2a. Graph the solutions of the linear equation $y = -2x + 1$. Then explain how the graph is different from the graph in the example.

The graph slants downward as you move

from left to right.

Unit 2   40   Lesson 2

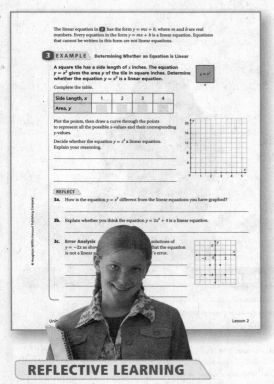

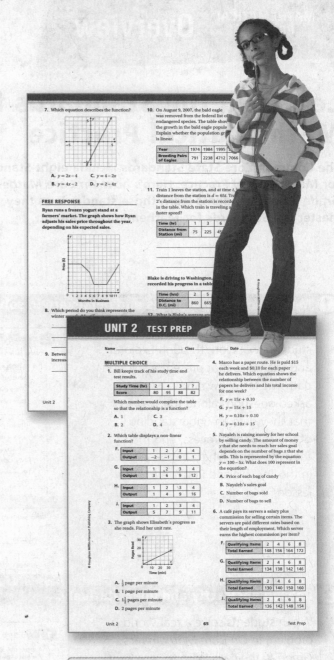

REFLECTIVE LEARNING

Students learn to be reflective thinkers through the follow-up questions after each Explore and Example in a lesson. The Reflect questions challenge students to really think about the mathematics they have just encountered and to share their understanding with the class.

TEST PREP

At the end of a unit, students have an opportunity to practice the material in multiple choice and free response formats common on standardized tests.

PROBLEM SOLVING CONNECTIONS

Special features that focus on problem solving occur near the ends of units. These features help students pull together the mathematical concepts and skills taught in a unit and apply them to real-world situations.

Learning the Standards for Mathematical Practice

The Common Core State Standards include eight Standards for Mathematical Practice. Here's how *On Core Mathematics Grade 8* helps students learn those standards as they master the Standards for Mathematical Content.

① Make sense of problems and persevere in solving them.

In *On Core Mathematics Grade 8*, students will work through Explores and Examples that present a solution pathway to follow. Students are asked questions along the way so that they gain an understanding of the solution process, and then they will apply what they've learned in the Try This and Practice for the lesson.

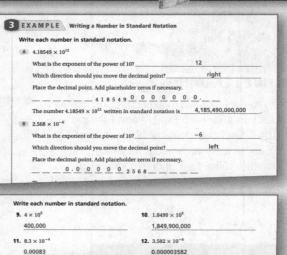

② Reason abstractly and quantitatively.

When students solve a real-world problem in *On Core Mathematics Grade 8*, they will learn to represent the situation symbolically by translating the problem into a mathematical expression or equation. Students will use these mathematical models to solve the problem and then state the answer in terms of the problem context. Students will reflect on the solution process in order to check their answers for reasonableness and to draw conclusions.

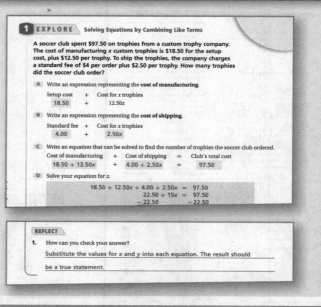

③ Construct viable arguments and critique the reasoning of others.

Throughout *On Core Mathematics Grade 8* students will be asked to make conjectures, construct mathematical arguments, explain their reasoning, and justify their conclusions. Reflect questions offer opportunities for cooperative learning and class discussion. Students will have additional opportunities to critique reasoning in Error Analysis problems.

2b. **Conjecture** Do you think that the value of r in the point $(1, r)$ is always the unit rate for any situation? Explain.

No; a situation may have variable rates of change or in a non-proportional

relationship, the point $(1, r)$ will not include r as the unit rate.

7. **Error Analysis** A student claims that the equation $y = 7$ is not a linear equation because it does not have the form $y = mx + b$. Do you agree or disagree? Why?

Disagree; the equation can be written in the form $y = mx + b$ where m is 0,

and the graph of the solutions is a horizontal line.

④ Model with mathematics.

On Core Mathematics Grade 8 presents problems in a variety of contexts such as as science, business, and everyday life. Students will use mathematical models such as expressions, equations, tables, and graphs to represent the information in the problem and to solve the problem. Then students will interpret their results in the problem context.

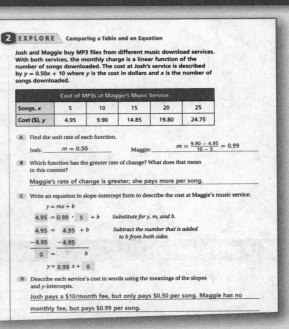

2 EXPLORE Comparing a Table and an Equation

Josh and Maggie buy MP3 files from different music download services. With both services, the monthly charge is a linear function of the number of songs downloaded. The cost at Josh's service is described by $y = 0.50x + 10$ where y is the cost in dollars and x is the number of songs downloaded.

Cost of MP3s at Maggie's Music Service					
Songs, x	5	10	15	20	25
Cost (\$), y	4.95	9.90	14.85	19.80	24.75

A Find the unit rate of each function.

Josh: $m = 0.50$ Maggie: $m = \dfrac{9.90 - 4.95}{10 - 5} = 0.99$

B Which function has the greater rate of change? What does that mean in this context?

Maggie's rate of change is greater; she pays more per song.

C Write an equation in slope-intercept form to describe the cost at Maggie's music service.

$y = mx + b$

$4.95 = 0.99 \cdot 5 + b$ Substitute for y, m, and b.

$4.95 = 4.95 + b$ Subtract the number that is added to b from both sides.

$\underline{-4.95 \quad -4.95}$

$0 = b$

$y = 0.99 x + 0$

D Describe each service's cost in words using the meanings of the slopes and y-intercepts.

Josh pays a \$10/month fee, but only pays \$0.50 per song. Maggie has no

monthly fee, but pays \$0.99 per song.

⑤ Use appropriate tools strategically.

Students will use a variety of tools in *On Core Mathematics Grade 8*, including manipulatives, paper and pencil, and technology. Students might use manipulatives to develop concepts, paper and pencil to practice skills, and technology (such as graphing calculators, spreadsheets, or geometry software) to investigate more complicated mathematical ideas.

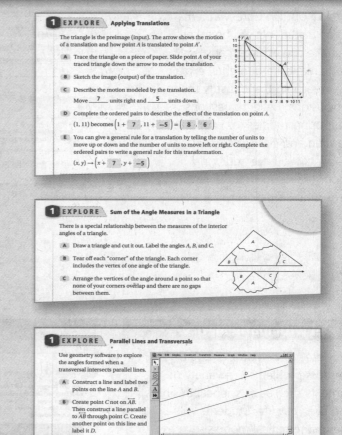

1 EXPLORE   Applying Translations

The triangle is the preimage (input). The arrow shows the motion of a translation and how point *A* is translated to point *A'*.

A Trace the triangle on a piece of paper. Slide point *A* of your traced triangle down the arrow to model the translation.

B Sketch the image (output) of the translation.

C Describe the motion modeled by the translation.

   Move __7__ units right and __5__ units down.

D Complete the ordered pairs to describe the effect of the translation on point *A*.

   $(1, 11)$ becomes $\left(1 + \boxed{7}, 11 + \boxed{-5}\right) = \left(\boxed{8}, \boxed{6}\right)$

E You can give a general rule for a translation by telling the number of units to move up or down and the number of units to move left or right. Complete the ordered pairs to write a general rule for this transformation.

   $(x, y) \rightarrow \left(x + \boxed{7}, y + \boxed{-5}\right)$

1 EXPLORE   Sum of the Angle Measures in a Triangle

There is a special relationship between the measures of the interior angles of a triangle.

A Draw a triangle and cut it out. Label the angles *A*, *B*, and *C*.

B Tear off each "corner" of the triangle. Each corner includes the vertex of one angle of the triangle.

C Arrange the vertices of the angle around a point so that none of your corners overlap and there are no gaps between them.

1 EXPLORE   Parallel Lines and Transversals

Use geometry software to explore the angles formed when a transversal intersects parallel lines.

A Construct a line and label two points on the line *A* and *B*.

B Create point *C* not on $\overleftrightarrow{AB}$. Then construct a line parallel to $\overleftrightarrow{AB}$ through point *C*. Create another point on this line and label it *D*.

⑥ Attend to precision.

Precision refers not only to the correctness of arithmetic calculations, algebraic manipulations, and geometric reasoning but also to the proper use of mathematical language, symbols, and units to communicate mathematical ideas. Throughout *On Core Mathematics Grade 8* students will demonstrate their skills in these areas when asked to calculate, describe, show, explain, prove, and predict.

REFLECT

4a. Scientists captured and released a whale shark that weighed about 6×10^5 units. Circle the best choice for the units this measurement is given in: (ounces)/pounds/tons.

4b. Explain how you chose a unit of measurement in **4a.**

   4×10^4 is 40,000 and 6×10^5 is 600,000; 6×10^5 is about 15 times 4×10^4 and I know that there are 16 ounces in 1 pound, so it makes sense that the measurement would be in ounces.

2c. Use your answers to **2a** and **2b** to explain whey there is only one cube root of a positive number.

   For the product of 3 equal factors to be positive, the factors must be positive.

In *On Core Mathematics Grade 8,* students will look for patterns or regularity in mathematical structures such as expressions, equations, operations, geometric figures, and diagrams. Students will use these patterns to generalize beyond a specific case and to make connections between related problems.

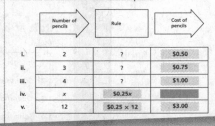

2 EXPLORE   Applying Properties of Integer Exponents

A Complete the following equations.

$3 \cdot 3 \cdot 3 \cdot 3 \cdot 3 = 3^{\boxed{5}}$

$(3 \cdot 3 \cdot 3 \cdot 3) \cdot 3 = 3^{\boxed{4}} \cdot 3^{\boxed{1}} = 3^{\boxed{5}}$

$(3 \cdot 3 \cdot 3) \cdot (3 \cdot 3) = 3^{\boxed{3}} \cdot 3^{\boxed{2}} = 3^{\boxed{5}}$

What pattern do you see when multiplying two powers with the same base?

The result has the same base with an exponent equal to the sum of the

exponents in the powers.

Use your pattern to complete this equation: $5^2 \cdot 5^5 = 5^{\boxed{7}}$

Conjecture Write a general rule for the result of $a^m \cdot a^n$. $\underline{a^m \cdot a^n = a^{m+n}}$

1 EXPLORE   Understanding Relationships

Carlos needs to buy some new pencils from the school supply cabinet at school. Carlos asks his classmates if they know how much pencils cost. Angela says she bought 2 pencils for $0.50. Paige bought 3 pencils for $0.75, and Spencer bought 4 pencils for $1.00.

Carlos thinks about the rule for the price of a pencil as a machine. When he puts the number of pencils he wants to buy into the machine, the machine applies a rule and tells him the total cost of that number of pencils.

	Number of pencils	Rule	Cost of pencils
i.	2	?	$0.50
ii.	3	?	$0.75
iii.	4	?	$1.00
iv.	x	$0.25x$	
v.	12	0.25×12	$3.00

UNIT 1

Expressions and the Number System

Unit Vocabulary

UNIT 1

Expressions and the Number System

Unit Focus

In this unit, you will learn more about the nature of expressions and the number system. You will learn how to use the properties of integer exponents. You will also learn how to write very small and very large numbers in scientific notation, including performing operations (+, −, ×, ÷) using scientific notation. You will use your knowledge of exponents to find square roots and cube roots. Lastly, you will learn to determine which numbers are rational and which are irrational. You will then compare the approximation of irrational numbers using decimals and the number line.

Unit at a Glance

COMMON CORE

Lesson		Standards for Mathematical Content
1-1	Integer Exponents	CC.8.EE.1
1-2	Scientific Notation	CC.8.EE.3
1-3	Operations with Scientific Notation	CC.8.EE.4
1-4	Square Roots and Cube Roots	CC.8.EE.2
1-5	Rational Numbers	CC.8.NS.1
1-6	Irrational Numbers	CC.8.NS.2, CC.8.EE.2
	Problem Solving Connections	
	Test Prep	

© Houghton Mifflin Harcourt Publishing Company

Unit 1   1   Expressions and the Number System

Unpacking the Common Core State Standards

Use the table to help you understand the Standards for Mathematical Content that are taught in this unit. Refer to the lessons listed after each standard for exploration and practice.

COMMON CORE Standards for Mathematical Content	What It Means For You
CC.8.NS.1 Know that numbers that are not rational are called irrational. Understand informally that every number has a decimal expansion; for rational numbers show that the decimal expansion repeats eventually, and convert a decimal expansion which repeats eventually into a rational number. Lesson 1-5	You will learn the definition of an irrational number. You will write rational numbers as decimals.
CC.8.NS.2 Use rational approximations of irrational numbers to compare the size of irrational numbers, locate them approximately on a number line diagram, and estimate the value of expressions (e.g., π^2). Lesson 1-6	You will approximate the value of numbers like $\sqrt{2}$ and locate them on a number line. Then you will order irrational numbers by approximating their values and comparing their locations on a number line.
CC.8.EE.1 Know and apply the properties of integer exponents to generate equivalent numerical expressions. Lesson 1-1	You will look for patterns and make conjectures about properties of exponents. You will explore three properties of exponents and simplify expressions involving powers with positive and negative exponents.
CC.8.EE.2 Use square root and cube root symbols to represent solutions to equations of the form $x^2 = p$ and $x^3 = p$, where p is a positive rational number. Evaluate square roots of small perfect squares and cube roots of small perfect cubes. Know that $\sqrt{2}$ is irrational. Lessons 1-4, 1-6	You will find square roots and cube roots. You will explore why the square root of a number yields two values while the cube root of a number yields only one value.
CC.8.EE.3 Use numbers expressed in the form of a single digit times an integer power of 10 to estimate very large or very small quantities, and to express how many times as much one is than the other. Lesson 1-2	You will learn how to write very small and very large numbers in scientific notation. You will learn that, in scientific notation, positive powers of 10 correspond to numbers greater than 1 and negative exponents correspond to numbers less than 1. You will compare numbers written in scientific notation.
CC.8.EE.4 Perform operations with numbers expressed in scientific notation, including problems where both decimal and scientific notation are used. Use scientific notation and choose units of appropriate size for measurements of very large or very small quantities. ... Interpret scientific notation that has been generated by technology. Lesson 1-3	You will perform operations ($+$, $-$, $\times$, $\div$) with numbers written in scientific notation. You will learn how to use a calculator to input and perform operations with numbers written in scientific notation.

Unpacking the Common Core State Standards

This page lists and explains the Standards for Mathematical Content that are addressed in this unit. For information about the Standards for Mathematical Practice, which are integrated throughout the text, see Teacher Edition pages vii–xiii.

Notes

_____

_____

_____

_____

_____

_____

_____

_____

_____

_____

Integer Exponents

Essential question: *How can you develop and use properties of integer exponents?*

COMMON CORE Standards for Mathematical Content

CC.8.EE.1 Know and apply the properties of integer exponents to generate equivalent numerical expressions.

Prerequisites

base

exponent

order of operations

Math Background

A number written in exponential form has base a raised to an exponent b in the form a^b, with b also sometimes referred to as a *power*. Exponents are a shorthand version for writing numbers. For example, the expanded form of 3 raised to the 4th power is written as $3 \times 3 \times 3 \times 3$. Using an exponent, this is written as 3^4. The base is 3. The exponent is 4 because the base is multiplied 4 times by itself. The order of operations is (1) Parentheses, (2) Exponents, (3) Multiplication and Division, and (4) Addition and Subtraction. Always work from left to right when using the order of operations.

INTRODUCE

Connect to prior learning by asking students to give examples of numbers written with exponents such as 3^2 and 2^3. Explain to students that exponential form is like an abbreviation. For example, it is much easier to write 2^5 than it is to write $2 \times 2 \times 2 \times 2 \times 2$. Tell students that in this lesson they will examine patterns and learn properties of integer exponents. Using these properties makes operations with numbers in exponential form more efficient.

TEACH

1 EXPLORE

Questioning Strategies

- How can you use your knowledge of expanded form to evaluate each exponential number? **The exponent tells you the number of times to multiply the base by itself.**

- What pattern can you use to evaluate negative exponents? **As the value of the exponent decreases, the value of the power is divided by the base. A number with a negative exponent should be written as the inverse of the number with a positive exponent.**

Teaching Strategies

The concept of exponents can be confusing at first. Show students that they can write the same values as powers in expanded form. For example, 7^4 is called "7 raised to the 4th power" or "7 multiplied by itself 4 times". This can be written as $7 \times 7 \times 7 \times 7 = 2401$.

2 EXPLORE

Questioning Strategies

- In each property what happens to the base? **The base stays the same.**

- In Part B, in what order must you subtract the exponents? **The bottom exponent is subtracted from the top exponent.**

Avoid Common Errors

Students may confuse the Product Rule of Exponents $a^m \cdot a^n$ with the Power Rule of Exponents $(a^m)^n$. Remind them to add exponents for $a^m \cdot a^n$, and multiply exponents for $(a^m)^n$. If they forget, remind them to write the rule again.

1-1

Name_____ Class_____ Date_____

Integer Exponents

Essential question: *How can you develop and use the properties of integer exponents?*

1 EXPLORE   Using Patterns of Integer Exponents

The table below shows powers of 5, 4, and 3.

$5^4 = 625$	$5^3 = 125$	$5^2 = 25$	$5^1 = 5$	$5^0 = 1$	$5^{-1} = \frac{1}{5}$	$5^{-2} = \frac{1}{25}$
$4^4 = 256$	$4^3 = 64$	$4^2 = 16$	$4^1 = 4$	$4^0 = 1$	$4^{-1} = \frac{1}{4}$	$4^{-2} = \frac{1}{16}$
$3^4 = 81$	$3^3 = 27$	$3^2 = 9$	$3^1 = 3$	$3^0 = 1$	$3^{-1} = \frac{1}{3}$	$3^{-2} = \frac{1}{9}$

A What pattern do you see in the powers of 5?

As the exponent decreases by 1, the value of the power is divided by 5.

B What pattern do you see in the powers of 4?

As the exponent decreases by 1, the value of the power is divided by 4.

C Complete the table for the values of $5^0, 5^{-1}, 5^{-2}$.   See table above.

D Complete the table for the values of $4^0, 4^{-1}, 4^{-2}$.   See table above.

E Complete the table for the values of $3^0, 3^{-1}, 3^{-2}$.   See table above.

F **Conjecture** Write a general rule for the values of a^0 and a^{-n} based on the patterns in the table.
$a^0 = 1;\ a^{-n} = \frac{1}{a^n}$

TRY THIS!

Find the value of each power.

1a. 6^{-4}
$\frac{1}{1296}$

1b. 12^0
1

1c. 8^{-1}
$\frac{1}{8}$

1d. 7^{-3}
$\frac{1}{343}$

1e. 347^0
1

1f. 15^{-2}
$\frac{1}{225}$

1g. 20^2
400

1h. 6^{-5}
$\frac{1}{7776}$

2 EXPLORE   Applying Properties of Integer Exponents

A Complete the following equations.

$3 \cdot 3 \cdot 3 \cdot 3 \cdot 3 = 3^{\boxed{5}}$

$(3 \cdot 3 \cdot 3 \cdot 3) \cdot 3 = 3^{\boxed{4}} \cdot 3^{\boxed{1}} = 3^{\boxed{5}}$

$(3 \cdot 3 \cdot 3) \cdot (3 \cdot 3) = 3^{\boxed{3}} \cdot 3^{\boxed{2}} = 3^{\boxed{5}}$

What pattern do you see when multiplying two powers with the same base?

The result has the same base with an exponent equal to the sum of the

exponents in the powers.

Use your pattern to complete this equation: $5^2 \cdot 5^5 = 5^{\boxed{7}}$

Conjecture Write a general rule for the result of $a^m \cdot a^n$. $a^m \cdot a^n = a^{m+n}$

B Complete the following equation: $\dfrac{4^5}{4^3} = \dfrac{4 \cdot 4 \cdot 4 \cdot 4 \cdot 4}{4 \cdot 4 \cdot 4} = \dfrac{\cancel{4} \cdot \cancel{4} \cdot \cancel{4} \cdot 4 \cdot 4}{\cancel{4}_1 \cdot \cancel{4}_1 \cdot \cancel{4}_1} = 4 \cdot 4 = 4^{\boxed{2}}$

What pattern do you see when dividing two powers with the same base?

The result has the same base with an exponent equal to the difference

of the exponent in the numerator and exponent in the denominator.

Use your pattern to complete this equation: $\dfrac{6^8}{6^3} = 6^{\boxed{5}}$.

Conjecture Write a general rule for the result of $\dfrac{a^m}{a^n}$. $\dfrac{a^m}{a^n} = a^{m-n}$

C Complete the following equations:

$(5^3)^2 = (5 \cdot 5 \cdot 5)^{\boxed{2}}$

$= (5 \cdot 5 \cdot 5) \cdot (5 \cdot 5 \cdot 5)$

$= 5^{\boxed{6}}$

What pattern do you see when raising a power to a power?

The result has the same base with an exponent equal to the product of

the exponents.

Use your pattern to complete this equation: $(7^2)^4 = 7^{\boxed{8}}$.

Conjecture Write a general rule for the result of $(a^m)^n$. $(a^m)^n = a^{m \cdot n}$

Questioning Strategies

- By the order of operations, which operation should you use first? **Evaluate the terms in the parentheses.**

- Do any of the numbers have a common base? **Yes, the base of 3.**

- How can you use the properties of exponents with the base 3 terms? **Add the exponents and keep the base the same.**

Teaching Strategies

Remind students of the order of operations: Parentheses, Exponents, Multiplication and Division, Addition and Subtraction (PEMDAS -Please Excuse My Dear Aunt Sally). Operate from left to right. Have students work through the example by highlighting the operation they will evaluate first, second, and so on.

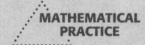 **MATHEMATICAL PRACTICE** **Highlighting the Standards**

This Example is an opportunity to address Standard 7 (Look for and make use of structure). Students are asked to identify patterns in integer exponents. Students use this pattern of behavior in values involving integer exponents to identify the structure of integer exponents, and summarize those patterns of behavior with properties. Students apply the properties of exponents to evaluate exponents and to simplify more complex expressions involving integer exponents.

CLOSE

Essential Question

How can you develop and use properties of integer exponents?

Possible answer: You can use the properties of integer exponents as a shorthand method of evaluating exponents and simplifying expressions using the order of operations. The Product Rule is $a^m \cdot a^n = a^{m+n}$, the Quotient Rule is $\frac{a^m}{a^n} = a^{m-n}$, and the Power Rule is $(a^m)^n = a^{m \times n}$.

Summarize

Have students answer the following prompt in their journals: How can you use expanded form to prove the properties of integer exponents? Give examples to justify your answer.

PRACTICE

Where skills are taught	Where skills are practiced
1 EXPLORE	EXS. 1–6
2 EXPLORE	EXS. 7–18
3 EXAMPLE	EXS. 19–22

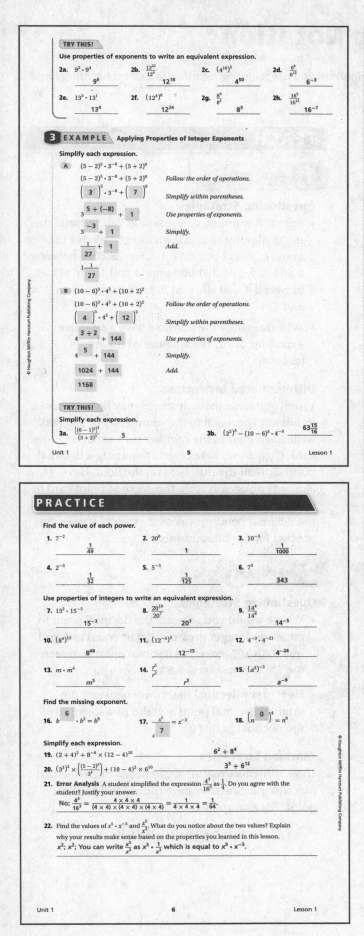

TRY THIS!

Use properties of exponents to write an equivalent expression.

2a. $9^2 \cdot 9^4$ 9^6

2b. $\dfrac{12^{22}}{12^4}$ 12^{18}

2c. $(4^{10})^5$ 4^{50}

2d. $\dfrac{6^9}{6^{12}}$ 6^{-3}

2e. $13^3 \cdot 13^1$ 13^4

2f. $(12^4)^6$ 12^{24}

2g. $\dfrac{8^9}{8^4}$ 8^5

2h. $\dfrac{16^5}{16^{12}}$ 16^{-7}

3 EXAMPLE   Applying Properties of Integer Exponents

Simplify each expression.

A $(5-2)^5 \cdot 3^{-8} + (5+2)^0$

$(5-2)^5 \cdot 3^{-8} + (5+2)^0$ *Follow the order of operations.*

$\left(\boxed{3} \right)^5 \cdot 3^{-8} + \left(\boxed{7} \right)^0$ *Simplify within parentheses.*

$3^{\boxed{5 + (-8)}} + \boxed{1}$ *Use properties of exponents.*

$3^{\boxed{-3}} + \boxed{1}$ *Simplify.*

$\dfrac{1}{\boxed{27}} + \boxed{1}$ *Add.*

$1\dfrac{1}{27}$

B $(10-6)^3 \cdot 4^2 + (10+2)^2$

$(10-6)^3 \cdot 4^2 + (10+2)^2$ *Follow the order of operations.*

$\left(\boxed{4} \right)^3 \cdot 4^2 + \left(\boxed{12} \right)^2$ *Simplify within parentheses.*

$4^{\boxed{3+2}} + 144$ *Use properties of exponents.*

$4^{\boxed{5}} + 144$ *Simplify.*

$\boxed{1024} + 144$ *Add.*

$\boxed{1168}$

TRY THIS!

Simplify each expression.

3a. $\dfrac{[(6-1)^2]^2}{(3+2)^3}$ 5

3b. $(2^2)^3 - (10-6)^3 \cdot 4^{-5}$ $63\dfrac{15}{16}$

© Houghton Mifflin Harcourt Publishing Company

PRACTICE

Find the value of each power.

1. 7^{-2} $\dfrac{1}{49}$

2. 20^0 1

3. 10^{-3} $\dfrac{1}{1000}$

4. 2^{-5} $\dfrac{1}{32}$

5. 5^{-3} $\dfrac{1}{125}$

6. 7^3 343

Use properties of integers to write an equivalent expression.

7. $15^2 \cdot 15^{-5}$ 15^{-3}

8. $\dfrac{20^{10}}{20^7}$ 20^3

9. $\dfrac{14^4}{14^9}$ 14^{-5}

10. $(8^4)^{12}$ 8^{48}

11. $(12^{-5})^3$ 12^{-15}

12. $4^{-3} \cdot 4^{-21}$ 4^{-24}

13. $m \cdot m^4$ m^5

14. $\dfrac{r^5}{r^2}$ r^3

15. $(a^3)^{-3}$ a^{-9}

Find the missing exponent.

16. $b^{\boxed{6}} \cdot b^2 = b^8$

17. $\dfrac{x^5}{x^{\boxed{7}}} = x^{-2}$

18. $\left(n^{\boxed{0}} \right)^4 = n^0$

Simplify each expression.

19. $(2+4)^2 + 8^{-6} \times (12-4)^{10}$ $6^2 + 8^4$

20. $(3^3)^2 \times \left(\dfrac{(5-2)^3}{3^4} \right) + (10-4)^2 \times 6^{10}$ $3^5 + 6^{12}$

21. Error Analysis A student simplified the expression $\dfrac{4^3}{16^3}$ as $\dfrac{1}{4}$. Do you agree with the student? Justify your answer.

No; $\dfrac{4^3}{16^3} = \dfrac{4 \times 4 \times 4}{(4 \times 4) \times (4 \times 4) \times (4 \times 4)} = \dfrac{1}{4 \times 4 \times 4} = \dfrac{1}{64}$.

22. Find the values of $x^5 \cdot x^{-3}$ and $\dfrac{x^5}{x^3}$. What do you notice about the two values? Explain why your results make sense based on the properties you learned in this lesson.

x^2; x^2; You can write $\dfrac{x^5}{x^3}$ as $x^5 \cdot \dfrac{1}{x^3}$ which is equal to $x^5 \cdot x^{-3}$.

© Houghton Mifflin Harcourt Publishing Company

1-2 Scientific Notation

Essential question: *How can you use scientific notation to express very large and very small quantities?*

COMMON Standards for
CORE Mathematical Content

CC.8.EE.3 Use numbers expressed in the form of a single digit times an integer power of 10 to estimate very large or very small quantities, and to express how much larger or smaller one is than the other.

Vocabulary
scientific notation

Prerequisites
Properties of exponents of integers

Math Background
Scientific notation is a method used to express very large and very small numbers in terms of a decimal number between 1 and 10 (including 1, but not 10) multiplied by a power of 10. For example, in scientific notation 85,488 equals 8.5488×10^4 and 0.0783 equals 7.83×10^{-2}. The power of 10 indicates the number of places that the decimal will move to equal the number in standard notation. In scientific notation, numbers greater than 1 are expressed with a positive exponent, and numbers less than 1 are expressed with a negative exponent.

INTRODUCE

Connect to prior learning by reviewing powers of 10 with students. Explain that powers of 10 are used in scientific notation to express extremely large or extremely small numbers, such as those used in science. Tell students that they will convert numbers in standard notation to scientific notation and vice versa.

TEACH

1 EXPLORE

Questioning Strategies
- For each number, where would you relocate the decimal point to create an integer greater than or equal to 1 and less than 10? **For 250,000 between 2 and 5; for 41,200 between 4 and 1; for 133.25 between 1 and the first 3; for 0.95 between 9 and 5.**
- Why does only the minnow have a negative exponent of 10? **The number of pounds is less than 1.**

Differentiated Instruction
Visual and kinesthetic learners may benefit from a hands-on approach to the numbers. For 250,000, write each digit in the number on a separate index card. Create one index card containing a decimal point. Spread the numbers on the floor. Have students physically walk the decimal point card to its new location and count the number of places the decimal point moves as they walk. Repeat this process for the other numbers.

2 EXAMPLE

Questioning Strategies
- Where would you relocate the decimal point to create an integer greater than or equal to 1 and less than 10? **Move the decimal point between the 6 and 8 to create 6.88.**
- How many decimal places are between the original decimal point and the new location of the decimal point? **9**

Teaching Strategies
Have students draw an arc between each decimal place to indicate they have moved the decimal point. For example:

6.880000000

Scientific Notation

COMMON CORE

CC.8.EE.3

Essential question: *How can you use scientific notation to express very large and very small quantities?*

Scientific notation is a method of expressing very large and very small numbers as a product of a number greater than or equal to 1 and less than 10, and a power of 10.

1 EXPLORE Using Scientific Notation

The weights of various sea creatures are shown in the table. You can write the weights in scientific notation.

Sea Creature	Blue Whale	Whale Shark	Eel	Minnow
Weight (lbs)	250,000	41,200	133.25	0.95

Write the weight of the blue whale in scientific notation.

A Move the decimal point in 250,000 to the left as many places as necessary to find a number that is greater than or equal to 1 and less than 10.

What number did you find? _____ 2.5

B Divide 250,000 by your answer to A . Write your answer as a power of 10.

100,000; 10^5

C Combine your answers to A and B to represent 250,000.

250,000 = 2.5×10^5

Write the weight of the minnow in scientific notation.

D Move the decimal point in 0.95 to the right as many places as necessary to find a number that is greater than or equal to 1 and less than 10.

What number did you find? _____ 9.5

E Divide 0.95 by your answer to D . Write your answer as a power of 10.

0.1 or $\frac{1}{10}$; 10^{-1}

F Combine your answers to D and E to represent 0.95.

0.95 = 9.5×10^{-1}

REFLECT

1a. What do you notice about the sign of the exponent for weights greater than one pound?

The exponent is positive for a weight greater than one pound.

1b. What do you notice about the sign of the exponent for weights less than one pound?

The exponent is negative for a weight less than one pound.

To translate between standard notation and scientific notation, you can count the number of places the decimal point moves.

Writing Numbers in Scientific Notation

When the number is greater than or equal to 1, use a positive exponent.	$84,000 = 8.4 \times 10^4$	*The decimal point moves 4 places.*
When the number is less than 1, use a negative exponent.	$0.0783 = 7.83 \times 10^{-2}$	*The decimal point moves 2 places.*

2 EXAMPLE Writing a Number in Scientific Notation

An estimate of the world population in 2010 was 6,880,000,000. Write the world's population in scientific notation.

To write 6,880,000,000 in scientific notation, move the decimal point as many places as necessary to find a number that is greater than or equal to 1 and less than 10.

Place the decimal point: 6·8 8 0 0 0 0 0 0 0

Which direction did you move the decimal point? _____ left

What number did you find? _____ 6.88

How many places did you move the decimal point? _____ 9

When 6,880,000,000 is written in scientific notation, should the exponent of the power of 10 be positive or negative? Explain.

Positive; you multiply 6.88 by a power of 10 greater than 1 to get 6,880,000,000.

The world's population, 6,880,000,000, written in scientific notation is

6.88×10^9

To translate between scientific notation and standard notation, you can move the decimal point the number of places indicated by the exponent in the pwoer of 10. When the exponent is positive, move the decimal point to the right. When the exponent is negative, move the decimal point to the left.

Notes

Questioning Strategies

- What is the power of 10? **The power of 10 is 12 in Part A and —6 in Part B.**

- What does the sign of the power of 10 tell you when moving the decimal point? **For positive powers of 10, move the decimal point to the right. For negative powers of 10, move the decimal point to the left.**

- What place holder do you use after you run out of numbers when moving the decimal point? **Use zeroes as place holders.**

Avoid Common Errors

Remind students that positive powers of 10 always move the decimal point to the right when converting from scientific notation to standard notation. Negative powers of 10 always move the decimal point to the left.

4 EXAMPLE

Questioning Strategies

- What is the integer part of each number? **The integers are 4 and 2.**

- How can you use the properties of integer exponents to compare the powers of 10 for the given numbers? **Use the quotient rule:**
$\frac{10^4}{10^2} = 10^{4-2} = 10^2 = 100.$

Teaching Strategies

To reinforce the connection between standard and scientific notation, have students write each weight in standard notation, divide, and then write the answer in scientific notation.

> **MATHEMATICAL PRACTICE** **Highlighting the Standards**
>
> This Example is an opportunity to address Standard 2 (Model with mathematics). Students are asked to model very large and very small numbers using scientific notation. They will connect scientific notation with rules of exponents.

CLOSE

Essential Question

How can you use scientific notation to express very large and very small quantities?

Possible answer: Scientific notation expresses very large and very small numbers in terms of a decimal number between 1 and 10 multiplied by a power of 10. To determine the power of 10, simply count the number of decimal places between the original decimal point and the location of the decimal point in the decimal number. Numbers larger than 1 will have a positive exponent. Numbers smaller than 1 will have a negative exponent.

Summarize

Have students answer the following prompt in their journals: What are examples of very large and very small numbers that you encounter in everyday life? How would you write these numbers using scientific notation?

PRACTICE

Where skills are taught	Where skills are practiced
1 EXPLORE	EXS. 1–8
2 EXAMPLE	EXS. 1–8
3 EXAMPLE	EXS. 9–16
4 EXAMPLE	EXS. 17–22

3 **EXAMPLE**   Writing a Number in Standard Notation

Write each number in standard notation.

A 4.18549×10^{12}

What is the exponent of the power of 10? _____12_____

Which direction should you move the decimal point? _____right_____

Place the decimal point. Add placeholder zeros if necessary.

_ _ _ _ _ _ 4 1 8 5 4 9 0 0 0 0 0 0 0 . _ _

The number 4.18549×10^{12} written in standard notation is ___4,185,490,000,000___

B 2.568×10^{-6}

What is the exponent of the power of 10? _____−6_____

Which direction should you move the decimal point? _____left_____

Place the decimal point. Add placeholder zeros if necessary.

_ _ 0 . 0 0 0 0 0 2 5 6 8 _ _ _ _

The number 2.568×10^{-6} written in standard notation is ___0.000002568___

4 **EXAMPLE**   Comparing Numbers in Scientific Notation

The approximate weight of a whale shark is 4×10^4 pounds. The approximate weight of a common dolphin is 2×10^2 pounds. How many times as great as the weight of the whale shark is the weight of the dolphin?

First compare the values between 1 and 10.

The 4 in 4×10^4 is ___2___ times as great as the 2 in 2×10^2.

Next compare the powers of 10.

10^4 is ___100___ times as great as 10^2.

Circle the most reasonable answer.

The weight of the whale shark is 2 / 20 /(200)/ 2000 times as great as the weight of the dolphin.

REFLECT

4a. Scientists captured and released a whale shark that weighed about 6×10^5 units. Circle the best choice for the units this measurement is given in:(ounces)/pounds/tons.

4b. Explain how you chose a unit of measurement in **4a.**

4×10^4 is 40,000 and 6×10^5 is 600,000; 6×10^5 is about 15 times 4×10^4

and I know that there are 16 ounces in 1 pound, so it makes sense that the

measurement would be in ounces.

PRACTICE

Write each number in scientific notation.

1. 58,927

5.8927×10^4

2. 1,304,000,000

1.304×10^9

3. 0.000487

4.87×10^{-4}

4. 0.000028

2.8×10^{-5}

5. 0.000059

5.9×10^{-5}

6. 6,730,000

6.73×10^6

7. 13,300

1.33×10^4

8. 0.0417

4.17×10^{-2}

Write each number in standard notation.

9. 4×10^5

400,000

10. 1.8499×10^9

1,849,900,000

11. 8.3×10^{-4}

0.00083

12. 3.582×10^{-6}

0.000003582

13. 2.97×10^{-2}

0.0297

14. 6.41×10^3

6,410

15. 8.456×10^7

84,560,000

16. 9.06×10^{-5}

0.0000906

Circle the correct answer.

17. 8×10^5 is 2/20/200/(2,000) times as great as 4×10^2.

18. 9×10^{10} is 30 / 300 /(3,000)/ 30,000 times as great as 3×10^7.

19. 4×10^{-5} is 0.02/(0.2)/2/20 times as great as 2×10^{-4}.

20. 4×10^{-12} is 0.00001 /(0.0001)/ 10 / 1000 times as great as 4×10^{-8}.

21. The mass of a proton is about 1.7×10^{-24} g. The mass of a neutron is about the same as a proton. The nucleus of an atom of carbon has 6 protons and 6 neutrons. The mass of the nucleus is about 2×10^{-28} units. Circle the best choice for the units this measurement is given in: g /(kg)/tons.

22. The air distance between Los Angeles, California, and New York City, New York, is about 3.9×10^3 units. Circle the best choice for the units this measurement is given in: cm / m /(km).

© Houghton Mifflin Harcourt Publishing Company

Notes

Operations with Scientific Notation

Essential question: *How do you add, subtract, multiply, and divide using scientific notation?*

COMMON CORE Standards for Mathematical Content

CC.8.EE.4 Perform operations with numbers expressed in scientific notation, including problems where both a decimal and scientific notation are used. Use scientific notation and choose units of appropriate size for measurements of very large or very small quantities. Interpret scientific notation that has been generated by technology.

Materials
Scientific calculator

Prerequisites
Properties of exponents
Scientific notation

Math Background
The properties of exponents are used when performing operations with numbers in scientific notation:

1. Product Rule: $a^m \cdot a^n = a^{m+n}$
   example: $5^3 \cdot 5^{-2} = 5^{3+(-2)} = 5^1$

2. Quotient Rule: $\frac{a^m}{a^n} = a^{m-n}$
   example: $\frac{5^3}{5^{-2}} = 5^{3-(-2)} = 5^5$

3. Power Rule: $(a^m)^n = a^{m \times n}$
   example: $(5^3)^{-2} = 5^{3 \cdot -2} = 5^{-6}$

INTRODUCE

Connect to prior learning by asking students to give examples of numbers written in standard notation and scientific notation. Discuss with students how tedious operations on very large numbers such as 1,408,582,895 and 20,855,392,858 can be. Tell students that they will perform operations by hand as well as by using a calculator on very large and very small numbers expressed in scientific notation.

TEACH

1 EXPLORE

Teaching Strategy
Make sure students understand that writing numbers with a common power of 10 to add or subtract them might result in the numbers no longer being in proper scientific notation. Remind students to be sure that the final answer is in proper scientific notation.

Questioning Strategies
- How can you make sure each number in the table has the same power of 10? **The common exponent is 8. Move the decimal point the required number of places in each multiplier to change the exponent to 8.**

- How do you use the multipliers and the powers of 10 to find the final answer? **In this case, add the multipliers and write the answer with a power of 10^8. Then make sure the final answer is expressed in proper scientific notation.**

- What is another way to add the numbers? **Rewrite each number in standard notation, find the sum, and then rewrite the answer in scientific notation.**

2 EXPLORE

Questioning Strategies
- In order to compare the numbers, must both the measurements be in the same or different notations? **To compare the numbers they must be in the same format.**

- What do you do with the multipliers? **Divide 2.025 by 2.25.**

- How can you use properties of exponents to divide the powers of 10? **Subtract the bottom exponent from the top exponent.**

TRY THIS

To multiply using scientific notation, students should multiply the multipliers, then use the product rule to add the powers of 10. Finally, write the answer in scientific notation.

Name_____ Class_____ Date_____

1-3

Operations with Scientific Notation

Essential question: *How do you add, subtract, multiply, and divide using scientific notation?*

1 EXPLORE Adding and Subtracting with Scientific Notation

The table below shows the population of the three largest countries in North America. Find the total population of the three countries.

Country	United States	Canada	Mexico
Population	3.1×10^8	3.38×10^7	1.1×10^8

Method 1:

A First write each population with the same power of 10.

United States: 3.1×10^8

Canada: 0.338×10^8

Mexico: 1.1×10^8

B Add the multipliers for each population. $3.1 + 0.338 + 1.1 = 4.538$

C Write the final answer in scientific notation. ___ 4.538×10^8 ___

Method 2:

D First write each number in standard notation.

United States: 310,000,000

Canada: 33,800,000

Mexico: 110,000,000

E Find the sum of the numbers in standard notation.

$310,000,000 + 33,800,000 + 110,000,000 = 453,800,000$

F Write the answer in scientific notation. 4.538×10^8

TRY THIS!

1a. Using the population table above, how many more people live in Mexico than in Canada?

$1.1 \times 10^8 - 3.38 \times 10^7 = 1.1 \times 10^8 - 0.338 \times 10^8$
$= 0.762 \times 10^8$
$= 7.62 \times 10^7$

2 EXPLORE Multiplying and Dividing with Scientific Notation

When the sun makes an orbit around the center of the Milky Way, it travels 2.025×10^{14} kilometers. The orbit takes 225 million years. At what rate does the Sun travel around the Milky Way? Write your answer in scientific notation.

A Set up a division problem to represent the situation.

$\text{Rate} = \dfrac{\text{Distance}}{\text{Time}}$

$\text{Rate} = \dfrac{2.025 \times 10^{14} \text{ kilometers}}{225,000,000 \text{ years}}$

B Write 225 million years in scientific notation. ___ 2.25×10^8 ___

C Write the expression for rate with years in scientific notation.

$\text{Rate} = \dfrac{2.025 \times 10^{14} \text{ kilometers}}{2.25 \times 10^8 \text{ years}}$

D Find the quotient by dividing the multipliers.

$2.025 \div 2.25 = 0.9$

E Use the laws of exponents to divide the powers of 10.

$\dfrac{10^{14}}{10^8} = 10^{14-8} = 10^6$

F Combine the answers from D and E to write the rate in scientific notation.

$0.9 \times 10^6 = 9.0 \times 10^5$ km per year

TRY THIS!

2a. Light from the Sun travels at a speed of 1.86×10^5 miles per second. It takes sunlight about 4.8×10^3 seconds to reach Saturn. Find the approximate distance from the Sun to Saturn. Write your answer in scientific notation.

$d = rt$

$= \left(1.86 \times 10^5\right)\left(4.8 \times 10^3\right)$

$= \left(1.86\right)(4.8) \times \left(10^5\right)(10^3)$

$= 8.928 \times 10^{5+3}$

$= 8.928 \times 10^8$ miles

Questioning Strategies

- What does "E" mean on your calculator? This refers to the power of 10. For example, "E9" means $\times 10^9$.

Avoid Common Errors

Students may try to use the "ENTER" key after each addend. Remind students that when they use the "E" key, the calculator will use the properties of integer exponents and correct order of operations.

MATHEMATICAL PRACTICE **Highlighting the Standards**

This Example is an opportunity to address Standard 5 (Use appropriate tools strategically.). When using pen and paper, students will apply properties of integer exponents when performing operations with numbers in scientific notation. When using technology, students will use calculators to input and perform operations on numbers in scientific notation.

CLOSE

Essential Question
How do you add, subtract, multiply, and divide using scientific notation?
Possible answer: If powers are the same, you can add or subtract the multipliers of numbers in scientific notation and keep the same power. You can multiply or divide the multipliers of each number and use properties of integer exponents for the powers. You can also convert numbers to standard notation, perform the operation, and then convert the result to scientific notation. Lastly, you can use a calculator.

Summarize
Have students answer the following prompt in their journals: Explain how properties of integer exponents are used to operate with numbers in scientific notation.

PRACTICE

Where skills are taught	Where skills are practiced
1 EXPLORE	EXS. 1–6
2 EXPLORE	EXS. 7–10
3 EXAMPLE	EXS. 11–17

On many scientific calculators, you can enter numbers in scientific notation by using a function labeled "ee" or "EE". Usually, the letter "E" takes the place of "×10". So, the number 4.1×10^9 would appear as 4.1E9 on the calculator.

3 EXAMPLE Scientific Notation on a Calculator

The table below shows the approximate populations for the three continents with the greatest populations. What is the total population of these three continents? Use your calculator to find the answer.

Continent	Asia	Africa	Europe
Population	4.1×10^9	1.0×10^9	7.28×10^8

Find $4.1 \times 10^9 + 1.0 \times 10^9 + 7.28 \times 10^8$.

Enter 4.1E9 + 1E 9 + 7.28 E 8 on your calculator.

Write the results from your calculator. 5,828,000,000 or 5.828E9

Write this number in scientific notation. 5.828×10^9

The total population of the three continents is 5.828×10^9 people.

TRY THIS!

Write each number using calculator notation.

1a. 7.5×10^5
  7.5E5
1b. 3×10^{-7}
  3E−7
1c. 2.7×10^{13}
  2.7E13

Write each number using scientific notation.

1d. 4.5E−1
  4.5×10^{-1}
1e. 5.6E12
  5.6×10^{12}
1f. 6.98E−8
  6.98×10^{-8}

PRACTICE

Add or subtract. Write your answer in scientific notation.

1. $3.2 \times 10^5 + 4.9 \times 10^8$
  4.9032×10^8
2. $4.378 \times 10^{12} + 7.701 \times 10^7$
  $4.37807701 \times 10^{12}$

3. $2.3 \times 10^8 - 2.12 \times 10^3$
  2.2999788×10^8
4. $4.55 \times 10^{15} - 7.4 \times 10^{11}$
  4.54926×10^{15}

5. $6.35 \times 10^3 + 1.65 \times 10^6$
  1.65635×10^6
6. $5 \times 10^3 - 1.23 \times 10^2$
  4.877×10^3

© Houghton Mifflin Harcourt Publishing Company

Multiply or divide. Write your answer in scientific notation.

7. $(1.8 \times 10^9)(6.78 \times 10^{12})$
  1.2204×10^{22}
8. $(5.092 \times 10^{21})(3.38 \times 10^6)$
  1.721096×10^{28}

9. $\dfrac{8.4 \times 10^{21}}{4.2 \times 10^{14}}$
  2.0×10^7
10. $\dfrac{3.46 \times 10^{17}}{2 \times 10^9}$
  1.73×10^8

11. A newborn baby has about 26,000,000,000 cells. An adult has about 1.9×10^3 times as many cells as a newborn. About how many cells does an adult have? Write your answer in scientific notation.

4.94×10^{13} cells

12. The edge of a cube measures 3.5×10^{-2} meters. What is the volume of the cube in cubic meters? Write your answer in scientific notation.

4.2875×10^{-5} cubic meters

13. The smallest state in the United States is Rhode Island with a land area of about 2.9×10^{10} square feet. The largest state is Alaska whose land area is about 5.5×10^2 as great as the land area of Rhode Island. What is the land area of Alaska in square feet? Write your answer in scientific notation.

1.595×10^{13} ft^2

14. Astronomers estimate that the diameter of the Andromeda galaxy is approximately 2.2×10^5 light-years. A light-year is the distance light travels in a vacuum in 1 year. One light-year is approximately 5.9×10^{12} miles. What is the diameter of the Andromeda galaxy in miles? Write your answer in scientific notation.

1.298×10^{18} miles

The table below shows the approximate populations of three countries.

Country	China	France	Australia
Population	1.33×10^9	6.48×10^7	2.15×10^7

15. How many more people live in France than in Australia? Write your answer in scientific notation.

4.33×10^7 people

16. The area of Australia is about 2.95×10^6 square miles. What is the approximate average number of people per square mile in Australia?

about 7 people per square mile

17. What is the ratio of the population of China to the population of France? What does this mean?

20.52; there are about 20 people in China for every 1 person in France.

© Houghton Mifflin Harcourt Publishing Company

Notes

Square Roots and Cube Roots

Essential question: *How do you evaluate square roots and cube roots?*

COMMON CORE **Standards for Mathematical Content**

CC.8.EE.2 Use square root and cube root symbols to represent solutions to equations of the form $x^2 = p$ and $x^3 = p$, where p is a positive rational number. Evaluate square roots of small perfect squares and cube roots of small perfect cubes. ... Know that $\sqrt{2}$ is irrational ...

Vocabulary

square root

principal square root

perfect square

cube root

perfect cube

Prerequisites

Evaluating exponents

Math Background

The square root of a positive number, p, is $\pm x$ if $x^2 = p$. There are two square roots for every positive number. The $\sqrt{}$ indicates the principal square root. When a number is a perfect square, its square roots are integers. For example, 25 is a perfect square; the square root of 25 is ± 5 because $(5)(5) = 25$ and $(-5)(-5) = 25$.

INTRODUCE

Connect to prior learning by asking students to give examples of numbers written in exponential notation such as 5^2 and 10^3. Remind students that they can evaluate these exponents by multiplying the base times itself the number of times indicated by the exponent. For example, $5^2 = 5 \cdot 5 = 25$ and $10^3 = 10 \cdot 10 \cdot 10 = 1000$. Tell students that in this lesson they will work in the reverse order: finding square roots and cube roots. For example, instead of finding 5^2 they will find $\sqrt{25}$ and, instead of finding 10^3 they will find $\sqrt[3]{1000}$.

TEACH

1 EXPLORE

Questioning Strategies

- What method can you use to find the relationship between the side length and the total number of tiles? **The side length squared equals the total number of tiles.**

- How can you use square root to describe the relationship between the total number of tiles and the number of tiles along one side of the figure? **The total number of tiles is a perfect square. The square root of the total number of tiles is the number of tiles along one side of the figure.**

- In this case, why does only one square root make sense? **Only the positive square root makes sense because a length cannot be negative.**

TRY THIS

Students may have difficulty finding the square root of a fraction. For 1b, encourage them to think "What fraction multiplied by itself is $\frac{1}{16}$? In the numerator, 1 times 1 is 1; in the denominator, 4 times 4 is 16. So, the square root of $\frac{1}{16}$ must be $\frac{1}{4}$."

2 EXPLORE

Questioning Strategies

- What is the relationship between the side length of the cube and total number of unit cubes that form the cube? **The total number of unit cubes is equal to the cube of the number of unit cubes along one side of the shape.**

- How can you use the cube root sign to represent the number of unit cubes along one side? **The cube root of the total number of unit cubes equals the number of unit cubes along one side.**

TRY THIS

Students may have difficulty finding the cube root of a fraction. For 2e, encourage them to think "What fraction used as a factor three times is $\frac{1}{8}$? In the numerator, 1 times 1 times 1 is 1; in the denominator, 2 times 2 times 2 is 8. So, the cube root of $\frac{1}{8}$ must be $\frac{1}{2}$."

Square Roots and Cube Roots

1-4

COMMON CORE
CC.8.EE.2

Essential question: *How do you evaluate square roots and cube roots?*

1 EXPLORE Finding the Square Root of Perfect Squares

There are 9 square tiles used to make a square mosaic. There are 3 tiles along each side of the mosaic.

Another square mosaic is made using 64 square tiles. How many tiles are on each side of this mosaic?

A Use what you know about the mosaic made with 9 tiles to find the relationship between number of tiles on each side and the total number of square tiles.

The mosaic is 3 tiles long and 3 tiles wide. The relationship

is $3^2 = 9$. The total number of tiles is the side length squared.

B Use this relationship to find the number of tiles along the side of a square mosaic made of 64 square tiles.

$64 = 8^2$ or 8×8; side length = 8 square tiles

C In this context, the total number of tiles is the number of tiles along each side of the mosaic squared. When the total number of tiles is 9, the number of tiles along a side is 3. Because $3^2 = 9$, we call 3 a *square root* of 9. This is written as $3 = \sqrt{9}$.

Use this notation to write the square root of 64: $\sqrt{64} = $ __8__

TRY THIS!

Evaluate each square root.

1a. $\sqrt{169}$ __13__

1b. $\sqrt{\frac{1}{16}}$ __$\frac{1}{4}$__

1c. $\sqrt{81}$ __9__

1d. $\sqrt{\frac{1}{400}}$ __$\frac{1}{20}$__

The **square root** of a positive number p is x if $x^2 = p$. There are two square roots for every positive number. For example, the square roots of 36 are 6 and -6 because $6^2 = 36$ and $(-6)^2 = 36$. The square roots of $\frac{1}{25}$ are $\frac{1}{5}$ and $-\frac{1}{5}$. You can write the square roots of $\frac{1}{25}$ as $\pm \frac{1}{5}$. The symbol $\sqrt{\ }$ indicates the positive, or **principal square root**.

A number that is a **perfect square** has square roots that are integers. The number 81 is a perfect square because its square roots are 9 and -9.

© Houghton Mifflin Harcourt Publishing Company

2 EXPLORE Finding the Cube Root

A cube shaped toy is made of 27 small cubes. There are 3 cubes along each edge of the toy.

Another cube shaped toy is made using 8 small cubes. How many small cubes are on each edge of this toy?

A Use what you know about the toy made with 27 small cubes to find the relationship between number of cubes on each edge and the total number of cubes.

The toy is 3 cubes long, 3 cubes wide, and 3 cubes tall. The

relationship is $3^3 = 27$. The total number of small cubes is the

side length cubed.

B Use this relationship to find the number of small cubes along each edge of a toy made of 8 small cubes.

$8 = 2^3$ or $2 \times 2 \times 2$. Side length = 2 small cubes.

C In this situation, the total number of small cubes is the number of small cubes along each edge of the toy cubed. When the total number of small cubes is 27, the number of small cubes along each edge is 3. Because $3^3 = 27$, we call 3 a *cube root* of 27. This is written as $\sqrt[3]{27} = 3$.

Use this notation to write the cube root of 8: $\sqrt[3]{8} = $ __2__

REFLECT

2a. The product of 3 equal positive factors is (positive)/ negative.

2b. The product of 3 equal negative factors is positive /(negative).

2c. Use your answers to **2a** and **2b** to explain whey there is only one cube root of a positive number.

For the product of 3 equal factors to be positive, the factors must

be positive.

TRY THIS!

Evaluate each cube root.

2d. $\sqrt[3]{125}$ __5__

2e. $\sqrt[3]{\frac{1}{8}}$ __$\frac{1}{2}$__

2f. $\sqrt[3]{1000}$ __10__

2g. $\sqrt[3]{\frac{1}{343}}$ __$\frac{1}{7}$__

© Houghton Mifflin Harcourt Publishing Company

Notes

Questioning Strategies

- How many square roots of 121 are there? Two
- How do you solve $121 = x^2$? Find the principal square root of 121, which is 11, and give the answer both positive and negative signs.
- How many cube roots are there for 729? One
- How do you solve $729 = x^3$? Find the principal cube root of 729, which is 9. Because 729 is positive, the cube root can only be positive.

Avoid Common Errors

Students may be tempted to find two cube roots since they found two square roots. Review how signed numbers in multiplication work for three factors. A cube root of a positive number can't be negative because $(-)(-)(-) = (-)$.

MATHEMATICAL PRACTICE **Highlighting the Standards**

This Example is an opportunity to address Standard 4 (Model with mathematics). Students are asked to identify the relationships between side length and total number of tiles or cubes in square or cube models. Students use the models to analyze their answers for reasonability, realizing that answers representing distance or length cannot be negative.

CLOSE

Essential Question

How do you evaluate square roots and cube roots?
Possible answer: The square root of a positive number p is $\pm x$ if $x^2 = p$. There are two square roots for every positive number. The cube root of a positive number p is x if $x^3 = p$. There is one cube root for every positive number.

Summarize

Have students construct models of squares and cubes using ruler, paper, and tape. Explain to students that they can refer to these models in the future if they need to be reminded about square roots and cube roots.

PRACTICE

Where skills are taught	Where skills are practiced
1 EXPLORE	EXS. 1–6, 13, 15, 16, 18, 22
2 EXPLORE	EXS. 7–12, 14, 17, 23
3 EXAMPLE	EXS. 19–21

The **cube root** of a positive number p is x if $x^3 = p$. There is one cube root for every positive number. For example, the cube root of 8 is 2 because $2^3 = 8$. The cube root of $\frac{1}{27}$ is $\frac{1}{3}$ because $\left(\frac{1}{3}\right)^3 = \frac{1}{27}$. The symbol $\sqrt[3]{}$ indicates the cube root. A number that is a **perfect cube** has a cube root that is an integer. The number 125 is a perfect cube because its cube root is 5.

3 EXAMPLE Solving Equations Using Square Roots and Cube Roots

Solve each equation for x.

A $x^2 = 121$

$\sqrt{x^2} = \sqrt{121}$ *Solve for x by taking the square root of both sides.*

$x = \sqrt{121}$ *Think: What number squared equals 121?*

$x = \pm\ \boxed{11}$ *Use ± to show both square roots.*

The solutions are __11__ and __−11__.

B $x^2 = \frac{16}{169}$

$\sqrt{x^2} = \sqrt{\frac{16}{169}}$ *Solve for x by taking the square root of both sides.*

$x = \sqrt{\frac{16}{169}}$ *Think: What number squared equals $\frac{16}{169}$?*

$x = \pm\ \frac{\boxed{4}}{\boxed{13}}$ *Use ± to show both square roots.*

The solutions are __$\frac{4}{13}$__ and __$-\frac{4}{13}$__.

C $729 = x^3$

$\sqrt[3]{729} = \sqrt[3]{x^3}$ *Solve for x by taking the cube root of both sides.*

$\sqrt[3]{729} = x$ *Think: What number cubed equals 729?*

$\boxed{9} = x$

The solution is __9__.

D $x^3 = \frac{8}{125}$

$\sqrt[3]{x^3} = \sqrt[3]{\frac{8}{125}}$ *Solve for x by taking the cube root of both sides.*

$x = \sqrt[3]{\frac{8}{125}}$ *Think: What number cubed equals $\frac{8}{125}$?*

$x = \frac{\boxed{2}}{\boxed{5}}$

The solution is __$\frac{2}{5}$__.

PRACTICE

Find the square roots of each number.

1. 144 ___±12___ 2. 256 ___±16___ 3. $\frac{1}{81}$ ___$\pm\frac{1}{9}$___

4. $\frac{49}{900}$ ___$\pm\frac{7}{30}$___ 5. 400 ___±20___ 6. $\frac{1}{100}$ ___$\pm\frac{1}{10}$___

Find the cube root of each number.

7. 216 ___6___ 8. 8000 ___20___ 9. $\frac{27}{125}$ ___$\frac{3}{5}$___

10. $\frac{1}{27}$ ___$\frac{1}{3}$___ 11. $\frac{27}{64}$ ___$\frac{3}{4}$___ 12. 512 ___8___

Simplify each expression.

13. $\sqrt{16} + \sqrt{25}$ ___9___ 14. $\sqrt[3]{125} + 10$ ___15___ 15. $\sqrt{25} + 10$ ___15___

16. $8 - \sqrt{64}$ ___0___ 17. $\sqrt[3]{\frac{16}{2}} + 1$ ___3___ 18. $\sqrt{\frac{16}{4}} + \sqrt{4}$ ___4___

19. The foyer of Ann's house is a square with an area of 36 square feet. What is the length of each side of the foyer?

   6 feet

20. A chessboard has 32 black squares and 32 white squares arranged in a square. How many squares are along each side of the chessboard?

   8 squares

21. A cubic aquarium holds 27 cubic feet of water. What is the length of each edge of the cube?

   3 feet

22. **Reasoning** How can you check your answer when you find the square root(s) of a number?

   Multiply the square root by itself. The product should be the number you

   started with.

23. **Reasoning** Can you arrange 12 small squares to make a larger square? Can you arrange 20 small cubes to make a larger cube? Explain how this relates to perfect squares and perfect cubes.

   No; 12 is not a perfect square. No; 20 is not a perfect cube.

Notes

Rational Numbers

Essential question: *How do you write rational numbers as decimals and fractions?*

COMMON CORE **Standards for Mathematical Content**

CC.8.NS.1 Know that numbers that are not rational are called *irrational*. Understand informally that every number has a decimal expansion; for rational numbers show that the decimal expansion repeats eventually, and convert a decimal expansion which repeats eventually into a rational number.

Materials

Scientific calculator

Vocabulary

rational number

terminating decimal

repeating decimal

Vocabulary

Square roots

Math Background

Real numbers consist of rational numbers and irrational numbers. A rational number can be written as a ratio a to b for integers a and b, where $b \neq 0$. Irrational numbers such as π and $\sqrt{7}$ cannot be expressed as a rational number. Every real number can be expressed in decimal form. Rational numbers have decimal equivalents that terminate or repeat a pattern. Irrational numbers have decimal equivalents that neither terminate nor repeat a pattern. They must be approximated in decimal form.

INTRODUCE

Connect to prior learning by asking students how to convert fractions into decimals. Ask students what the decimal equivalent is for $\frac{1}{2}$. They should easily be able to answer 0.5. Tell students that in this lesson they will write rational numbers as decimals and fractions.

TEACH

1 EXAMPLE

Questioning Strategies

- How do you use division to find the decimal form of a fraction? **Divide the numerator by the denominator.**

- What two types of decimal equivalents do you see in this example? **One stops short (terminates) and the other repeats.**

- Do you see the same types of decimal equivalents in the Try This answers? **Yes**

Teaching Strategies

Students can use a calculator to find numerous decimal equivalents and make conjectures about the two types of decimal equivalents for rational numbers.

2 EXAMPLE

Questioning Strategies

- What is the first step when writing a decimal number as a fraction? **Write the decimal number over a power of 10, and simplify.**

- For a repeating decimal, how can you set up an equation to write the decimal as a fraction? **Let x equal the repeating decimal. Multiply both sides of the equation by a power of 10, where the exponent for the power of 10 equals the number of digits that repeat in the repeating decimal. Because x equals the repeating decimal, subtract x from one side of the equation and the repeating decimal from the other. This results in an equation that can be solved by division.**

Rational Numbers

Name_____ Class_____ Date_____

Essential question: *How do you write rational numbers as decimals and as fractions?*

A **rational number** is a number that can be written as a ratio in the form $\frac{a}{b}$, where a and b are integers and b is not 0.

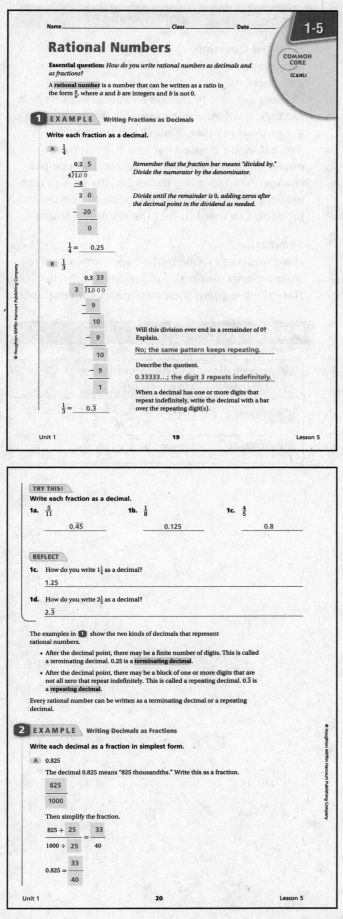

1 EXAMPLE Writing Fractions as Decimals

Write each fraction as a decimal.

A $\frac{1}{4}$

$$4\overline{)1.00}$$ = 0.2 5

−8

2 0

− 20

0

Remember that the fraction bar means "divided by." Divide the numerator by the denominator.

Divide until the remainder is 0, adding zeros after the decimal point in the dividend as needed.

$\frac{1}{4} = 0.25$

B $\frac{1}{3}$

$$3\overline{)1.000}$$ = 0.3 33

− 9

10

− 9

10

− 9

1

Will this division ever end in a remainder of 0? Explain.

No; the same pattern keeps repeating.

Describe the quotient.

0.33333...; the digit 3 repeats indefinitely.

When a decimal has one or more digits that repeat indefinitely, write the decimal with a bar over the repeating digit(s).

$\frac{1}{3} = 0.\overline{3}$

© Houghton Mifflin Harcourt Publishing Company

Unit 1   19   Lesson 5

TRY THIS!

Write each fraction as a decimal.

1a. $\frac{5}{11}$ **1b.** $\frac{1}{8}$ **1c.** $\frac{4}{5}$

0.$\overline{45}$ 0.125   0.8

REFLECT

1c. How do you write $1\frac{1}{4}$ as a decimal?

1.25

1d. How do you write $2\frac{1}{3}$ as a decimal?

2.$\overline{3}$

The examples in **1** show the two kinds of decimals that represent rational numbers.

• After the decimal point, there may be a finite number of digits. This is called a **terminating decimal**. 0.25 is a **terminating decimal**.

• After the decimal point, there may be a block of one or more digits that are not all zero that repeat indefinitely. This is called a repeating decimal. 0.$\overline{3}$ is a **repeating decimal**.

Every rational number can be written as a terminating decimal or a repeating decimal.

2 EXAMPLE Writing Decimals as Fractions

Write each decimal as a fraction in simplest form.

A 0.825

The decimal 0.825 means "825 thousandths." Write this as a fraction.

$$\frac{825}{1000}$$

Then simplify the fraction.

$$\frac{825 \div 25}{1000 \div 25} = \frac{33}{40}$$

$$0.825 = \frac{33}{40}$$

© Houghton Mifflin Harcourt Publishing Company

Unit 1   20   Lesson 5

Avoid Common Errors

Students may automatically assume that 100 is the power of 10 to use when converting a repeating decimal into a fraction. Remind students to count the number of decimal places that repeat in order to determine the power of 10 to use.

⋰ **MATHEMATICAL PRACTICE**   **Highlighting the Standards**

This example is an opportunity to address Standard 2 (Reason abstractly and quantitatively). Students are asked to think of numbers abstractly when converting repeating decimals to fractions. By using a variable to represent a repeating decimal, students write an equation and use abstract methods and representations to solve for the same variable in fraction form.

CLOSE

Essential Question

How do you write rational numbers as decimals and fractions?

Possible answer: To change a rational number to a fraction, divide the numerator by the denominator. If a rational number changes to terminating decimal, write the decimal as a fraction over a power of 10 and simplify. If the rational number changes to a repeating decimal, write an equation where x equals the repeating decimal, and use properties to solve so that the result is a fraction.

Summarize

Have students explain in their own words how to write rational numbers as fractions and decimals. Have them support their statements with examples.

PRACTICE

Where skills are taught	Where skills are practiced
1 EXAMPLE	EXS. 1–6, 13–19, 21–22, 24–26
2 EXAMPLE	EXS. 7–12, 20, 23

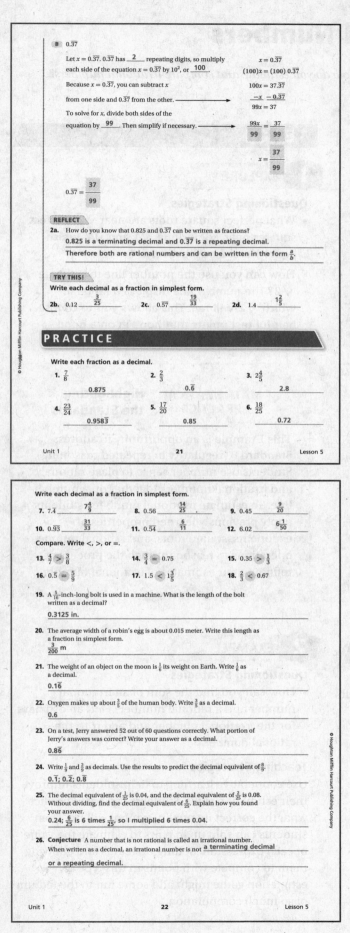

B $0.\overline{37}$

Let $x = 0.\overline{37}$. $0.\overline{37}$ has __2__ repeating digits, so multiply each side of the equation $x = 0.\overline{37}$ by 10^2, or __100__.

$x = 0.\overline{37}$

$(100)x = (100) 0.\overline{37}$

Because $x = 0.\overline{37}$, you can subtract x from one side and $0.\overline{37}$ from the other.

$100x = 37.\overline{37}$

$\underline{-x \quad -0.\overline{37}}$

$99x = 37$

To solve for x, divide both sides of the equation by __99__. Then simplify if necessary.

$\dfrac{99x}{99} = \dfrac{37}{99}$

$x = \dfrac{37}{99}$

$0.\overline{37} = \dfrac{37}{99}$

REFLECT

2a. How do you know that 0.825 and $0.\overline{37}$ can be written as fractions?

0.825 is a terminating decimal and $0.\overline{37}$ is a repeating decimal.

Therefore both are rational numbers and can be written in the form $\frac{a}{b}$.

TRY THIS!

Write each decimal as a fraction in simplest form.

2b. 0.12 __$\frac{3}{25}$__   **2c.** $0.\overline{57}$ __$\frac{19}{33}$__   **2d.** 1.4 __$1\frac{2}{5}$__

PRACTICE

Write each fraction as a decimal.

1. $\frac{7}{8}$ ____0.875____   **2.** $\frac{2}{3}$ ____$0.\overline{6}$____   **3.** $2\frac{4}{5}$ ____2.8____

4. $\frac{23}{24}$ ____$0.958\overline{3}$____   **5.** $\frac{17}{20}$ ____0.85____   **6.** $\frac{18}{25}$ ____0.72____

Write each decimal as a fraction in simplest form.

7. $7.\overline{4}$ __$7\frac{4}{9}$__   **8.** 0.56 __$\frac{14}{25}$__   **9.** 0.45 __$\frac{9}{20}$__

10. $0.\overline{93}$ __$\frac{31}{33}$__   **11.** $0.\overline{54}$ __$\frac{6}{11}$__   **12.** 6.02 __$6\frac{1}{50}$__

Compare. Write <, >, or =.

13. $\frac{4}{7}$ > $\frac{3}{8}$ **14.** $\frac{3}{4}$ = 0.75   **15.** 0.35 > $\frac{1}{3}$

16. $0.\overline{5}$ = $\frac{5}{9}$ **17.** 1.5 < $1\frac{3}{5}$ **18.** $\frac{2}{3}$ < 0.67

19. A $\frac{5}{16}$-inch-long bolt is used in a machine. What is the length of the bolt written as a decimal?

0.3125 in.

20. The average width of a robin's egg is about 0.015 meter. Write this length as a fraction in simplest form.

$\frac{3}{200}$ m

21. The weight of an object on the moon is $\frac{1}{6}$ its weight on Earth. Write $\frac{1}{6}$ as a decimal.

$0.1\overline{6}$

22. Oxygen makes up about $\frac{3}{5}$ of the human body. Write $\frac{3}{5}$ as a decimal.

0.6

23. On a test, Jerry answered 52 out of 60 questions correctly. What portion of Jerry's answers was correct? Write your answer as a decimal.

$0.8\overline{6}$

24. Write $\frac{1}{9}$ and $\frac{2}{9}$ as decimals. Use the results to predict the decimal equivalent of $\frac{8}{9}$.

$0.\overline{1}$; $0.\overline{2}$; $0.\overline{8}$

25. The decimal equivalent of $\frac{1}{25}$ is 0.04, and the decimal equivalent of $\frac{2}{25}$ is 0.08. Without dividing, find the decimal equivalent of $\frac{6}{25}$. Explain how you found your answer.

0.24; $\frac{6}{25}$ is 6 times $\frac{1}{25}$, so I multiplied 6 times 0.04.

26. Conjecture A number that is not rational is called an irrational number. When written as a decimal, an irrational number is not __a terminating decimal__

__or a repeating decimal.__

Irrational Numbers

Essential question: *How do you estimate and compare irrational numbers?*

COMMON CORE **Standards for Mathematical Content**

CC.8.EE.2 …Use square root and cube root symbols to represent solutions to equations of the form $x^2 = p$ and $x^3 = p$, where p is a positive rational number. Evaluate square roots of small perfect squares and cube roots of small perfect cubes… Know that $\sqrt{2}$ is irrational.

CC.8.NS.2 Use rational approximations of irrational numbers to compare the size of irrational numbers, locate them approximately on a number line diagram, and estimate the value of expressions (e.g., π^2).

Vocabulary
irrational numbers

Prerequisites
Rational numbers

Math Background
You can estimate irrational numbers that are written as square roots of non-perfect squares by using square roots of perfect squares as a reference. For example, because $\sqrt{4} < \sqrt{5} < \sqrt{9}$, you know that $2 < \sqrt{5} < 3$. For a closer estimation, find the square of selected test points between 2 and 3. For example, $2.2^2 = 4.84$ and $2.3^2 = 5.29$, so the answer must be between 2.2 and 2.3. Then try 2.21 and 2.25, and so on. So, $\sqrt{5} \approx 2.236$.

INTRODUCE

Connect to prior learning by asking students to give examples of the square roots of perfect squares. Tell students that in this lesson they will approximate the square roots of numbers that are not perfect squares using estimation and a number line.

TEACH

1 EXPLORE

Questioning Strategies
- What perfect square roots are near $\sqrt{2}$? **Perfect squares near $\sqrt{2}$ include $\sqrt{1}$ and $\sqrt{4}$, which equal 1 and 2, respectively.**
- How can you use the number line to estimate $\sqrt{2}$? **The number line displays a range in which $\sqrt{2}$ will fall. This allows you to choose helpful test points that hone in on a good estimate.**

MATHEMATICAL PRACTICE — **Highlighting the Standards**

This Example is an opportunity to address Standard 8 (regularity in repeated reasoning). Students use number sense to place rational and irrational numbers together on a number line. To estimate irrational numbers, students apply previously learned properties of exponents, square roots, and rational number operations to reason through the process of refining their estimates of irrational numbers.

---

2 EXAMPLE

Questioning Strategies
- How can you find the sum of an irrational number and a rational number? **Find an estimate for the irrational number and add it to the rational number.**

Teaching Strategies
Use cooperative learning to help students improve their estimation skills. Students can try to predict what the correct inequality symbol will be. Then students can split up in pairs to estimate the value of each expression. Setting up teams and allowing them to compete with points in this type of estimation game might add some fun to the tedium of so much computation.

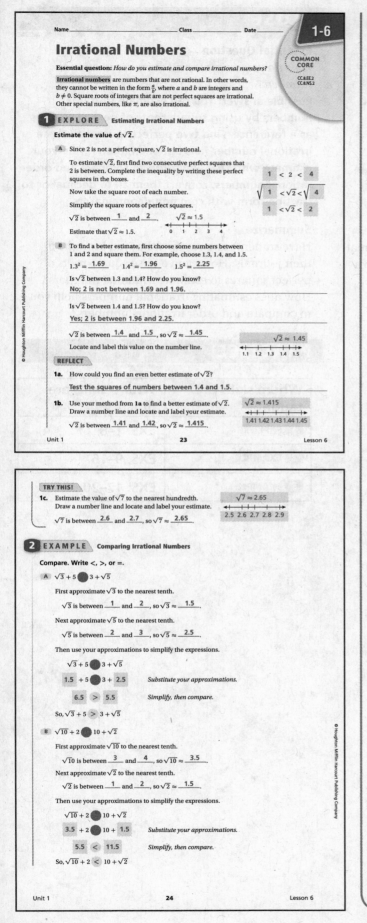

Name _____ **Class** _____ **Date** _____

1-6

COMMON CORE
CC.8.EE.2
CC.8.NS.2

Irrational Numbers

Essential question: *How do you estimate and compare irrational numbers?*

Irrational numbers are numbers that are not rational. In other words, they cannot be written in the form $\frac{a}{b}$, where a and b are integers and $b \neq 0$. Square roots of integers that are not perfect squares are irrational. Other special numbers, like π, are also irrational.

1 EXPLORE Estimating Irrational Numbers

Estimate the value of $\sqrt{2}$.

A Since 2 is not a perfect square, $\sqrt{2}$ is irrational.

To estimate $\sqrt{2}$, first find two consecutive perfect squares that 2 is between. Complete the inequality by writing these perfect squares in the boxes.

Now take the square root of each number.

Simplify the square roots of perfect squares.

$1 < 2 < 4$

$\sqrt{1} < \sqrt{2} < \sqrt{4}$

$1 < \sqrt{2} < 2$

$\sqrt{2}$ is between __1__ and __2__. $\sqrt{2} \approx 1.5$

Estimate that $\sqrt{2} \approx 1.5$.

B To find a better estimate, first choose some numbers between 1 and 2 and square them. For example, choose 1.3, 1.4, and 1.5.

$1.3^2 = $ __1.69__ $1.4^2 = $ __1.96__ $1.5^2 = $ __2.25__

Is $\sqrt{2}$ between 1.3 and 1.4? How do you know?

No; 2 is not between 1.69 and 1.96.

Is $\sqrt{2}$ between 1.4 and 1.5? How do you know?

Yes; 2 is between 1.96 and 2.25.

$\sqrt{2}$ is between __1.4__ and __1.5__, so $\sqrt{2} \approx$ __1.45__.

Locate and label this value on the number line.

$\sqrt{2} \approx 1.45$
1.1 1.2 1.3 1.4 1.5

REFLECT

1a. How could you find an even better estimate of $\sqrt{2}$?

Test the squares of numbers between 1.4 and 1.5.

1b. Use your method from **1a** to find a better estimate of $\sqrt{2}$. Draw a number line and locate and label your estimate.

$\sqrt{2} \approx 1.415$
1.41 1.42 1.43 1.44 1.45

$\sqrt{2}$ is between __1.41__ and __1.42__, so $\sqrt{2} \approx$ __1.415__.

TRY THIS!

1c. Estimate the value of $\sqrt{7}$ to the nearest hundredth. Draw a number line and locate and label your estimate.

$\sqrt{7} \approx 2.65$
2.5 2.6 2.7 2.8 2.9

$\sqrt{7}$ is between __2.6__ and __2.7__, so $\sqrt{7} \approx$ __2.65__.

2 EXAMPLE Comparing Irrational Numbers

Compare. Write <, >, or =.

A $\sqrt{3} + 5 \bigcirc 3 + \sqrt{5}$

First approximate $\sqrt{3}$ to the nearest tenth.

$\sqrt{3}$ is between __1__ and __2__, so $\sqrt{3} \approx$ __1.5__.

Next approximate $\sqrt{5}$ to the nearest tenth.

$\sqrt{5}$ is between __2__ and __3__, so $\sqrt{5} \approx$ __2.5__.

Then use your approximations to simplify the expressions.

$\sqrt{3} + 5 \bigcirc 3 + \sqrt{5}$

$1.5 + 5 \bigcirc 3 + 2.5$ *Substitute your approximations.*

$6.5 \boxed{>} 5.5$ *Simplify, then compare.*

So, $\sqrt{3} + 5 > 3 + \sqrt{5}$

B $\sqrt{10} + 2 \bigcirc 10 + \sqrt{2}$

First approximate $\sqrt{10}$ to the nearest tenth.

$\sqrt{10}$ is between __3__ and __4__, so $\sqrt{10} \approx$ __3.5__.

Next approximate $\sqrt{2}$ to the nearest tenth.

$\sqrt{2}$ is between __1__ and __2__, so $\sqrt{2} \approx$ __1.5__.

Then use your approximations to simplify the expressions.

$\sqrt{10} + 2 \bigcirc 10 + \sqrt{2}$

$3.5 + 2 \bigcirc 10 + 1.5$ *Substitute your approximations.*

$5.5 \boxed{<} 11.5$ *Simplify, then compare.*

So, $\sqrt{10} + 2 < 10 + \sqrt{2}$

Questioning Strategies

- How do you express all the numbers so that you can compare them? **Write fractions as decimals and write irrational numbers as approximate decimal numbers.**

- Why do you need a better estimate than 1.5 for $\sqrt{3}$ in this example? **Because one of the numbers to compare is equal to 1.5, we need an estimate for $\sqrt{3}$ that can tell us whether $\sqrt{3}$ is less than or greater than 1.5.**

Technology

Students can use a graphing calculator to order real numbers. Have students enter each number into a list and sort the list.

Essential Question

How do you estimate and compare irrational numbers?

Possible answer: You can estimate irrational numbers by using square roots of perfect squares as a reference. Find two perfect squares that the irrational number falls between, then refine your estimate with trial and error. To compare and order rational numbers, convert them all to decimal or to fraction form with common denominators.

Summarize

Have students answer the following prompts in their journals: How can you use square roots of perfect squares to estimate irrational numbers? How does estimating irrational numbers help you to compare and order irrational numbers?

PRACTICE

Where skills are taught	Where skills are practiced
1 EXPLORE	EXS. 1–8
2 EXAMPLE	EXS. 9–16
3 EXAMPLE	EXS. 17–20

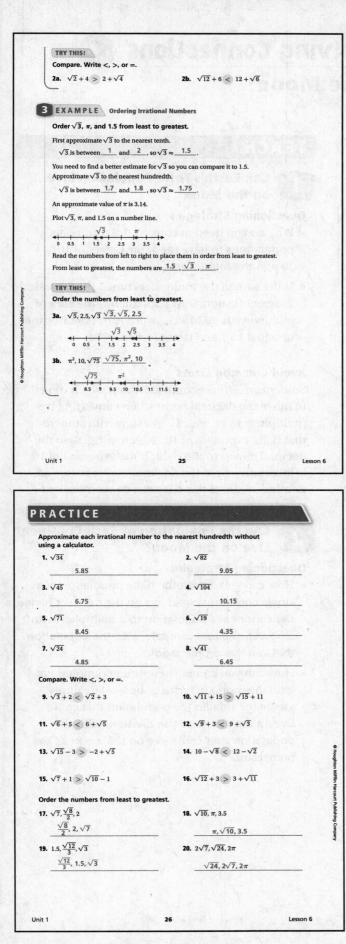

TRY THIS!

Compare. Write <, >, or =.

2a. $\sqrt{2} + 4$ $\boxed{>}$ $2 + \sqrt{4}$

2b. $\sqrt{12} + 6$ $\boxed{<}$ $12 + \sqrt{6}$

3 EXAMPLE Ordering Irrational Numbers

Order $\sqrt{3}$, π, and 1.5 from least to greatest.

First approximate $\sqrt{3}$ to the nearest tenth.

$\sqrt{3}$ is between ___1___ and ___2___, so $\sqrt{3} \approx$ ___1.5___.

You need to find a better estimate for $\sqrt{3}$ so you can compare it to 1.5.
Approximate $\sqrt{3}$ to the nearest hundredth.

$\sqrt{3}$ is between ___1.7___ and ___1.8___, so $\sqrt{3} \approx$ ___1.75___.

An approximate value of π is 3.14.

Plot $\sqrt{3}$, π, and 1.5 on a number line.

Read the numbers from left to right to place them in order from least to greatest.

From least to greatest, the numbers are ___1.5___, ___$\sqrt{3}$___, ___π___.

TRY THIS!

Order the numbers from least to greatest.

3a. $\sqrt{5}$, 2.5, $\sqrt{3}$ $\sqrt{3}, \sqrt{5}, 2.5$

3b. π^2, 10, $\sqrt{75}$ $\sqrt{75}, \pi^2, 10$

PRACTICE

Approximate each irrational number to the nearest hundredth without using a calculator.

1. $\sqrt{34}$

_____5.85_____

2. $\sqrt{82}$

_____9.05_____

3. $\sqrt{45}$

_____6.75_____

4. $\sqrt{104}$

_____10.15_____

5. $\sqrt{71}$

_____8.45_____

6. $\sqrt{19}$

_____4.35_____

7. $\sqrt{24}$

_____4.85_____

8. $\sqrt{41}$

_____6.45_____

Compare. Write <, >, or =.

9. $\sqrt{3} + 2$ $\boxed{<}$ $\sqrt{2} + 3$

10. $\sqrt{11} + 15$ $\boxed{>}$ $\sqrt{15} + 11$

11. $\sqrt{6} + 5$ $\boxed{<}$ $6 + \sqrt{5}$

12. $\sqrt{9} + 3$ $\boxed{<}$ $9 + \sqrt{3}$

13. $\sqrt{15} - 3$ $\boxed{>}$ $-2 + \sqrt{5}$

14. $10 - \sqrt{8}$ $\boxed{<}$ $12 - \sqrt{2}$

15. $\sqrt{7} + 1$ $\boxed{>}$ $\sqrt{10} - 1$

16. $\sqrt{12} + 3$ $\boxed{>}$ $3 + \sqrt{11}$

Order the numbers from least to greatest.

17. $\sqrt{7}, \frac{\sqrt{8}}{2}, 2$

_____$\frac{\sqrt{8}}{2}, 2, \sqrt{7}$_____

18. $\sqrt{10}, \pi, 3.5$

_____$\pi, \sqrt{10}, 3.5$_____

19. $1.5, \frac{\sqrt{12}}{3}, \sqrt{3}$

_____$\frac{\sqrt{12}}{3}, 1.5, \sqrt{3}$_____

20. $2\sqrt{7}, \sqrt{24}, 2\pi$

_____$\sqrt{24}, 2\sqrt{7}, 2\pi$_____

© Houghton Mifflin Harcourt Publishing Company

Notes

Problem Solving Connections 🌎
Living on the Moon!

COMMON CORE **Standards for Mathematical Content**

CC.8.EE.1 Know and apply the properties of integer exponents to generate equivalent numerical expressions.

CC.8.EE.3 Use numbers expressed in the form of a single-digit times an integer power of 10 to estimate very large or very small quantities and to express how many times as much one is than the other.

CC.8.EE.4 Perform operations with numbers expressed in scientific notation, including problems where both the decimal and scientific notation are used...

Materials
Scientific calculators

INTRODUCE

Ask students: Can you estimate the world's population and express it in scientific notation? Do you think all of the Earth's population could live on the moon? Explain to students that this project will help them answer these questions by comparing the world's population to the population that could live on the moon.

TEACH

1 Can Earth's Total Population Live on the Moon?

Questioning Strategies

- Why do you need to convert the continents' populations to have the same power of 10? **To add the multipliers.**

- Is the sum of the multipliers times 10^7 expressed in scientific notation? Explain. **No, the sum of multipliers is 903.7901, which is not greater than or equal to 1 and is not less than 10.**

Avoid Common Errors

Students might get confused about which direction to move the decimal point when converting the multipliers to go with 10^8. Review with students that if the exponent of 10 is decreasing, then the decimal moves to the right. If the exponent of 10 is increasing, then the decimal moves to the left. Remind students that they can convert back to standard notation to verify their answers.

2 Can the Population of Each Continent Live on the Moon?

Questioning Strategies

- How can you determine if the population of a single continent could live on the moon? **Change the continent's population to a multiplier with a power of 9 and compare with the population that can live on the moon.**

- How can you compare continent populations with the moon in terms of how many times greater or smaller the population that could live on the moon is? **Use division, with the population that could live on the moon as the numerator.**

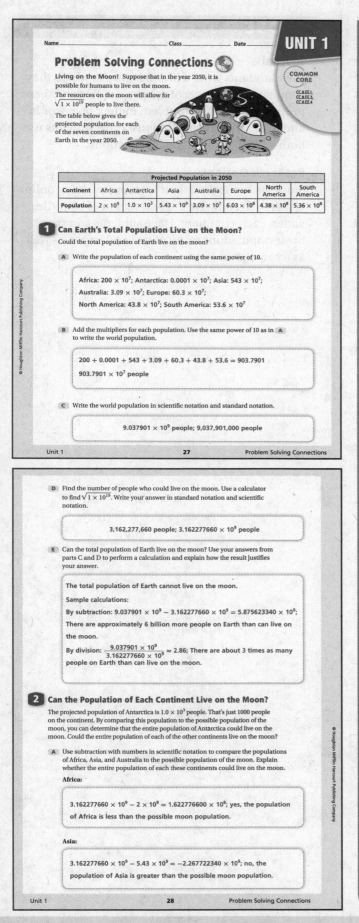

Name _____ Class _____ Date _____

UNIT 1

Problem Solving Connections 🌙

COMMON CORE
CC.8.EE.1,
CC.8.EE.3,
CC.8.EE.4

Living on the Moon! Suppose that in the year 2050, it is possible for humans to live on the moon. The resources on the moon will allow for $\sqrt{1 \times 10^{19}}$ people to live there.

The table below gives the projected population for each of the seven continents on Earth in the year 2050.

Projected Population in 2050							
Continent	Africa	Antarctica	Asia	Australia	Europe	North America	South America
Population	2×10^9	1.0×10^3	5.43×10^9	3.09×10^7	6.03×10^8	4.38×10^8	5.36×10^8

1 Can Earth's Total Population Live on the Moon?

Could the total population of Earth live on the moon?

A Write the population of each continent using the same power of 10.

> Africa: 200×10^7; Antarctica: 0.0001×10^7; Asia: 543×10^7;
> Australia: 3.09×10^7; Europe: 60.3×10^7;
> North America: 43.8×10^7; South America: 53.6×10^7

B Add the multipliers for each population. Use the same power of 10 as in **A** to write the world population.

> $200 + 0.0001 + 543 + 3.09 + 60.3 + 43.8 + 53.6 = 903.7901$
> 903.7901×10^7 people

C Write the world population in scientific notation and standard notation.

> 9.037901×10^9 people; $9,037,901,000$ people

D Find the number of people who could live on the moon. Use a calculator to find $\sqrt{1 \times 10^{19}}$. Write your answer in standard notation and scientific notation.

> $3,162,277,660$ people; 3.162277660×10^9 people

E Can the total population of Earth live on the moon? Use your answers from parts C and D to perform a calculation and explain how the result justifies your answer.

> The total population of Earth cannot live on the moon.
>
> Sample calculations:
>
> By subtraction: $9.037901 \times 10^9 - 3.162277660 \times 10^9 = 5.875623340 \times 10^9$;
> There are approximately 6 billion more people on Earth than can live on the moon.
>
> By division: $\dfrac{9.037901 \times 10^9}{3.162277660 \times 10^9} \approx 2.86$; There are about 3 times as many people on Earth than can live on the moon.

2 Can the Population of Each Continent Live on the Moon?

The projected population of Antarctica is 1.0×10^3 people. That's just 1000 people on the continent. By comparing this population to the possible population of the moon, you can determine that the entire population of Antarctica could live on the moon. Could the entire population of each of the other continents live on the moon?

A Use subtraction with numbers in scientific notation to compare the populations of Africa, Asia, and Australia to the possible population of the moon. Explain whether the entire population of each these continents could live on the moon.

Africa:

> $3.162277660 \times 10^9 - 2 \times 10^9 = 1.622776600 \times 10^8$; yes, the population of Africa is less than the possible moon population.

Asia:

> $3.162277660 \times 10^9 - 5.43 \times 10^9 = -2.267722340 \times 10^9$; no, the population of Asia is greater than the possible moon population.

Teaching Strategies

Students may have difficulty knowing when to compare with subtraction and when to compare with division. Remind students to look for the words "how much greater" or "how much smaller" to indicate subtraction, and to look for the words "how many times as…" to indicate division.

3 What is the Population Density on the Moon?

Questioning Strategies

- What does population density measure? **The average number of people per area unit of land, such as 500 people per square mile. It tells how densely populated a place is.**

- What assumption is made when you use only land area rather than total area to find the population density of Earth? **It assumes that people do not live in the ocean.**

- How can you explain why the population density of Earth is less than the population density of most major cities? **Population density is an average, and Earth has many land areas that are not heavily populated as well as many land areas that are. Most major cities do not have much land area that is not heavily populated.**

Technology

You may wish to allow students to use calculators to find and compare population densities. Comparing population densities of nearby communities, cities, and states is good practice and can be motivating for students.

CLOSE

Journal

Have students write a journal entry in which they summarize each part of the project. Remind them to state the project's problem in their own words and to describe their solutions. Have students use both scientific and standard notations.

Research Options

Students can extend their learning by doing online research to compare the population of countries within each continent. Have students compare these populations using pencil and paper, as well as a calculator.

Australia:

$3.162277660 \times 10^9 - 0.0309 \times 10^9 = 3.131377660 \times 10^9$; yes, the population of Australia is less than the possible moon population.

B Use division with numbers in scientific notation to compare the populations of Europe, North America, and South America to the possible population of the moon. Explain whether the entire population of each these continents could live on the moon.

Europe:

$\dfrac{3.162277660 \times 10^9}{6.03 \times 10^8} \approx 5.24$; yes, the possible moon population is more than 5 times the population of Europe.

North America:

$\dfrac{3.162277660 \times 10^9}{4.38 \times 10^8} \approx 7.22$; yes, the possible moon population is more than 7 times the population of North America.

South America:

$\dfrac{3.162277660 \times 10^9}{5.36 \times 10^8} \approx 5.9$; yes, the possible moon population is almost 6 times the population of South America.

C Name the continent(s) for which the entire population could live on the moon.

Africa, Antarctica, Australia, Europe, North America, South America

---

3　What is the Population Density on the Moon?

Population density is a measure of the number of people per a given area. For example, the population density of Boston, Massachusettes, is about 5,000 people per square kilometer.

The land surface area of Earth is 1.4894×10^8 square kilometers. The surface area of the moon is 3.793×10^7 square kilometers. Assume that humans are able to colonize the entire surface area of the moon. If $\sqrt{1 \times 10^{19}}$ people lived on the moon, would the population density be greater on Earth or on the moon?

A Find the average population density of Earth by dividing the total population of Earth by the land surface area of Earth.

$$\dfrac{9.037901 \times 10^9}{1.4894 \times 10^8} \approx 60.68$$

There are about __61__ people per square kilometer on Earth.

B Find the average population density of the moon by dividing the possible population of the moon by the surface area of the moon.

$$\dfrac{3.162277660 \times 10^9}{3.793 \times 10^7} \approx 83.37$$

There would be about __83__ people per square kilometer on the moon.

C Use your answers from **A** and **B** to explain whether Earth or the moon would have a greater population density.

The population density on the moon would be greater.

D Extension　Make a conjecture about why the population density of a city like Boston is greater than the population density of Earth.

There are many regions of Earth that are not populated, but population

density is an average.

Notes

UNIT 1 TEST PREP

Standard	Items
CC.8.EE.1	1, 2, 16
CC.8.EE.2	7–9, 13, 17
CC.8.EE.3	4, 6
CC.8.EE.4	3, 5
CC.8.NS.1	11, 12
CC.8.NS.2	10, 14, 15

TEST PREP DOCTOR ⊕

Multiple Choice: Item 4

- Students who answered **F** did not express the answer in proper scientific notation.
- Students who answered **G** may have added the exponents instead of subtracting the exponents.
- Students who answered **J** may have multiplied the numbers instead of dividing them.

Multiple Choice: Item 10

- Students who answered **F** found the reciprocal of 3 instead of the square root of 3.
- Students who answered **H** just removed the square root sign.
- Students who answered **J** found the decimal portion of $\sqrt{3}$, but then squared 3 to find the whole number portion of the decimal.

Free Response: Item 12

- Students who did not include 2 as a rational number may not have recognized that 2 can be written as the fraction $\frac{2}{1}$.
- Students who did not include $0.\overline{3}$ may not remember that rational numbers include repeating decimals.
- Students who included $\sqrt{11}$ as a rational number may not realize that only the square root of a perfect square is a rational number.

Free Response: Item 16

- Students who answered $4 \cdot 6$ may not have noticed that 6 is an exponent, or may not understand exponents.
- Students who answered $4^2 \cdot 4^3$ may misunderstand the product of powers to involve the product of exponents instead of the sum of exponents.

Name _____ Class _____ Date _____

MULTIPLE CHOICE

1. An industrial machine creates $4^3 \cdot 4^5$ products every year. How many products does the machine create each year?

   A. 4   C. 64

   B. 16   (D.) 65,536

2. Simplify the expression:
   $$(2^2)^4 - \left(\frac{(7-1)^9}{6^2}\right) + (20-17)^3 \times 3^8$$

   F. $2^6 - 6^{11} + 3^{11}$ (H.) $2^8 - 6^7 + 3^{11}$

   G. $4^6 - 6^{11} + 3^5$ J. $8^6 - 36^{11} + 9^{11}$

Use the table for 3 and 4.

Weights of Large Animals			
Animal	African Bush Elephant	Polar Bear	Ostrich
Weight (lbs)	27,000	2,000	343.92

3. What is the weight of the ostrich written scientific notation?

   A. 0.34392×10^4 pounds

   (B.) 3.4392×10^2 pounds

   C. 3.4392×10^3 pounds

   D. 34.392×10^4 pounds

4. How many times as great as the weight of the polar bear is the weight of the African bush elephant?

   F. 0.135×10^2 pounds

   G. 1.35×10^7 pounds

   (H.) 1.35×10^1 pounds

   J. 5.4×10^7 pounds

5. In 2009, the population of California was estimated as 3.696×10^7 people. The population of Florida was estimated as 1.854×10^7 people. What was the total estimated population for these two states?

   (A) 5.550×10^7 people

   B. 5.550×10^5 people

   C. 1.842×10^7 people

   D. 1.842×10^1 people

6. In 2009, the population of the United States was estimated as 3.07×10^8 people. The population of Maryland was estimated as 5.7×10^6 people. About how many times greater is the population of the U.S. than the population of Maryland?

   F. 2 times

   G. 5 times

   (H.) 50 times

   J. 200 times

7. A square section of a kitchen floor is made of 49 square tiles. How many tiles are on each side of the square section of the kitchen floor?

   A. 4.9 tiles   C. 36 tiles

   (B.) 7 tiles   D. 42 tiles

8. A sculpture of a giant cube contains 1331 cubes within it. How many smaller cubes are along each edge of the sculpture?

   (F.) 11 cubes   H. 36 cubes

   G. 13 cubes   J. 133 cubes

9. Chen is building a birdhouse. The bottom part is a cube with a volume of $\frac{1}{8}$ cubic foot. What is the length of each edge of the cube in feet?

   (A) $\frac{1}{2}$ foot

   B. $\frac{1}{3}$ foot

   C. $\frac{1}{64}$ foot

   D. $\frac{1}{512}$ foot

10. Which is approximately equal to $\sqrt{3}$?

    F. $\frac{1}{3}$

    (G.) 1.732050808...

    H. 3.0

    J. 9.732050808...

11. Which fraction is equivalent to $0.\overline{15}$?

    A. $\frac{1}{15}$ C. $\frac{10}{15}$

    (B.) $\frac{15}{99}$ D. $\frac{15}{1}$

FREE RESPONSE

12. Explain whether each of the following numbers is rational.

    $2, \frac{1}{13}, \sqrt{11}, 0.\overline{3}$

    2 and $\frac{1}{13}$ are rational because they can

    be written as ratios of integers; $\sqrt{11}$

    is not rational because it is not the

    square root of a perfect square; $0.\overline{3}$

    is rational because it can be written

    as the fraction $\frac{1}{3}$.

13. Find a number greater than 1 and less than 1000 that is both a perfect square and a perfect cube. Give the principal square root and the cube root of your number.

    Possible answers: 64, 8, 4; 729, 27, 9

14. Explain how you know that $\sqrt{2}$ is less than $2\sqrt{2}$ without performing any calculations.

    Since $\sqrt{2}$ is positive, 2 times $\sqrt{2}$ is

    positive. Multiplying $\sqrt{2}$ by 2 results

    in a greater number.

15. Explain how you know whether $\sqrt{38}$ is closer to 6 or 7 without using a calculator.

    38 is closer to 36 than to 49, so $\sqrt{38}$ is

    closer to 6 than to 7.

16. Give two ways to write 4^6 as a product of powers.

    Sample answer: $4^2 \cdot 4^4$, $4^3 \cdot 4^3$

17. Chris needs to install carpet in a square room. The floor of the room has an area of about 876 square feet. Chris must order a whole number of square yards of carpet.

    a. About how many feet long is the room?

       about 30 feet long

    b. How many square yards of carpet should Chris order? Explain your reasoning.

       30 feet = 10 yards; 10 yards ×

       10 yards = 100 square yards

© Houghton Mifflin Harcourt Publishing Company

UNIT 2

Functions

Unit Vocabulary

UNIT 2

Functions

Unit Focus

Functions give us a way to describe relationships that happen in our lives. A function can describe the cost of a cell phone plan, predict how long it will take to drive to the beach, or help you choose the best payment plan.

In this unit, you will learn how to use a table, write a mathematical expression, or create a graph to describe the relationship between two things. You will see how each of these representations can give you important information about the relationship, and how you can use this information to make decisions.

Unit at a Glance

COMMON CORE

Lesson		Standards for Mathematical Content
2-1	Functions, Tables, and Graphs	CC.8.F.1
2-2	Graphing Linear Functions	CC.8.EE.5, CC.8.F.3
2-3	Rate of Change and Slope	CC.8.EE.5
2-4	Slope-Intercept Form	CC.8.EE.6, CC.8.F.3
2-5	Writing Equations to Describe Functions	CC.8.F.3, CC.8.F.4
2-6	Comparing Functions	CC.8.EE.5, CC.8.F.2, CC.8.F.4
2-7	Analyzing Graphs	CC.8.F.5
	Problem Solving Connections	
	Test Prep	

Unpacking the Common Core State Standards

Use the table to help you understand the Common Core State Standards that are taught in this unit. Refer to the lessons listed after each standard for exploration and practice.

COMMON CORE Standards for Mathematical Content	What It Means For You
CC.8.EE.5 Graph proportional relationships, interpreting the unit rate as the slope of the graph. Compare two different proportional relationships represented in different ways. Lessons 2-2, 2-3, 2-6	You will learn how to recognize constant rates and to apply your understanding of rates to analyzing real-world situations.
CC.8.EE.6 Use similar triangles to explain why the slope m is the same between any two distinct points on a non-vertical line in the coordinate plane; **derive the equation $y = mx$ for a line through the origin and the equation $y = mx + b$ for a line intercepting the vertical axis at b.** Lesson 2-4	Equations can describe functional relationships. If you understand what the equation describes, you can use that information to understand a problem situation.
CC.8.F.1 Understand that a function is a rule that assigns to each input exactly one output. The graph of a function is the set of ordered pairs consisting of an input and the corresponding output. Lesson 2-1	A function is a special type of relationship between input values and output values. You can generate ordered pairs of input and output values in order to graph a function.
CC.8.F.2 Compare properties of two functions each represented in a different way (algebraically, graphically, numerically in tables, or by verbal descriptions). Lesson 2-6	You will learn to translate between different representations of functions such as tables, graphs, equations, and verbal descriptions.
CC.8.F.3 Interpret the equation $y = mx + b$ as defining a linear function, whose graph is a straight line; give examples of functions that are not linear. Lessons 2-2, 2-4, 2-5	The graph of a linear function is a straight line. The graph of a non-linear function is not a straight line. Every linear function can be described by a linear equation. The equation $y = mx + b$ is a linear equation in slope-intercept form.
CC.8.F.4 Construct a function to model a linear relationship between two quantities. Determine the rate of change and initial value of the function from a description of a relationship or from two (x, y) values, including reading these from a table or from a graph. Interpret the rate of change and initial value of a linear function in terms of the situation it models, and in terms of its graph or a table of values. Lessons 2-5, 2-6	You will learn to identify the slope of a line and the y-intercept using a table, graph, equation, or verbal description. The slope of a line is the rate of change of the situation modeled by a linear function. The y-intercept is the initial value of the function.

Unpacking the Common Core State Standards

This page lists and explains the Standards for Mathematical Content that are addressed in this unit. For information about the Standards for Mathematical Practice, which are integrated throughout the text, see Teacher Edition pages vii–xiii.

Additional Standards in This Unit

CC.8.F.5 Describe qualitatively the functional relationship between two quantities by analyzing a graph (e.g., where the function is increasing or decreasing, linear or nonlinear). Sketch a graph that exhibits the qualitative features of a function that has been described verbally. Lesson 2-7

Notes

_____

_____

_____

_____

_____

_____

_____

_____

_____

_____

Functions, Tables, and Graphs

Essential question: *How do you represent a function with a table or graph?*

CC.8.F.1 Understand that a function is a rule that assigns to each input exactly one output. The graph of a function is the set of ordered pairs consisting of an input and the corresponding output.

Vocabulary
input
output
function

Prerequisites
Graphing equations

Math Background
A function is a relationship between two variables such that any input value corresponds to *exactly* one output value. In the graph of a function, the input variable is represented by the *x*-axis (horizontal) and the output variable is represented by the *y*-axis (vertical). Any letters can be used for the input and output variables, but without context, variables *x* and *y* are typically used.

INTRODUCE

Real-world examples that are relevant to students are the best way to engage them as you introduce functions. There are many relationships in students' lives that can be modeled by functions. For example, ask students whether the amount of sleep they get the night before a test will affect their performance on the test. Ask about other things that might impact their performance on a test, such as the amount of time spent studying.

TEACH

1 EXPLORE

Questioning Strategies
- What do the numbers that go into the machine represent? **pencils**
- What do the numbers that come out of the machine represent? **cost**
- Where do you get the information for the first three rows of the table? **It is given in the problem.**
- How can you tell what the rule is? **Possible answer: Find a pattern in the consecutive values in the cost column, adding 0.25. Test it as a rule by multiplying 0.25 by the number of pencils.**

TRY THIS

Students used patterns in the table to find the rule in the Explore. In the Try This, students are asked to use number sense and inverse operations to find a rule.

> MATHEMATICAL **Highlighting the**
> PRACTICE **Standards**
>
> This Example is an opportunity to address Standard 4 (Model with mathematics). Students are asked to write equations that describe the relationship between given quantities. To extend the application of this standard, ask students to suggest other situations in real life that can be described with equations and/or tables.

Avoid Common Errors
Students may get in a rush and think they know the rule from looking at only the first one or two pairs of corresponding values in a table. Remind them that it must work for all the values, and encourage them to verify that their rule holds for all known values.

Functions, Tables, and Graphs

Essential question: *How do you represent a function with a table or graph?*

2-1

COMMON CORE
CC.8.F.1

1 EXPLORE Understanding Relationships

Carlos needs to buy some new pencils from the school supply cabinet at school. Carlos asks his classmates if they know how much pencils cost. Angela says she bought 2 pencils for $0.50. Paige bought 3 pencils for $0.75, and Spencer bought 4 pencils for $1.00.

Carlos thinks about the rule for the price of a pencil as a machine. When he puts the number of pencils he wants to buy into the machine, the machine applies a rule and tells him the total cost of that number of pencils.

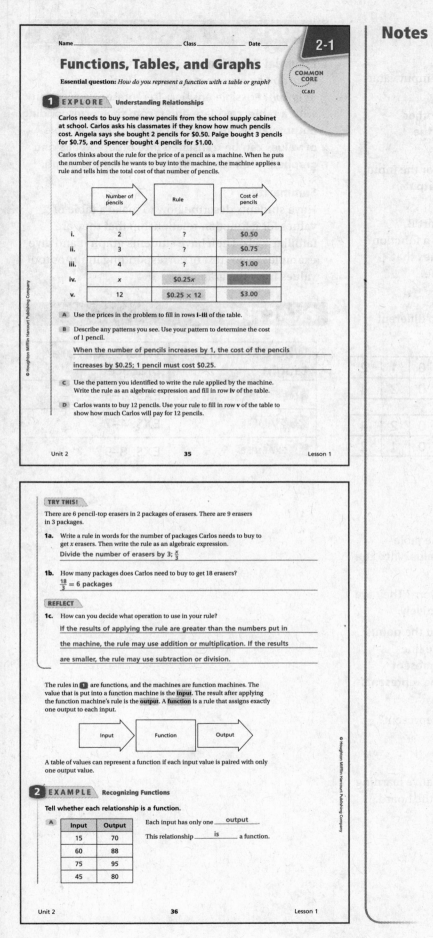

	Number of pencils	Rule	Cost of pencils
i.	2	?	$0.50
ii.	3	?	$0.75
iii.	4	?	$1.00
iv.	x	$0.25x$	
v.	12	0.25×12	$3.00

A Use the prices in the problem to fill in rows **i–iii** of the table.

B Describe any patterns you see. Use your pattern to determine the cost of 1 pencil.

When the number of pencils increases by 1, the cost of the pencils

increases by $0.25; 1 pencil must cost $0.25.

C Use the pattern you identified to write the rule applied by the machine. Write the rule as an algebraic expression and fill in row **iv** of the table.

D Carlos wants to buy 12 pencils. Use your rule to fill in row **v** of the table to show how much Carlos will pay for 12 pencils.

© Houghton Mifflin Harcourt Publishing Company

TRY THIS!

There are 6 pencil-top erasers in 2 packages of erasers. There are 9 erasers in 3 packages.

1a. Write a rule in words for the number of packages Carlos needs to buy to get x erasers. Then write the rule as an algebraic expression.

Divide the number of erasers by 3; $\frac{x}{3}$

1b. How many packages does Carlos need to buy to get 18 erasers?

$\frac{18}{3} = 6$ packages

REFLECT

1c. How can you decide what operation to use in your rule?

If the results of applying the rule are greater than the numbers put in

the machine, the rule may use addition or multiplication. If the results

are smaller, the rule may use subtraction or division.

The rules in **1** are functions, and the machines are function machines. The value that is put into a function machine is the **input**. The result after applying the function machine's rule is the **output**. A **function** is a rule that assigns exactly one output to each input.

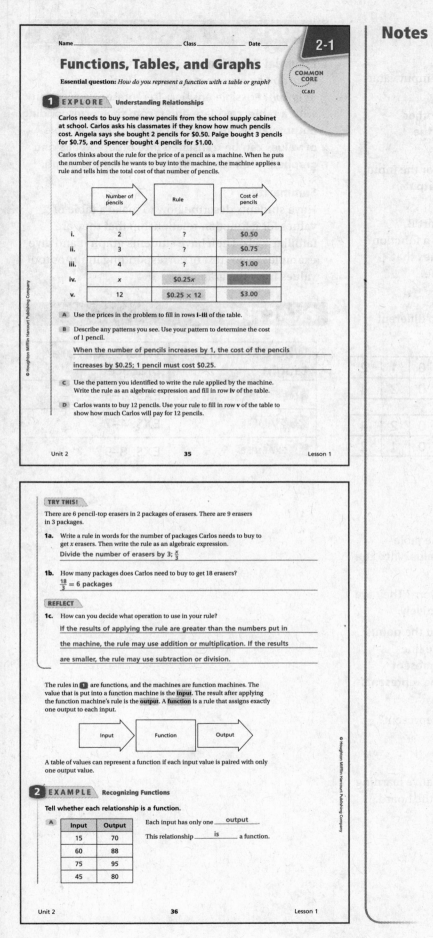

A table of values can represent a function if each input value is paired with only one output value.

2 EXAMPLE Recognizing Functions

Tell whether each relationship is a function.

A

Input	Output
15	70
60	88
75	95
45	80

Each input has only one ___output___.

This relationship ___is___ a function.

© Houghton Mifflin Harcourt Publishing Company

Questioning Strategies

• In part A, what is the output for the input value of 15? **70**

• Can the input value of 15 have any other corresponding output value? **not if the relationship is a function**

• In part B, what is the output value for the input 14? **There are two corresponding outputs: 60 and 57.**

• How can you tell that the table in part B represents a relationship that is *not* a function? **There are two different output values that correspond to one single input value.**

Teaching Strategies

Point out that a function *can* have two different inputs that both have the same output.

Function:	Input	−2	−1	0	1	2
	Output	4	2	0	2	4

Not a Function:	Input	4	2	0	2	4
	Output	−2	−1	0	1	2

3 EXAMPLE

Questioning Strategies

• What does the middle column of the table display? **the substitution of input values into the function rule**

• Where do the ordered pairs come from? **They are the input and output values, respectively.**

• What is the difference between what the points on the graph represent and what the line through them represents? **Points represent specific input-output values. The line represents all possible input-output values.**

• What do the arrowheads on a line represent? **The relationship continues.**

Differentiated Instruction

Use kinesthetic strategies and cooperative learning by having students work in groups at the board.

CLOSE

Essential Question

How do you represent a function with a table or graph? **Possible answer: To represent a function with a table, calculate and record the corresponding output values for different input values. A table of values can be translated into ordered pairs and graphed. Look for a pattern to sketch the graph.**

Summarize

Have students describe how to make a table of values for a function relationship that they are familiar with. Then have students graph it and give examples in context of corresponding input-output values from the graph.

PRACTICE

Where skills are taught	Where skills are practiced
1 EXPLORE	EXS. 1–3
2 EXAMPLE	EXS. 4–7
3 EXAMPLE	EXS. 8–9

Input	Output
14	60
13	55
14	57
15	52

The input ____14____ has more than one output.

This relationship ____is not____ a function.

The input values (x) and output values (y) of a function can be displayed in a table or written as ordered pairs (x, y). These ordered pairs can be graphed in the coordinate plane to show a graph of the function.

Some function rules can be written as equations such as $y = 2x$. By substituting values for x, you can generate corresponding y-values. The ordered pairs (x, y) are solutions of the equation.

3 EXAMPLE Graphing a Function

Graph the function $y = 2x + 3$.

Create a table of values.

x	$2x + 3$	y
−4	2(−4) + 3	−5
−1	2(−1) + 3	1
0	2(0) + 3	3
2	2(2) + 3	7
3	2(3) + 3	9

Write ordered pairs.

(x, y)
(−4 , −5)
(−1 , 1)
(0 , 3)
(2 , 7)
(3 , 9)

Graph the ordered pairs.

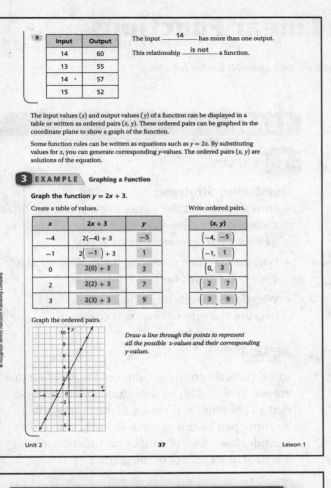

Draw a line through the points to represent all the possible x-values and their corresponding y-values.

© Houghton Mifflin Harcourt Publishing Company

Unit 2   37   Lesson 1

PRACTICE

Fill in each table. In the row with x as the input, write a rule as an algebraic expression for the output. Then complete the last row of the table using the rule.

1.
Input	Output
Tickets	Cost ($)
2	40
5	100
7	140
8	160
x	20x
10	200

2.
Input	Output
Minutes	Pages Read
2	1
10	5
20	10
30	15
x	$\frac{x}{2}$
60	30

3.
Input	Output
Muffins	Cost ($)
1	2.25
3	6.75
6	13.50
12	27.00
x	2.25x
18	40.50

Tell whether each relationship is a function.

4.
Input	6	7	8	7	9
Output	75	80	87	88	95

____not a function____

5.
Input	1	2	3	4	5
Output	4	8	12	16	20

____function____

6. (1, 3), (2, 5), (3, 0), (4, −1), (5, 5)

____function____

7. (2, 7), (6, 4), (0, 3), (2, 6), (1, 5)

____not a function____

Graph each function on the coordinate plane.

8. $y = -2x$

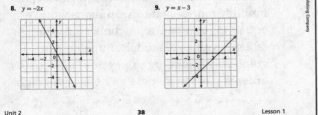

9. $y = x - 3$

© Houghton Mifflin Harcourt Publishing Company

Unit 2   38   Lesson 1

Graphing Linear Functions

Essential question: *How do you graph a linear function?*

COMMON CORE **Standards for Mathematical Content**

CC.8.EE.5 Graph proportional relationships, interpreting the unit rate as the slope of the graph. Compare two different proportional relationships represented in different ways.

CC.8.F.3 Interpret the equation $y = mx + b$ as defining a linear function, whose graph is a straight line; give examples of functions that are not linear.

Vocabulary

linear function

linear equation

Prerequisites

Ordered pairs

Graphing on a coordinate plane

Math Background

A function with a constant rate of change across its domain (the set of all input values) is called a *linear function*. The graph of a linear function is a line. Any function whose rate of change is variable is a non-linear function. A line is uniquely determined by its y-intercept, b, and rate of change (slope), m. Given these two values, an equation can be written that describes the line: $y = mx + b$. If the equation of a function cannot be written in this form, then the function is non-linear.

INTRODUCE

Compare the movements of a car on the highway to a car on a city street. In the city, a car may slow down and speed up as it navigates through its course. On a highway, however, a car may reach a certain speed and maintain that speed. Ideally with cruise control, it can travel at a constant rate for long distances. In this lesson, we learn to describe and graph functions that maintain constant rates.

TEACH

1 EXPLORE

Questioning Strategies

- How do you find the values to complete the table? **Multiply the time values by the rate 1.5 cm/h to get the total amounts of rain in cm.**

- Why are the time values on the horizontal axis? **Time is the input for this function.**

- Why do the points lie along a straight line? **because the rate of change is constant**

REFLECT

In 1a, students consider values of the function that are not in the table. Be sure students understand that all possible (x, y) values of the function will be contained by this same line. In 1b, students consider how the constant of the function affects the slant or steepness of the graph.

2 EXAMPLE

Questioning Strategies

- What common words in the problem tell you the operations to use in the equation? **"per" indicates a rate; "daily" indicates constant; "plus" indicates a sum.**

- How do you find values for the calories to complete the table? **Substitute the given weights (input) for x in the equation, and evaluate for y.**

> **MATHEMATICAL PRACTICE** **Highlighting the Standards**
>
> This Example is an opportunity to address Standard 4 (Model with mathematics). Students model function relationships with multiple representations. Students write equations to model a function, complete tables of values to model a function, and graph corresponding values from the table as ordered pairs to model functions with graphs.

Graphing Linear Functions

Essential question: *How do you graph a linear function?*

2-2

COMMON CORE

CC.8.EE.5
CC.8.F.3

1 EXPLORE Investigating Change

The U.S. Department of Agriculture defines heavy rain as rain that falls at a rate of 1.5 centimeters per hour.

A The table shows the total amount of rain that falls in various amounts of time during a heavy rain. Complete the table.

Time (h)	0	1	2	3	4	5
Total Amount of Rain (cm)	0	1.5	3	4.5	6	7.5

B Plot the ordered pairs from the table on the coordinate plane at the right.

C How much rain falls in 3.5 hours?

_____5.25 cm_____

D Plot the point corresponding to 3.5 hours of heavy rain.

E What do you notice about all of the points you plotted?

__All of the points lie along a straight line.__

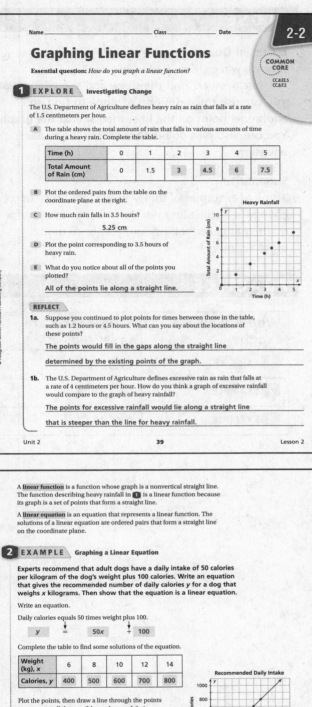

Heavy Rainfall

REFLECT

1a. Suppose you continued to plot points for times between those in the table, such as 1.2 hours or 4.5 hours. What can you say about the locations of these points?

__The points would fill in the gaps along the straight line__

__determined by the existing points of the graph.__

1b. The U.S. Department of Agriculture defines excessive rain as rain that falls at a rate of 4 centimeters per hour. How do you think a graph of excessive rainfall would compare to the graph of heavy rainfall?

__The points for excessive rainfall would lie along a straight line__

__that is steeper than the line for heavy rainfall.__

A **linear function** is a function whose graph is a nonvertical straight line. The function describing heavy rainfall in **1** is a linear function because its graph is a set of points that form a straight line.

A **linear equation** is an equation that represents a linear function. The solutions of a linear equation are ordered pairs that form a straight line on the coordinate plane.

2 EXAMPLE Graphing a Linear Equation

Experts recommend that adult dogs have a daily intake of 50 calories per kilogram of the dog's weight plus 100 calories. Write an equation that gives the recommended number of daily calories y for a dog that weighs x kilograms. Then show that the equation is a linear equation.

Write an equation.

Daily calories equals 50 times weight plus 100.

y $=$ $50x$ $+$ 100

Complete the table to find some solutions of the equation.

Weight (kg), x	6	8	10	12	14
Calories, y	400	500	600	700	800

Plot the points, then draw a line through the points to represent all the possible x-values and their corresponding y-values.

The equation is a linear equation because
__the graph of the solutions is a straight line.__

Recommended Daily Intake

TRY THIS!

2a. Graph the solutions of the linear equation $y = -2x + 1$. Then explain how the graph is different from the graph in the example.

__The graph slants downward as you move__

__from left to right.__

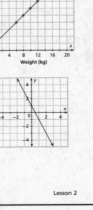

© Houghton Mifflin Harcourt Publishing Company

Questioning Strategies

- How is the change in the table of values in this example different from the change in Example 1? **In Example 1, each input value is multiplied by the same number to get the corresponding output value. In Example 3, each input value is multiplied by a different number to get the corresponding output value.**

- Why doesn't the graph fall on a line? **It is not a linear function because there is not a constant rate of change.**

Technology

Use a graphing calculator to explore functions that do and do not have a constant rate of change to explore linear and nonlinear functions. To prepare them for Exercise 7, ask students whether they think $y = 5$ is a linear function.

Essential Question

How do you graph a linear function?
Possible answer: Find the slope and the *y*-intercept. You can use the definition of slope to find an additional point on the line, then sketch the graph. You can also plot points that satisfy the linear equation.

Summarize

Think of examples of things in life that move or change at a constant rate. Discuss how to use mathematical equations and graphs to model these actions.

Where skills are taught	Where skills are practiced
1 EXPLORE	EXS. 1–4
2 EXAMPLE	EXS. 3–4
3 EXAMPLE	EXS. 1–7

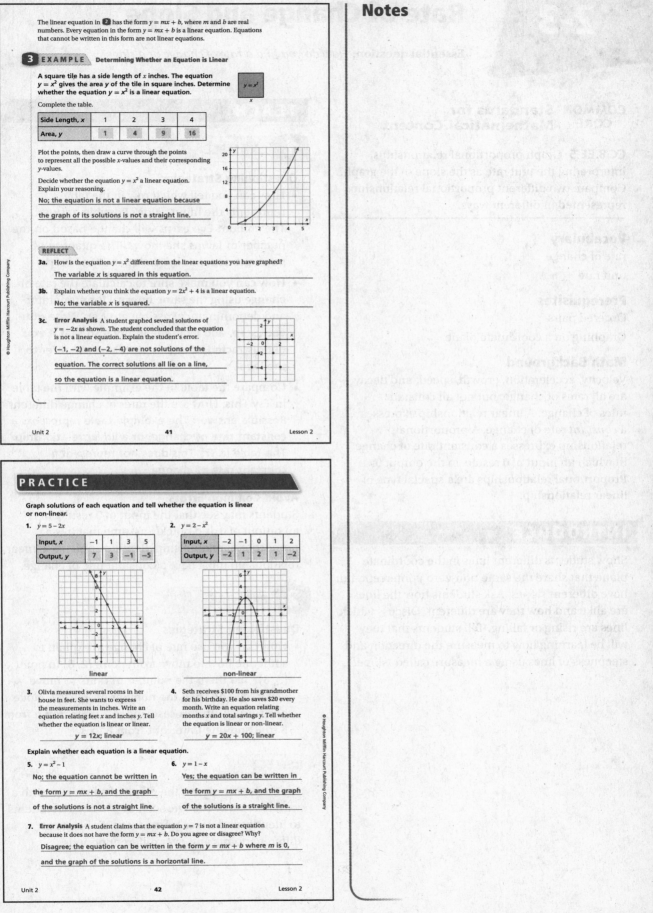

The linear equation in ② has the form $y = mx + b$, where m and b are real numbers. Every equation in the form $y = mx + b$ is a linear equation. Equations that cannot be written in this form are not linear equations.

3 EXAMPLE Determining Whether an Equation is Linear

A square tile has a side length of x inches. The equation $y = x^2$ gives the area y of the tile in square inches. Determine whether the equation $y = x^2$ is a linear equation.

Complete the table.

Side Length, x	1	2	3	4
Area, y	1	4	9	16

Plot the points, then draw a curve through the points to represent all the possible x-values and their corresponding y-values.

Decide whether the equation $y = x^2$ a linear equation. Explain your reasoning.

No; the equation is not a linear equation because

the graph of its solutions is not a straight line.

REFLECT

3a. How is the equation $y = x^2$ different from the linear equations you have graphed?

The variable x is squared in this equation.

3b. Explain whether you think the equation $y = 2x^2 + 4$ is a linear equation.

No; the variable x is squared.

3c. **Error Analysis** A student graphed several solutions of $y = -2x$ as shown. The student concluded that the equation is not a linear equation. Explain the student's error.

$(-1, -2)$ and $(-2, -4)$ are not solutions of the

equation. The correct solutions all lie on a line,

so the equation is a linear equation.

© Houghton Mifflin Harcourt Publishing Company

PRACTICE

Graph solutions of each equation and tell whether the equation is linear or non-linear.

1. $y = 5 - 2x$

Input, x	−1	1	3	5
Output, y	7	3	−1	−5

linear

2. $y = 2 - x^2$

Input, x	−2	−1	0	1	2
Output, y	−2	1	2	1	−2

non-linear

3. Olivia measured several rooms in her house in feet. She wants to express the measurements in inches. Write an equation relating feet x and inches y. Tell whether the equation is linear or linear.

$y = 12x$; linear

4. Seth receives $100 from his grandmother for his birthday. He also saves $20 every month. Write an equation relating months x and total savings y. Tell whether the equation is linear or non-linear.

$y = 20x + 100$; linear

Explain whether each equation is a linear equation.

5. $y = x^2 - 1$

No; the equation cannot be written in

the form $y = mx + b$, and the graph

of the solutions is not a straight line.

6. $y = 1 - x$

Yes; the equation can be written in

the form $y = mx + b$, and the graph

of the solutions is a straight line.

7. **Error Analysis** A student claims that the equation $y = 7$ is not a linear equation because it does not have the form $y = mx + b$. Do you agree or disagree? Why?

Disagree; the equation can be written in the form $y = mx + b$ where m is 0,

and the graph of the solutions is a horizontal line.

© Houghton Mifflin Harcourt Publishing Company

Notes

2-3

Rate of Change and Slope

Essential question: *How do you find a rate of change or a slope?*

COMMON CORE Standards for Mathematical Content

CC.8.EE.5 Graph proportional relationships, interpreting the unit rate as the slope of the graph. Compare two different proportional relationships represented in different ways.

Vocabulary

rate of change

unit rate

Prerequisites

Ordered pairs

Graphing on a coordinate plane

Math Background

Velocity, acceleration, growth, speed, and decay are all rates of change, but not all constant rates of change. A linear relationship expresses a *constant* rate of change. A proportional relationship expresses a constant rate of change in which an input of 0 results in the output 0. Proportional relationships are a special type of linear relationship.

INTRODUCE

Show students different lines in the coordinate plane that share the same non-zero *y*-intercept, but have different slopes. Ask students how the lines are alike and how they are different. Discuss which lines are rising or falling. Tell students that they will be learning how to measure the direction and steepness of lines using a measure called "slope."

TEACH

1 EXAMPLE

Questioning Strategies

• How can you tell which row in the table represents the input value? **Possible answer: The amount Eve earns will change based on the number of lawns she mows. The quantity of payment depends on the quantity of work.**

• How can you make sure to calculate the rate of change using the same interval for numerator and denominator? **Possible answer: Write out each step, and label the interval so that if you get distracted or interrupted, you can refer to the label.**

• Compare the table in the example with the table in Try This. How are the rates of change different? **Possible answer: The example table represents a constant rate of change, or a linear relationship. The table in Try This does not represent a constant rate of change.**

Avoid Common Errors

Students may see that the input of 0 results in an output of 0 and quickly assume that it is a proportional relationship. Remind students a linear relationship must have a constant rate of change.

2 EXPLORE

Questioning Strategies

• How can you use rate of change to explain to someone how to move from point (2, 8) to point (3, 6)? **Tell them the number of units to move vertically and then the number of units to move horizontally. In this case, move 2 units down from 8 to 6 and one unit right from 2 to 3.**

REFLECT

On the board, sketch the graph of a function with a variable rate of change, such as $y = x^2$. Ask students to identify and describe the rates of change at different points and over different periods.

Rate of Change and Slope

COMMON CORE
CC.8.EE.5

Essential question: *How do you find a rate of change or a slope?*

A **rate of change** is a ratio of the amount of change in the output to the amount of change in the input.

1 EXAMPLE Investigating Rates of Change

Eve keeps a record of the number of lawns she mows and the money she earns.

	Day 1	Day 2	Day 3	Day 4	Day 5
Number of Lawns	1	3	6	8	13
Amount Earned ($)	15	45	90	120	195

Input variable: __number of lawns__   Output variable: __amount earned__

Find the rates of change:

Day 1 to Day 2 $\dfrac{\text{change in \$}}{\text{change in lawns}} = \dfrac{45 - 15}{3 - 1} = \dfrac{30}{2} = 15$

Day 2 to Day 3 $\dfrac{\text{change in \$}}{\text{change in lawns}} = \dfrac{90 - 45}{6 - 3} = \dfrac{45}{3} = 15$

Day 3 to Day 4 $\dfrac{\text{change in \$}}{\text{change in lawns}} = \dfrac{120 - 90}{8 - 6} = \dfrac{30}{2} = 15$

Day 4 to Day 5 $\dfrac{\text{change in \$}}{\text{change in lawns}} = \dfrac{195 - 120}{13 - 8} = \dfrac{75}{5} = 15$

The rates of change are (constant)/ variable.

TRY THIS!

1. The table shows the approximate height of a football after it is kicked.

Time (s)	0	0.5	1.5	2
Height (ft)	0	18	31	26

Input variable: __time__   Output variable: __height__

Find the rates of change:

$\dfrac{18 - 0}{0.5 - 0} = 36; \dfrac{31 - 18}{1.5 - 0.5} = 13; \dfrac{26 - 31}{2 - 1.5} = -10$

The rates of change are constant /(variable).

© Houghton Mifflin Harcourt Publishing Company

You can also use a graph to find rates of change.

2 EXPLORE Using Graphs to Find Rates of Change

The graph shows the distance Nathan bicycled over time.
What is Nathan's rate of change?

A Find the rate of change from 1 hour to 2 hours.

$\dfrac{\text{change in distance}}{\text{change in hours}} = \dfrac{30 - 15}{2 - 1} = \dfrac{15}{1} = 15$ miles per hour

B Find the rate of change from 1 hour to 4 hours.

$\dfrac{\text{change in distance}}{\text{change in hours}} = \dfrac{60 - 15}{4 - 1} = \dfrac{45}{3} = 15$ miles per hour

C Recall that the graph of a proportional relationship is a straight line through the origin. Explain whether the relationship between Nathan's time and distance appears to be a proportional relationship.

__Yes; the graph appears to be a straight line through__

__the origin.__

D Find Nathan's unit rate.

__The graph goes through (1, 15), so the unit rate is 15 mi/h.__

E Compare the rate of change to the unit rate.

__They are the same.__

REFLECT

2a. Does it matter what interval you use when you find the rate of change of a proportional relationship? Explain.

__No; in a proportional relationship, the rate of change is constant.__

2b. **Conjecture** Do you think that the value of r in the point $(1, r)$ is always the unit rate for any situation? Explain.

__No; a situation may have variable rates of change or in a non-proportional__

__relationship, the point $(1, r)$ will not include r as the unit rate.__

© Houghton Mifflin Harcourt Publishing Company

Questioning Strategies

- This line passes through the origin. What is another point on the line with integer coordinates? **Possible Answer: (3, 1)**

- How can you use these two points to find the slope of the line? **Find the quotient of the change in *y*-coordinates and the change in corresponding *x*-coordinates.**

- How do you choose the points to use? **It is easiest if you choose points with integer coordinates.**

REFLECT

Questions 3a, 3b, and 3c summarize the different slopes that students may encounter when finding the slopes of lines, and what they indicate about the graph (from left to right).

- Positive slope: rising
- Negative slope: falling
- Zero (0 in numerator): horizontal
- Undefined (0 in denominator): vertical

MATHEMATICAL PRACTICE **Highlighting the Standards**

This Example is an opportunity to address Standard 5 (Use appropriate tools strategically). Students use the formula for slope to find the rate of change in a given context and to determine whether the rate of change is constant. They use the slope formula to understand the direction and extremity of the rate of change, mathematically and in context. Students use the slope formula to make connections with proportional relationships.

CLOSE

Essential Question

How do you find a rate of change or a slope?
Possible answer: Find the ratio of the change in output to the change in input by using points, an equation, or a graph.

Summarize

The rate of change tells us the average change of the function over a given period. It can yield velocity, speed, acceleration, rate of population growth, rate of decay, and other real life measures. In a linear function, the rate of change is constant and is called the *slope*. Non-linear functions have variable rates of change.

PRACTICE

Where skills are taught	Where skills are practiced
1 EXAMPLE	EXS. 1–2
2 EXPLORE	EXS. 3–4
3 EXAMPLE	EXS. 5–7

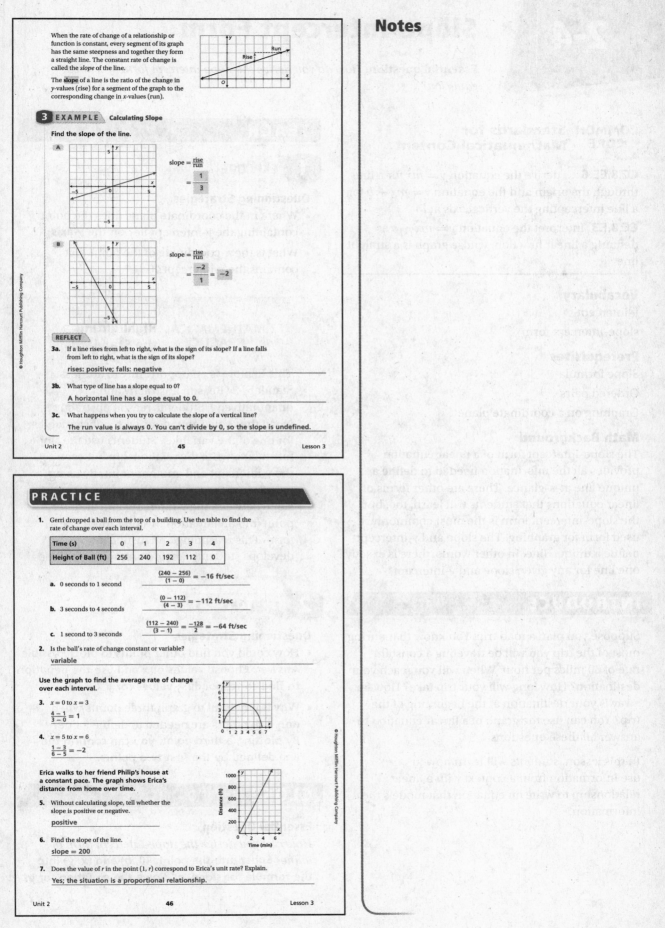

When the rate of change of a relationship or function is constant, every segment of its graph has the same steepness and together they form a straight line. The constant rate of change is called the *slope* of the line.

The **slope** of a line is the ratio of the change in *y*-values (rise) for a segment of the graph to the corresponding change in *x*-values (run).

3 EXAMPLE Calculating Slope

Find the slope of the line.

A

$$\text{slope} = \frac{\text{rise}}{\text{run}}$$

$$= \frac{1}{3}$$

B

$$\text{slope} = \frac{\text{rise}}{\text{run}}$$

$$= \frac{-2}{1} = -2$$

REFLECT

3a. If a line rises from left to right, what is the sign of its slope? If a line falls from left to right, what is the sign of its slope?

rises: positive; falls: negative

3b. What type of line has a slope equal to 0?

A horizontal line has a slope equal to 0.

3c. What happens when you try to calculate the slope of a vertical line?

The run value is always 0. You can't divide by 0, so the slope is undefined.

Unit 2   45   Lesson 3

PRACTICE

1. Gerri dropped a ball from the top of a building. Use the table to find the rate of change over each interval.

Time (s)	0	1	2	3	4
Height of Ball (ft)	256	240	192	112	0

a. 0 seconds to 1 second

$$\frac{(240 - 256)}{(1 - 0)} = -16 \text{ ft/sec}$$

b. 3 seconds to 4 seconds

$$\frac{(0 - 112)}{(4 - 3)} = -112 \text{ ft/sec}$$

c. 1 second to 3 seconds

$$\frac{(112 - 240)}{(3 - 1)} = \frac{-128}{2} = -64 \text{ ft/sec}$$

2. Is the ball's rate of change constant or variable?

variable

Use the graph to find the average rate of change over each interval.

3. $x = 0$ to $x = 3$

$$\frac{4 - 1}{3 - 0} = 1$$

4. $x = 5$ to $x = 6$

$$\frac{1 - 3}{6 - 5} = -2$$

Erica walks to her friend Philip's house at a constant pace. The graph shows Erica's distance from home over time.

5. Without calculating slope, tell whether the slope is positive or negative.

positive

6. Find the slope of the line.

slope = 200

7. Does the value of *r* in the point $(1, r)$ correspond to Erica's unit rate? Explain.

Yes; the situation is a proportional relationship.

Unit 2   46   Lesson 3

Slope-Intercept Form

Essential question: *How do you derive the slope-intercept form of a linear equation?*

COMMON CORE Standards for Mathematical Content

CC.8.EE.6 ... derive the equation $y = mx$ for a line through the origin and the equation $y = mx + b$ for a line intercepting the vertical axis at b.

CC.8.F.3 Interpret the equation $y = mx + b$ as defining a linear function, whose graph is a straight line

Vocabulary

y-intercept

slope-intercept form

Prerequisites

Slope formula

Ordered pairs

Graphing on a coordinate plane

Math Background

The slope-intercept form of a linear equation provides all the information needed to define a unique line at-a-glance. There are other forms of linear equations that students will learn, too, but the slope-intercept form is the most commonly used form for graphing. The slope and *y*-intercept define a unique line. In other words, there is exactly one line for any given slope and *y*-intercept.

INTRODUCE

Suppose you plan a road trip. You know that during most of the trip you will be traveling a constant rate of 60 miles per hour. When will you reach your destination? How long will your trip take? How far away is your destination at the beginning of the trip? You can use the graph of a linear equation to answer all these questions.

In this lesson, students will learn how to use information from a context with a linear relationship to write an equation that models the information.

TEACH

1 EXPLORE

Questioning Strategies

- Where in the coordinate plane does the point containing the *y*-intercept lie? **on the *y*-axis**

- What is the *x*-coordinate of the point that contains the *y*-intercept? **0**

MATHEMATICAL PRACTICE **Highlighting the Standards**

This Explore is an opportunity to address Standard 2 (Reason abstractly and quantitatively). Students reason abstractly when they solve equations with only variables for one of the variables. Students use the slope formula to write the relationship between the *y*-intercept and another point. By using properties of equality students transform the slope between the *y*-intercept and another point into an equation in slope-intercept form. This reasoning and justification develops students' abstract reasoning abilities.

---

2 EXPLORE

Questioning Strategies

- How could you find other points to plot? **Possible Answer: Choose values of *x* and use the equation to find corresponding values for *y*.**

- Why is it helpful to graph three points when only two points are needed to define a line? **By plotting a third point, you can confirm the line defined by the first two points.**

CLOSE

Essential Question

How can you derive the slope-intercept form of a line? **Substitute the points (0, *b*) and (*x*, *y*) into the formula for slope, *m*. Solve the equation for *y*.**

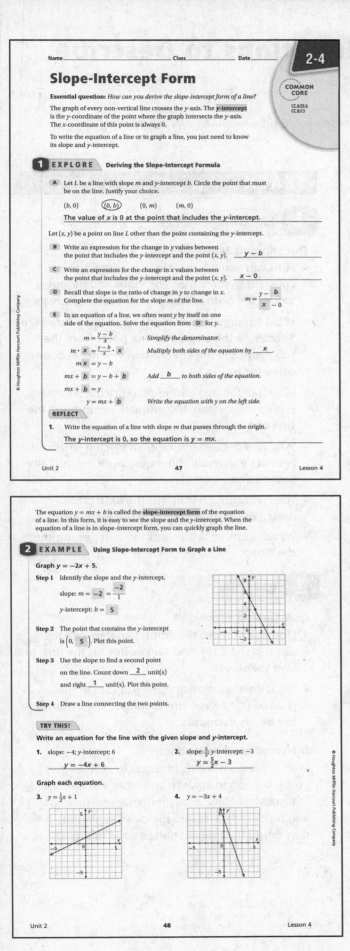

Name _____ **Class** _____ **Date** _____

2-4

Slope-Intercept Form

Essential question: *How can you derive the slope-intercept form of a line?*

COMMON CORE

CC.8.EE.6
CC.8.F.3

The graph of every non-vertical line crosses the y-axis. The **y-intercept** is the y-coordinate of the point where the graph intersects the y-axis. The x-coordinate of this point is always 0.

To write the equation of a line or to graph a line, you just need to know its slope and y-intercept.

1 EXPLORE   Deriving the Slope-Intercept Formula

A   Let L be a line with slope m and y-intercept b. Circle the point that must be on the line. Justify your choice.

$(b, 0)$ $(0, b)$ $(0, m)$ $(m, 0)$

The value of x is 0 at the point that includes the y-intercept.

Let (x, y) be a point on line L other than the point containing the y-intercept.

B   Write an expression for the change in y values between the point that includes the y-intercept and the point (x, y). $y - b$

C   Write an expression for the change in x values between the point that includes the y-intercept and the point (x, y). $x - 0$

D   Recall that slope is the ratio of change in y to change in x. Complete the equation for the slope m of the line. $m = \dfrac{y - b}{x - 0}$

E   In an equation of a line, we often want y by itself on one side of the equation. Solve the equation from D for y.

$m = \dfrac{y - b}{x}$ *Simplify the denominator.*

$m \cdot x = \dfrac{y - b}{x} \cdot x$ *Multiply both sides of the equation by x.*

$m x = y - b$

$mx + b = y - b + b$ *Add b to both sides of the equation.*

$mx + b = y$

$y = mx + b$ *Write the equation with y on the left side.*

REFLECT

1. Write the equation of a line with slope m that passes through the origin.

   The y-intercept is 0, so the equation is $y = mx$.

Unit 2   47   Lesson 4

The equation $y = mx + b$ is called the **slope-intercept form** of the equation of a line. In this form, it is easy to see the slope and the y-intercept. When the equation of a line is in slope-intercept form, you can quickly graph the line.

2 EXAMPLE   Using Slope-Intercept Form to Graph a Line

Graph $y = -2x + 5$.

Step 1 Identify the slope and the y-intercept.

slope: $m = -2 = \dfrac{-2}{1}$

y-intercept: $b = 5$

Step 2 The point that contains the y-intercept is $\left(0, \; 5\right)$. Plot this point.

Step 3 Use the slope to find a second point on the line. Count down ___2___ unit(s) and right ___1___ unit(s). Plot this point.

Step 4 Draw a line connecting the two points.

TRY THIS!

Write an equation for the line with the given slope and y-intercept.

1. slope: -4; y-intercept: 6

   $y = -4x + 6$

2. slope: $\frac{5}{2}$; y-intercept: -3

   $y = \frac{5}{2}x - 3$

Graph each equation.

3. $y = \frac{1}{2}x + 1$

4. $y = -3x + 4$

Unit 2   48   Lesson 4

Writing Equations to Describe Functions

Essential question: *How do you write an equation for a function given a table, graph, or description?*

COMMON CORE **Standards for Mathematical Content**

CC.8.F.3 Interpret the equation $y = mx + b$ as defining a linear function, whose graph is a straight line.

CC.8.F.4 Construct a function to model a linear relationship between two quantities. Determine the rate of change and initial value of the function from a description of a relationship or from two (x, y) values, including reading these from a table or from a graph. Interpret the rate of change and initial value of a linear function in terms of the situation it models, and in terms of its graph or a table of values.

Prerequisites

Linear functions

Slope-intercept form

Math Background

Information about a function can be given in tables, graphs, or words. We often need to translate information about a linear relationship into a linear function model in order to learn more about the situation. In whichever form the information about a linear relationship is given, you will need to gather the rate of change, or slope, and a point that the line goes through in order to write the linear function model.

INTRODUCE

Discuss with students different situations that involve a constant rate of change: walking or jogging at a constant rate of speed; hourly rate of pay; monthly membership dues, and so on. Include two different rates for the same type of situation, such as two different hourly pay rates. Tell students that they will be writing linear functions to model and compare situations with linear relationships.

TEACH

1 EXPLORE

Questioning Strategies

- How can you tell that the rate of change is constant in the table? **The input and output values are both increasing at regular intervals.**

- What strategy can you use to find the y-intercept? **Substitute the slope and one point from the table into the linear equation $y = mx + b$, and solve for b.**

- Which of the two phone-plan pricing structures is better if you talk 100 minutes per month? **the first one**

- Which of the two phone-plan pricing structures is better if you talk 500 minutes per month? **the second one**

- Which number represents the base price regardless of minutes used? **the y-intercept**

- Which number represents the cost per minute? **the slope**

2 EXPLORE

Questioning Strategies

- How can you use the graph to determine the slope of the line? **Find two points on the line, and find the slope.**

- What does a negative slope indicate in this situation? **As Katie drives longer, the distance to the beach decreases.**

Differentiated Instruction

With students working together in groups, give each group a graph to analyze and write a linear function to represent. Have each group present their graph and results to the rest of the class, explaining how they found the information to write the function.

Name_____ Class_____ Date_____

Writing Equations to Describe Functions

COMMON
CORE
CC.8.F.3
CC.8.F.4

Essential question: *How do you write an equation for a function given a table, graph, or description?*

1 EXPLORE   Writing an Equation for a Function from a Table

Elizabeth can choose from several monthly cell phone plans. The cost of each plan is a linear function of the number of minutes that are included in the plan. Write an equation in slope-intercept form that represents the function.

Minutes Included, x	100	200	300	400	500
Cost of Plan ($), y	18	28	38	48	58

A Choose any two ordered pairs from the table to find the slope.

$$m = \frac{y_2 - y_1}{x_2 - x_1} = \frac{28 - 18}{200 - 100} = \frac{10}{100} = 0.10$$ Sample calculations shown.

B Use the equation $y = mx + b$ and any point from the table.
Substitute values for y, m, and x into the equation and solve for b.

$$y = mx + b$$

$18 = 0.10 \cdot 100 + b$ *Substitute for y, m, and b.*

$18 = 10 + b$ *Simplify on the right side.*

$\underline{-10 \quad -10}$ *Subtract the number that is added to b from both sides.*

$8 = b$

C Use the slope and y-intercept values to write an equation in slope-intercept form.

$y = 0.10\,x + 8$

REFLECT

1a. Use the equation to predict the cost of a cell phone plan that includes 175 minutes.

$y = 0.10(175) + 8 = 25.5;\ \$25.50$

1b. What is the base price for any cell phone plan, regardless of how many minutes are included?

$8; There is an \$8 fee included in each plan's cost.

© Houghton Mifflin Harcourt Publishing Company

TRY THIS!

1c. **What if?** Elizabeth's cell phone company changed the prices for each of their plans. Write an equation in slope-intercept form that represents the function.

Minutes Included, x	100	200	300	400	500
Cost of Plan ($), y	30	35	40	45	50

$y = 0.05x + 25$

2 EXPLORE   Writing an Equation for a Function from a Graph

Kate is planning a trip to the beach. She used an estimated average speed to make a graph showing the progress she expects to make on her trip. Write an equation in slope-intercept form that represents the function.

A Choose two points on the graph to find the slope. Sample calculations shown.

$$m = \frac{y_2 - y_1}{x_2 - x_1} = \frac{0 - 300}{5 - 0} = \frac{-300}{5} = -60$$

B Read the y-intercept from the graph.

$b = 300$

C Use your slope and y-intercept values to write an equation in slope-intercept form.

$y = -60x + 300$

REFLECT

2a. What does the value of the slope represent in this context?

Kate expects to travel at an average speed of 60 mi/h.

2b. Is the slope positive or negative? What does the sign of the slope mean in this context?

Negative; Slope is negative because Kate is decreasing her distance to the beach.

2c. Describe the meaning of the y-intercept.

When time is 0 hours, Kate is 300 miles from the beach. This means Kate starts her trip 300 miles away from her destination.

© Houghton Mifflin Harcourt Publishing Company

Questioning Strategies

- How can you find the slope of this function when you don't have a rule or a graph? **Write the information as two ordered pairs (temperature, chirps): (59, 76) and (65, 100).**

- Does it matter which point you use to solve for b? **No, either point will give the same answer.**

Teaching Strategies

Ask students to suggest situations that could be modeled with a linear function. Use their descriptions to create mathematical models. Prepare a couple of examples to get things started.

:**MATHEMATICAL PRACTICE** **Highlighting the Standards**

These examples provide an opportunity to address Standard 7 (Look for and make use of structure). Students are asked to identify a linear relationship in tables, graphs, and real-world situations, and write a function to model the linear relationship. The structure of a linear function is the same regardless of how it is presented. Students learn to translate the information they are given into the information that is needed in order to write the linear function model.

CLOSE

Essential Question

How do you find a rate of change or a slope?
Possible answer: Find the ratio of the change in output to the change in input by using points, an equation, or a graph.

Summarize

The rate of change tells us the average change of the function over a given period. It can yield velocity, speed, acceleration, rate of population growth, rate of decay, and other real life measures. In a linear function, the rate of change is constant and is called the *slope*. Non-linear functions have variable rates of change.

PRACTICE

Where skills are taught	Where skills are practiced
1 EXAMPLE	EXS 1–4
2 EXPLORE	EXS 5–7
3 EXAMPLE	EXS 8–9

3 EXPLORE Writing an Equation for a Function from a Description

The rate at which crickets chirp is a linear function of temperature. At 59 °F, they chirp 76 times per minute, and at 65 °F, they chirp 100 times per minute. Write an equation in slope-intercept form that represents the function.

A Identify the input and output variables in this relationship.

Input variable: __temperature__   Output variable: __chirps per minute__

B Write the information given in the problem as ordered pairs.

At 59 °F, crickets chirp 76 times per minute: $(59, 76)$

At 65 °F, crickets chirp 100 times per minute: $(65, 100)$

C Find the slope.

$$m = \frac{y_2 - y_1}{x_2 - x_1} = \frac{100 - 76}{65 - 59} = \frac{24}{6} = 4$$

D Use the equation $y = mx + b$ and one of the ordered pairs. Substitute values for y, m, and x into the equation and solve for b.

$y = mx + b$

$100 = 4 \cdot 65 + b$ *Substitute for y, m, and b.*

$100 = 260 + b$ *Simplify on the right side.*

$\underline{-260 \quad -260}$ *Subtract the number that is added to b from both sides.*

$-160 = \qquad b$

E Write an equation in slope-intercept form.

$y = 4x - 160$

REFLECT

3a. Predict the number of chirps per minute when the temperature is 72 °F.

$y = 4(72) - 160 = 128$

3b. Without graphing, tell whether the graph of this function rises or falls from left to right. What does the sign of the slope mean in this context?

Slope is positive, so the graph rises from left to right. This means that crickets

chirp at faster rates as the temperature increases.

PRACTICE

The table shows the temperature at different altitudes. The temperature is a linear function of the altitude.

Altitude (ft), x	0	2,000	4,000	6,000	8,000	10,000	12,000
Temperature (°F), y	59	51	43	35	27	19	11

1. Find the slope of the function.

$m = \frac{51 - 59}{2,000 - 0} = \frac{-8}{2,000} = -0.004$

2. Find the y-intercept of the function.

$b = 59$

3. Write an equation in slope-intercept form that represents the function.

$y = -0.004x + 59$

4. Use your equation to determine the temperature at an altitude of 5,000 feet.

$y = -0.004(5000) + 59 = 39$ °F

The graph shows a scuba diver's ascent over time.

5. Use the graph to find the slope of the line. Tell what the slope means in this context.

$m = \frac{0 - (-5)}{80 - 0} = \frac{5}{80} = 0.0625$; the diver

ascends at a rate of 0.0625 m/s

Scuba Diver's Ascent

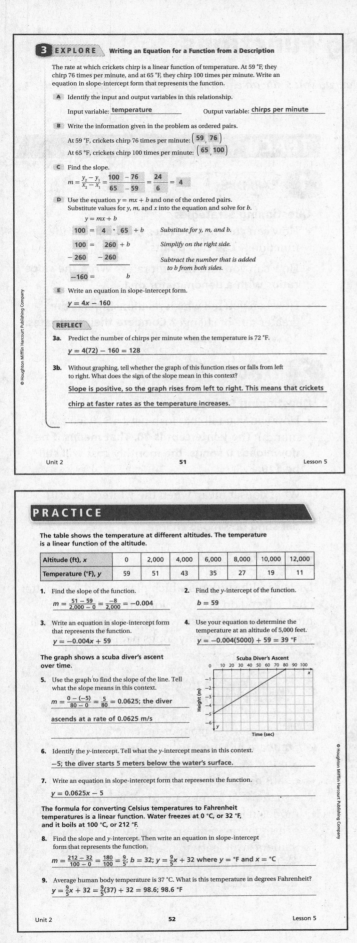

6. Identify the y-intercept. Tell what the y-intercept means in this context.

-5; the diver starts 5 meters below the water's surface.

7. Write an equation in slope-intercept form that represents the function.

$y = 0.0625x - 5$

The formula for converting Celsius temperatures to Fahrenheit temperatures is a linear function. Water freezes at 0 °C, or 32 °F, and it boils at 100 °C, or 212 °F.

8. Find the slope and y-intercept. Then write an equation in slope-intercept form that represents the function.

$m = \frac{212 - 32}{100 - 0} = \frac{180}{100} = \frac{9}{5}$; $b = 32$; $y = \frac{9}{5}x + 32$ where $y = $ °F and $x = $ °C

9. Average human body temperature is 37 °C. What is this temperature in degrees Fahrenheit?

$y = \frac{9}{5}x + 32 = \frac{9}{5}(37) + 32 = 98.6$; 98.6 °F

Comparing Functions

Essential question: *How do you write an equation for a function given a table, graph, or description?*

⠶ **COMMON** Standards for
⠶ **CORE** Mathematical Content

CC.8.EE.5 Graph proportional relationships, interpreting the unit rate as the slope of the graph. Compare two different proportional relationships represented in different ways.

CC.8.F.2 Compare properties of two functions each represented in a different way (algebraically, graphically, numerically in tables, or by verbal descriptions).

CC.8.F.4 Construct a function to model a linear relationship between two quantities. Determine the rate of change and initial value of the function from a description of a relationship or from two (x, y) values, including reading these from a table or from a graph. Interpret the rate of change and initial value of a linear function in terms of the situation it models, and in terms of its graph or a table of values.

Prerequisites

Linear functions
Slope-intercept form

Math Background

Comparing functions requires that we first write them in common terms, such as in slope-intercept form. Then we need to be able to interpret the like terms and different terms in relation to the context. Parallel lines represent situations with the same constant rate of change. Lines that intersect share the same input and output values at the intersection point only.

INTRODUCE

Suppose you want to subscribe to a music download service. Different services have different monthly fees and different rates for each downloaded song. How do you compare the options and choose the plan that's best for you? In this lesson you learn to compare these two types of situations.

TEACH

1 **EXPLORE**

Questioning Strategies

- How can you find the rates of change for the functions? **Use two points.**

- How can you find the unit rates? **Write the slope ratios with a denominator of 1.**

- How can you tell which relationship has the greater rate of change? **Compare their unit rates: 15 wpm < 20 wpm**

2 **EXPLORE**

Questioning Strategies

- How can you tell that Josh pays a $10 fee each month? **The *y*-intercept is 10. That means if he downloads 0 songs, the monthly cost will still be $10.**

- What does it mean when the *y*-intercept is 0? **There is no monthly fee in addition to the per-song download charge.**

REFLECT

Discuss with students which plan would be a better choice if you do not download many songs per month and which plan would be a better choice if you do download many songs per month.

⋰ **MATHEMATICAL** Highlighting
   PRACTICE the Standards

This Lesson is an opportunity to address Standard 4 (Model with mathematics). Students will learn to compare linear relationships whether they are modeled with equations or graphs. By creating an effective model, it is possible to analyze the outcome of a situation in different real-world settings. Students will learn to use the mathematical model as an effective problem-solving tool.

Comparing Functions

Essential question: *How can you use tables, graphs, and equations to compare functions?*

1 EXPLORE   Comparing a Table and a Graph

The table and graph show how many words Morgan and Brian typed correctly on a typing test. For both students, the relationship between words typed correctly and time is linear.

Morgan's Typing Test					
Time (min)	2	4	6	8	10
Words	30	60	90	120	150

Brian's Typing Test

A Find Morgan's unit rate.

$m = \dfrac{60 - 30}{4 - 2} = \dfrac{30}{2} = 15$; 15 words per minute

B Find Brian's unit rate.

$m = \dfrac{80 - 40}{4 - 2} = \dfrac{40}{2} = 20$; 20 words per minute

C Which student types more correct words per minute?

Brian types 5 more correct words per minute.

REFLECT

1a. Sketch a graph of Morgan's test results on the same coordinate grid as Brian's results. How are the graphs similar? How are they different?

Both graphs go through the origin. Brian's graph is steeper than

Morgan's because Brian's rate (slope) is greater.

1b. Katie types 17 correct words per minute. Explain how a graph of Katie's test results would compare to Morgan's and Brian's.

Katie's graph would go through the origin. Katie's graph would

be less steep than Brian's, but steeper than Morgan's.

1c. The equation that describes Jen's test results is $y = 24x$. Explain how a graph of Jen's test results would compare to Morgan's and Brian's.

Jen's graph would go through the origin. Jen's graph would be

steeper than Brian's and Morgan's.

2 EXPLORE   Comparing a Table and an Equation

Josh and Maggie buy MP3 files from different music download services. With both services, the monthly charge is a linear function of the number of songs downloaded. The cost at Josh's service is described by $y = 0.50x + 10$ where y is the cost in dollars and x is the number of songs downloaded.

Cost of MP3s at Maggie's Music Service					
Songs, x	5	10	15	20	25
Cost ($), y	4.95	9.90	14.85	19.80	24.75

A Find the unit rate of each function.

Josh: $m = 0.50$ Maggie: $m = \dfrac{9.90 - 4.95}{10 - 5} = 0.99$

B Which function has the greater rate of change? What does that mean in this context?

Maggie's rate of change is greater; she pays more per song.

C Write an equation in slope-intercept form to describe the cost at Maggie's music service.

$y = mx + b$

$4.95 = 0.99 \cdot 5 + b$ Substitute for y, m, and b.

$4.95 = 4.95 + b$ Subtract the number that is added to b from both sides.

$\underline{-\,4.95 \quad -\,4.95}$

$0 = b$

$y = 0.99 x + 0$

D Describe each service's cost in words using the meanings of the slopes and y-intercepts.

Josh pays a $10/month fee, but only pays $0.50 per song. Maggie has no

monthly fee, but pays $0.99 per song.

REFLECT

2a. How much does it cost at each service to download 20 songs?

Josh's: $y = 0.50(20) + 10 = \$20$; Maggie's: $y = 0.99(20) = \$19.80$

2b. You are trying to choose between these two music services. How could you decide which service is better for you?

If you plan to download fewer than 20 songs per month, Maggie's service is

cheaper. If you plan to download more than 20 songs, Josh's service is cheaper.

Questioning Strategies

- How can you determine the equation by looking at the graph? **Because 100 is the *y*-intercept, we know that *b* = 100. The slope shows 10 units ($) down for each 1 unit (mo) right, or $\frac{-10}{1}$, so the slope is −10. The equation is $y = -10x + 100$.**

- How can you determine the equation by reading the words? **An initial payment of $60 indicates a *y*-intercept of 60. Weekly payments of $20 indicate a slope of $\frac{-20}{1}$, or −20.**

Teaching Strategies

Present students with different functions and/or situations modeled with graphs, equations, tables, and descriptions. Have students work in groups to compare and contrast the linear functions. Ask them to make decisions based on the functions and real-world parameters.

Essential Question

How do you write an equation for a function given a table, graph, or description?

Possible answer: Find the slope, or rate of change, and the *y*-intercept. When working with a description, you must use key words to identify the rate. You can identify the *y*-intercept by looking for initial values or base rates. Use the slope-intercept formula to write the equation of the linear function.

Summarize

Information can be gathered from a variety of sources. A mathematical model is a tool that helps analyze the information. Knowing how to represent information involving constant rates with linear function models allows us to compare the relationships and make well-informed decisions.

PRACTICE

Where skills are taught	Where skills are practiced
1 EXPLORE	EXS. 1–4
2 EXPLORE	EXS. 1–4
3 EXPLORE	EXS. 5–8

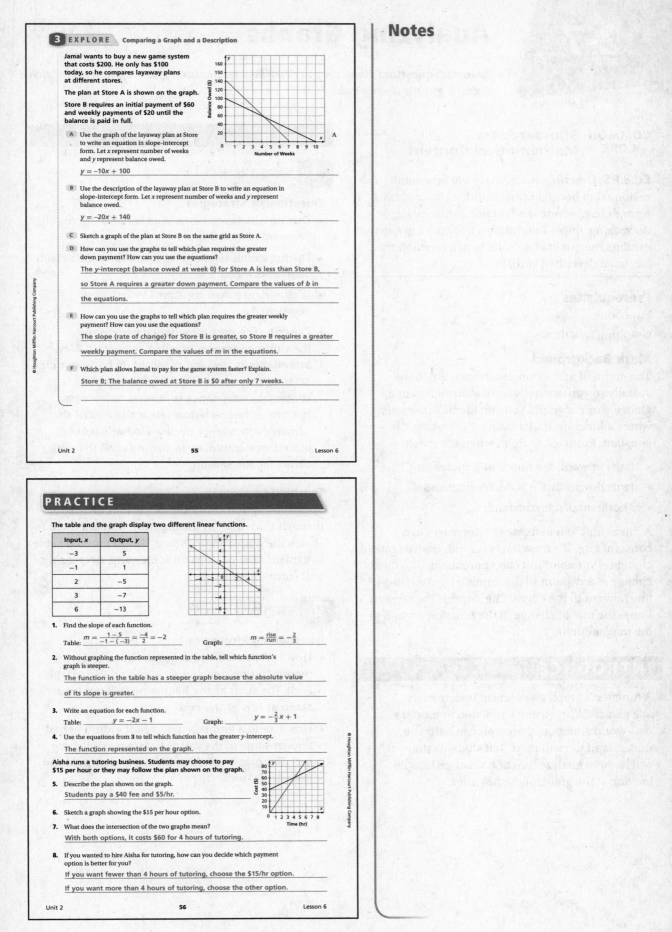

3 EXPLORE Comparing a Graph and a Description

Jamal wants to buy a new game system that costs $200. He only has $100 today, so he compares layaway plans at different stores.

The plan at Store A is shown on the graph.

Store B requires an initial payment of $60 and weekly payments of $20 until the balance is paid in full.

A Use the graph of the layaway plan at Store to write an equation in slope-intercept form. Let x represent number of weeks and y represent balance owed.

$y = -10x + 100$

B Use the description of the layaway plan at Store B to write an equation in slope-intercept form. Let x represent number of weeks and y represent balance owed.

$y = -20x + 140$

C Sketch a graph of the plan at Store B on the same grid as Store A.

D How can you use the graphs to tell which plan requires the greater down payment? How can you use the equations?

The y-intercept (balance owed at week 0) for Store A is less than Store B, so Store A requires a greater down payment. Compare the values of b in the equations.

E How can you use the graphs to tell which plan requires the greater weekly payment? How can you use the equations?

The slope (rate of change) for Store B is greater, so Store B requires a greater weekly payment. Compare the values of m in the equations.

F Which plan allows Jamal to pay for the game system faster? Explain.

Store B; The balance owed at Store B is $0 after only 7 weeks.

PRACTICE

The table and the graph display two different linear functions.

Input, x	Output, y
−3	5
−1	1
2	−5
3	−7
6	−13

1. Find the slope of each function.

   Table: $m = \dfrac{1-5}{-1-(-3)} = \dfrac{-4}{2} = -2$ Graph: $m = \dfrac{rise}{run} = -\dfrac{2}{3}$

2. Without graphing the function represented in the table, tell which function's graph is steeper.

   The function in the table has a steeper graph because the absolute value of its slope is greater.

3. Write an equation for each function.

   Table: $y = -2x - 1$ Graph: $y = -\dfrac{2}{3}x + 1$

4. Use the equations from 3 to tell which function has the greater y-intercept.

   The function represented on the graph.

Aisha runs a tutoring business. Students may choose to pay $15 per hour or they may follow the plan shown on the graph.

5. Describe the plan shown on the graph.

   Students pay a $40 fee and $5/hr.

6. Sketch a graph showing the $15 per hour option.

7. What does the intersection of the two graphs mean?

   With both options, it costs $60 for 4 hours of tutoring.

8. If you wanted to hire Aisha for tutoring, how can you decide which payment option is better for you?

   If you want fewer than 4 hours of tutoring, choose the $15/hr option.

   If you want more than 4 hours of tutoring, choose the other option.

Notes

Analyzing Graphs

Essential question: *How can you describe a relationship given a graph and sketch a graph given a description?*

COMMON CORE Standards for Mathematical Content

CC.8.F.5 Describe qualitatively the functional relationship between two quantities by analyzing a graph (e.g., where the function is increasing or decreasing, linear or nonlinear). Sketch a graph that exhibits the qualitative features of a function that has been described verbally.

Prerequisites

Functions

Graphing functions

Math Background

The graph of a function describes a function visually so you can get a lot of information at a glance. From a graph, you can identify intervals where a function is increasing, decreasing, or constant. From left to right, when the graph:

- slants upward, the function is increasing;
- slants downward, it is decreasing; and
- is horizontal, it is constant.

A linear function increases or decreases at a constant rate. If a function is curved, then its rate of change is variable. You can approximate the rate of change at any point in the domain by sketching a line tangent to the curve. The slope of the tangent line is the rate of change of the function's graph at the tangent point.

INTRODUCE

A function's graph gives lots of information at a glance. When using a function to model a real-world situation, the graph can help you understand the situation. Tell students they will learn to analyze function relationships by looking at the graph of the function.

TEACH

1 EXPLORE

Questioning Strategies

- During which segments is attendance increasing? **Segments 2 and 3**
- During which segments is attendance decreasing? **Segments 4 and 5**
- Is attendance ever constant? **yes, during Segment 1**
- Describe the park attendance pattern over the summer season. **Possible answer: In May, attendance is low and constant. In early summer, attendance increases quickly. As summer continues, attendance continues to increase, but not as fast as before. Near the end of the summer, attendance declines. After summer, attendance continues to decline until the park closes for the season.**

Teaching Strategies

Suggest situations to students, such as driving through town and on the highway, and ask them to sketch the graph on the board. They should be able to explain their reasons for increasing, decreasing, and constant intervals.

2 EXPLORE

Questioning Strategies

- How can you tell which graph shows a slower memorization rate at the beginning than at the end? **The slant at the beginning will not be as steep as it is at the end.**
- How would a graph be affected if a student had known some of the words before receiving the list? **The graph would start at a higher point on the vertical axis.**

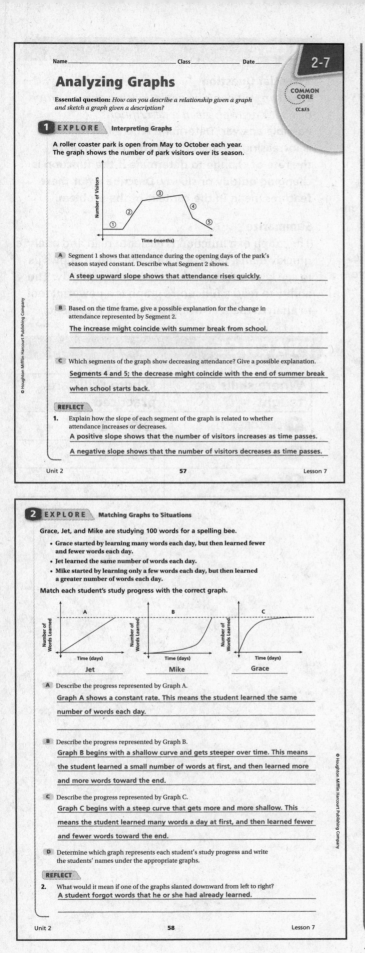

2-7

COMMON CORE
CC.8.F.5

Analyzing Graphs

Essential question: *How can you describe a relationship given a graph and sketch a graph given a description?*

1 EXPLORE   Interpreting Graphs

A roller coaster park is open from May to October each year. The graph shows the number of park visitors over its season.

A Segment 1 shows that attendance during the opening days of the park's season stayed constant. Describe what Segment 2 shows.

A steep upward slope shows that attendance rises quickly.

B Based on the time frame, give a possible explanation for the change in attendance represented by Segment 2.

The increase might coincide with summer break from school.

C Which segments of the graph show decreasing attendance? Give a possible explanation.

Segments 4 and 5; the decrease might coincide with the end of summer break when school starts back.

REFLECT

1. Explain how the slope of each segment of the graph is related to whether attendance increases or decreases.

A positive slope shows that the number of visitors increases as time passes.

A negative slope shows that the number of visitors decreases as time passes.

Unit 2   57   Lesson 7

2 EXPLORE   Matching Graphs to Situations

Grace, Jet, and Mike are studying 100 words for a spelling bee.

- Grace started by learning many words each day, but then learned fewer and fewer words each day.
- Jet learned the same number of words each day.
- Mike started by learning only a few words each day, but then learned a greater number of words each day.

Match each student's study progress with the correct graph.

A — Jet   B — Mike   C — Grace

A Describe the progress represented by Graph A.

Graph A shows a constant rate. This means the student learned the same number of words each day.

B Describe the progress represented by Graph B.

Graph B begins with a shallow curve and gets steeper over time. This means the student learned a small number of words at first, and then learned more and more words toward the end.

C Describe the progress represented by Graph C.

Graph C begins with a steep curve that gets more and more shallow. This means the student learned many words a day at first, and then learned fewer and fewer words toward the end.

D Determine which graph represents each student's study progress and write the students' names under the appropriate graphs.

REFLECT

2. What would it mean if one of the graphs slanted downward from left to right?

A student forgot words that he or she had already learned.

Unit 2   58   Lesson 7

Questioning Strategies

Can the graphs for the math tutoring situation vary or is there exactly one correct answer? The graph will be the same for the first week and the rate of increase may vary according to each student's interpretation of the words "gradually increases."

Teaching Strategies

Have students work in groups to create graphs given descriptions of real-world situations. Have groups present their graphs on the board and discuss how the graphs are alike and different. Discuss the information that would be needed in order to have exactly one correct graph for the situation.

MATHEMATICAL PRACTICE **Highlighting the Standards**

This Explore is an opportunity to address Standard 3 (Construct viable arguments and critique the reasoning of others). By comparing their graphs to those of others, students will gain insight into the different reasonings of other students. They will learn to distinguish between mistakes in reasoning and differences in interpretation. By explaining their own reasoning, students will learn to construct convincing arguments.

Essential Question

How can you describe a relationship given a graph or sketch a graph given a description?

Possible answer: Determine where the function is increasing, decreasing, or constant. Analyze the rate of change to determine if the function is changing quickly or slowly. Describe what these features mean in the context of the problem.

Summarize

The graph of a function is easier to read and analyze quickly than a table or a function rule. It allows us to see key features of the relationship quickly. The ability to read a function's graph is a powerful tool to analyze the real-world situation it represents.

PRACTICE

Where skills are taught	Where skills are practiced
1 EXPLORE	EXS. 1–3
2 EXPLORE	EXS. 4–6
3 EXPLORE	EXS. 4–6

3 EXPLORE Sketching a Graph for a Situation

Mrs. Sutton provides free math tutoring to her students every day after school. No one comes to tutoring sessions during the first week of school. Over the next two weeks, use of the tutoring service gradually increases.

A Sketch a graph showing the number of students who use the tutoring service over the first three weeks of school.

Sample answer:

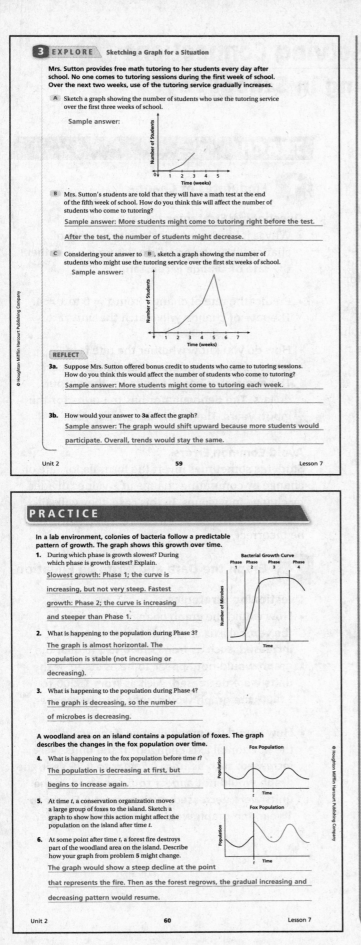

B Mrs. Sutton's students are told that they will have a math test at the end of the fifth week of school. How do you think this will affect the number of students who come to tutoring?

Sample answer: More students might come to tutoring right before the test.

After the test, the number of students might decrease.

C Considering your answer to B , sketch a graph showing the number of students who might use the tutoring service over the first six weeks of school.

Sample answer:

REFLECT

3a. Suppose Mrs. Sutton offered bonus credit to students who came to tutoring sessions. How do you think this would affect the number of students who come to tutoring?

Sample answer: More students might come to tutoring each week.

3b. How would your answer to **3a** affect the graph?

Sample answer: The graph would shift upward because more students would

participate. Overall, trends would stay the same.

© Houghton Mifflin Harcourt Publishing Company

Unit 2   59   Lesson 7

PRACTICE

In a lab environment, colonies of bacteria follow a predictable pattern of growth. The graph shows this growth over time.

1. During which phase is growth slowest? During which phase is growth fastest? Explain.

Slowest growth: Phase 1; the curve is

increasing, but not very steep. Fastest

growth: Phase 2; the curve is increasing

and steeper than Phase 1.

2. What is happening to the population during Phase 3?

The graph is almost horizontal. The

population is stable (not increasing or

decreasing).

3. What is happening to the population during Phase 4?

The graph is decreasing, so the number

of microbes is decreasing.

A woodland area on an island contains a population of foxes. The graph describes the changes in the fox population over time.

4. What is happening to the fox population before time *t*?

The population is decreasing at first, but

begins to increase again.

5. At time *t*, a conservation organization moves a large group of foxes to the island. Sketch a graph to show how this action might affect the population on the island after time *t*.

6. At some point after time *t*, a forest fire destroys part of the woodland area on the island. Describe how your graph from problem **5** might change.

The graph would show a steep decline at the point

that represents the fire. Then as the forest regrows, the gradual increasing and

decreasing pattern would resume.

© Houghton Mifflin Harcourt Publishing Company

Unit 2   60   Lesson 7

Problem Solving Connections 🌎
Does Staying in School Pay?

COMMON **Standards for**
CORE **Mathematical Content**

CC.8.EE.5 Graph proportional relationships, interpreting the unit rate as the slope of the graph. Compare two different proportional relationships represented in different ways.

CC.8.EE.6 ... derive the equation $y = mx$ for a line through the origin and the equation $y = mx + b$ for a line intercepting the vertical axis at b.

CC.8.F.1 Understand that a function is a rule that assigns to each input exactly one output. The graph of a function is the set of ordered pairs consisting of an input and the corresponding output.

CC.8.F.3 Interpret the equation $y = mx + b$ as defining a linear function, whose graph is a straight line ...

CC.8.F.4 Construct a function to model a linear relationship between two quantities ...

CC.8.F.5 Describe qualitatively the functional relationship between two quantities by analyzing a graph ... Sketch a graph that exhibits the qualitative features of a function that has been described verbally.

Materials
Scientific calculators

INTRODUCE

Ask students if they know how much it costs to go to college. Many will not know. Give students examples of complete costs for a year of study at different schools. Include a community college, a public university, and private university. Many people ask whether going to work after high school is better than investing in the exorbitant expenses of higher education. Tell students they will investigate the benefits of a college education to help them decide.

TEACH

1 Find Rates of Change

Questioning Strategies

- Why is it important to calculate the rate of change for each period? **to determine whether the rate of change is constant**

- Predict the rate of change from $x = 0$ to $x = 4$. **The rate of change will match the unit rate.**

- How do you know whether the rate is in terms of years per dollar or dollars per year? **The numerator has the units for the output, dollars. The denominator has the units for the input, years. The rate is dollars per year.**

Avoid Common Errors
Students sometimes invert the formula for rate of change by computing change in x-values divided by change in y-values. In this case, they will still find a constant rate of change, but the value will be incorrect.

2 Graph the Data and Write an Equation

Questioning Strategies

- How would the graph change if the scale of the vertical axis changed? **If the units were increased, such as from $5000 to $10,000, the graph would not appear to be as steep. If the units were decreased, such as from $5000 to $1000, the graph would appear to be steeper.**

- How would the graph change if the scale of the horizontal axis changed? **If the units were increased, such as from 0.5 year to 0.25 year, the graph would not appear to be as steep. If the units were decreased, such as from 0.5 year to 1 year, the graph would appear to be steeper.**

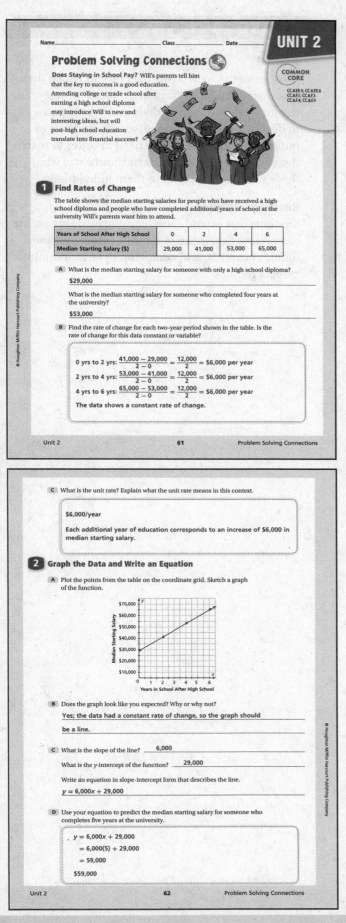

Problem Solving Connections

UNIT 2

COMMON CORE

CC.8.EE.5; CC.8.EE.6
CC.8.F.1; CC.8.F.3
CC.8.F.4; CC.8.F.5

Does Staying in School Pay? Will's parents tell him that the key to success is a good education. Attending college or trade school after earning a high school diploma may introduce Will to new and interesting ideas, but will post-high school education translate into financial success?

1 Find Rates of Change

The table shows the median starting salaries for people who have received a high school diploma and people who have completed additional years of school at the university Will's parents want him to attend.

Years of School After High School	0	2	4	6
Median Starting Salary ($)	29,000	41,000	53,000	65,000

A What is the median starting salary for someone with only a high school diploma?

$29,000

What is the median starting salary for someone who completed four years at the university?

$53,000

B Find the rate of change for each two-year period shown in the table. Is the rate of change for this data constant or variable?

0 yrs to 2 yrs: $\frac{41,000 - 29,000}{2 - 0} = \frac{12,000}{2} = \$6,000$ per year

2 yrs to 4 yrs: $\frac{53,000 - 41,000}{2 - 0} = \frac{12,000}{2} = \$6,000$ per year

4 yrs to 6 yrs: $\frac{65,000 - 53,000}{2 - 0} = \frac{12,000}{2} = \$6,000$ per year

The data shows a constant rate of change.

© Houghton Mifflin Harcourt Publishing Company

Unit 2   61   Problem Solving Connections

C What is the unit rate? Explain what the unit rate means in this context.

$6,000/year

Each additional year of education corresponds to an increase of $6,000 in median starting salary.

2 Graph the Data and Write an Equation

A Plot the points from the table on the coordinate grid. Sketch a graph of the function.

B Does the graph look like you expected? Why or why not?

Yes; the data had a constant rate of change, so the graph should be a line.

C What is the slope of the line? 6,000

What is the y-intercept of the function? 29,000

Write an equation in slope-intercept form that describes the line.

$y = 6,000x + 29,000$

D Use your equation to predict the median starting salary for someone who completes five years at the university.

$y = 6,000x + 29,000$

$= 6,000(5) + 29,000$

$= 59,000$

$59,000

© Houghton Mifflin Harcourt Publishing Company

Unit 2   62   Problem Solving Connections

3 Analyze Data

Questioning Strategies

• What is an equation for a graph that is shifted *down* from the graph of the original equation? $y = 6{,}000x + b$, where b is any value less than 29,000.

• What is an equation for a graph that increases more slowly than the original equation? $y = mx + 29{,}000$ where m is any value less than 6,000

 MATHEMATICAL PRACTICE **Highlighting the Standards**

This Project is an opportunity to address Standard 1 (Make sense of problems and persevere in solving them). The question requires multiple steps in the problem solving method. Students must invest time and thought to solve the problem and find a solution that they understand. Students should gain confidence in their ability to solve problems after seeing the problem through to its conclusion.

---

4 Answer the Questions

Questioning Strategies

• What household annual salary do you expect to reach in your future? **Answers will vary. Discuss.**

• Does staying in school pay? **Possible answer: Earning a higher education degree allows many more options for earning more money.**

Teaching Strategies

Earning over one million dollars may seem good enough to many students. Discuss lifetime expenses, such as mortgage/rent, utilities, car payments, insurance, health care, food, etc. How much do you expect to spend in a lifetime?

CLOSE

Journal

Have students write a journal entry in which they summarize the project. Remind them to state the project's problem in their own words and to describe their solution. Also, ask students to outline the main steps they used in order to reach their solution. Ask students to summarize what these conclusions mean to them individually.

Research Options

Students can extend their learning by doing online research to find average salaries associated with different careers, and what kind of education those careers require.

E   Use your equation to predict how many years of school after high school
Will would need to complete in ordered to expect a starting salary of about
$100,000.

$$y = 6,000x + 29,000$$

$$100,000 = 6,000x + 29,000$$

$$71,000 = 6,000x$$

$$\frac{71,000}{6,000} = x$$

$$11.83 \approx x$$

Will would need to complete about 12 years of school after high school.

F   Explain whether you think you could use the equation to determine how
many years of post-high school education would translate into a starting
salary of $1,000,000.

While you could solve the equation for x when $y = 1,000,000$, the

result ($x \approx 162$ years) is not realistic. Equations that model real-world

situations are often subject to limitations.

3 Analyze Data

A   Another study reports that the median starting salary for people with high
school diplomas is $32,000. This study still reports that each additional year of
education yields an additional $6,000 in starting salary. Sketch a graph of the
results from this study. How is the graph different from your original graph?

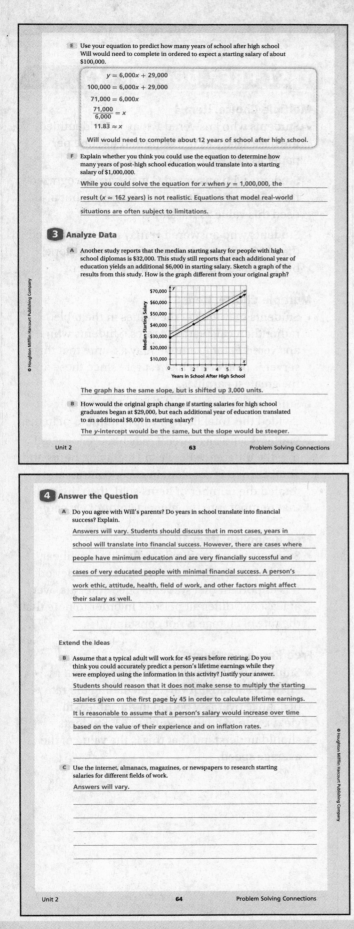

The graph has the same slope, but is shifted up 3,000 units.

B   How would the original graph change if starting salaries for high school
graduates began at $29,000, but each additional year of education translated
to an additional $8,000 in starting salary?

The y-intercept would be the same, but the slope would be steeper.

4 Answer the Question

A   Do you agree with Will's parents? Do years in school translate into financial
success? Explain.

Answers will vary. Students should discuss that in most cases, years in

school will translate into financial success. However, there are cases where

people have minimum education and are very financially successful and

cases of very educated people with minimal financial success. A person's

work ethic, attitude, health, field of work, and other factors might affect

their salary as well.

Extend the Ideas

B   Assume that a typical adult will work for 45 years before retiring. Do you
think you could accurately predict a person's lifetime earnings while they
were employed using the information in this activity? Justify your answer.

Students should reason that it does not make sense to multiply the starting

salaries given on the first page by 45 in order to calculate lifetime earnings.

It is reasonable to assume that a person's salary would increase over time

based on the value of their experience and on inflation rates.

C   Use the internet, almanacs, magazines, or newspapers to research starting
salaries for different fields of work.

Answers will vary.

COMMON CORE CORRELATION

Standard	Items
CC.8.EE.5	3, 10, 12
CC.8.EE.6	10
CC.8.F.1	1
CC.8.F.2	6, 11
CC.8.F.3	2, 7, 13
CC.8.F.4	4, 5
CC.8.F.5	8, 9

TEST PREP DOCTOR ✚

Multiple Choice: Item 4

- Students who answered **F** may have identified the base salary as the slope and the rate per paper as the y-intercept.

- Students who answered **G** may have recognized that 15 corresponds to the y-intercept, but also used this value as the slope.

- Students who answered **H** may have recognized that 0.10 will give the rate of change, or slope, but also used this value as the y-intercept.

Multiple Choice: Item 6

- Students may look at the values in the table rather than calculate the rates. Students who answered **F**, for example, may assume that this server is paid at the highest rate since these are the greatest earnings.

- Students who answered **G** may have simply divided the Total Earned by the number of items.

- Students who answered **J** may have recognized that the difference between Qualifying Items and Total Earned is constant in every column and totaled the number of items sold, then divided that number into the highest amount earned.

Free Response: Item 10

- Students who identified the function as linear, may have only checked the rate for one period. It is important that students check the rate over at least two different periods in order to note that the rate of change is not constant.

Free Response: Item 12

- Students may have different methods, but answers should not vary. Calculating the rate of change over any period in the table will yield a rate of change equal to 65. Students should understand that this is the value of the average speed.

UNIT 2 TEST PREP

Name _____ Class _____ Date _____

MULTIPLE CHOICE

1. Bill keeps track of his study time and test results.

Study Time (hr)	2	4	3	?
Score	80	95	88	82

Which number would complete the table so that the relationship is a function?

A. 1   **C.** 3

B. 2   **D.** 4

2. Which table displays a non-linear function?

F.

Input	1	2	3	4
Output	−2	−1	0	1

G.

Input	1	2	3	4
Output	3	6	9	12

H.

Input	1	2	3	4
Output	1	4	9	16

J.

Input	1	2	3	4
Output	5	7	9	11

3. The graph shows Elisabeth's progress as she reads. Find her unit rate.

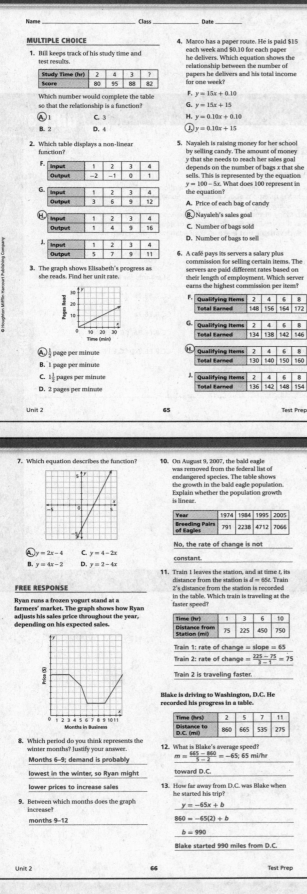

A. $\frac{1}{2}$ page per minute

B. 1 page per minute

C. $1\frac{1}{2}$ pages per minute

D. 2 pages per minute

4. Marco has a paper route. He is paid $15 each week and $0.10 for each paper he delivers. Which equation shows the relationship between the number of papers he delivers and his total income for one week?

F. $y = 15x + 0.10$

G. $y = 15x + 15$

H. $y = 0.10x + 0.10$

J. $y = 0.10x + 15$

5. Nayaleh is raising money for her school by selling candy. The amount of money y that she needs to reach her sales goal depends on the number of bags x that she sells. This is represented by the equation $y = 100 − 5x$. What does 100 represent in the equation?

A. Price of each bag of candy

B. Nayaleh's sales goal

C. Number of bags sold

D. Number of bags to sell

6. A café pays its servers a salary plus commission for selling certain items. The servers are paid different rates based on their length of employment. Which server earns the highest commission per item?

F.

Qualifying Items	2	4	6	8
Total Earned	148	156	164	172

G.

Qualifying Items	2	4	6	8
Total Earned	134	138	142	146

H.

Qualifying Items	2	4	6	8
Total Earned	130	140	150	160

J.

Qualifying Items	2	4	6	8
Total Earned	136	142	148	154

7. Which equation describes the function?

A. $y = 2x − 4$ **C.** $y = 4 − 2x$

B. $y = 4x − 2$ **D.** $y = 2 − 4x$

FREE RESPONSE

Ryan runs a frozen yogurt stand at a farmers' market. The graph shows how Ryan adjusts his sales price throughout the year, depending on his expected sales.

8. Which period do you think represents the winter months? Justify your answer.

Months 6–9; demand is probably

lowest in the winter, so Ryan might

lower prices to increase sales

9. Between which months does the graph increase?

months 9–12

10. On August 9, 2007, the bald eagle was removed from the federal list of endangered species. The table shows the growth in the bald eagle population. Explain whether the population growth is linear.

Year	1974	1984	1995	2005
Breeding Pairs of Eagles	791	2238	4712	7066

No, the rate of change is not

constant.

11. Train 1 leaves the station, and at time t, its distance from the station is $d = 65t$. Train 2's distance from the station is recorded in the table. Which train is traveling at the faster speed?

Time (hr)	1	3	6	10
Distance from Station (mi)	75	225	450	750

Train 1: rate of change = slope = 65

Train 2: rate of change = $\frac{225 − 75}{3 − 1} = 75$

Train 2 is traveling faster.

Blake is driving to Washington, D.C. He recorded his progress in a table.

Time (hrs)	2	5	7	11
Distance to D.C. (mi)	860	665	535	275

12. What is Blake's average speed?

$m = \frac{665 − 860}{5 − 2} = −65$; 65 mi/hr

toward D.C.

13. How far away from D.C. was Blake when he started his trip?

$y = −65x + b$

$860 = −65(2) + b$

$b = 990$

Blake started 990 miles from D.C.

UNIT 3

Equations

Unit Vocabulary

system of equations (3-3)

Equations

Unit Focus

Equations are used to model situations and relationships. They can help you answer questions about a situation. Some situations require more than one equation to completely describe all the relationships in the context. Many of these situations can be described by a system of equations in two variables. Solving a system of equations means finding values for each variable that make all the equations in the system true.

Unit at a Glance

COMMON CORE

Lesson	Standards for Mathematical Content
3-1 Solving Equations	CC.8.EE.7b
3-2 Analyzing Solutions	CC.8.EE.7a
3-3 Solving Systems Graphically	CC.8.EE.8a, CC.8.EE.8c
3-4 Solving Systems Algebraically	CC.8.EE.8b, CC.8.EE.8c
Problem Solving Connections	
Test Prep	

Unpacking the Common Core State Standards

Use the table to help you understand the Common Core State Standards that are taught in this unit. Refer to the lessons listed after each standard for exploration and practice.

COMMON CORE **Standards for Mathematical Content**	**What It Means For You**
CC.8.EE.7a Give examples of linear equations in one variable with one solution, infinitely many solutions, or no solutions. Show which of these possibilities is the case by successively transforming the given equation into simpler forms, until an equivalent equation of the form $x = a$, $a = a$, or $a = b$ results (where a and b are different numbers). Lesson 3-2	Some equations have only one solution. Other equations have so many solutions that you can't count them all. Other equations have no solution. You will learn to recognize how many solutions a particular equation has.
CC.8.EE.7b Solve linear equations with rational number coefficients, including equations whose solutions require expanding expressions using the distributive property and collecting like terms. Lesson 3-1	Simple one-step equations can be solved by applying only one property of equality. Other equations may require you to perform operations with fractions, decimals, or integers, to apply more than one property of equality, or to use other properties of operations, such as the distributive property.
CC.8.EE.8a Understand that solutions to a system of two linear equations in two variables correspond to points of intersection of their graphs, because points of intersection satisfy both equations simultaneously. Lesson 3-3	When you graph the solutions of a linear equation in two variables, the points fall on a line. To solve a system of two equations by graphing, you graph the solutions of each equation in the system. If a point lies on both lines at the same time (the lines intersect at one or more points), then that point is a solution of both equations.
CC.8.EE.8b Solve systems of two linear equations in two variables algebraically, and estimate solutions by graphing the equations. Solve simple cases by inspection. Lesson 3-4	Sometimes it is difficult to identify the solution of a system of equations by graphing. You can use graphing to estimate the solution, but you will need to use algebraic methods to solve the system.
CC.8.EE.8c Solve real-world and mathematical problems leading to two linear equations in two variables. Lessons 3-3, 3-4	Many real-world problems can be solved by writing and solving a system of linear equations. Learning to write and solve systems of equations will allow you to solve these kinds of problems.

Unpacking the Common Core State Standards

This page lists and explains the Standards for Mathematical Content that are addressed in this unit. For information about the Standards for Mathematical Practice, which are integrated throughout the text, see Teacher Edition pages vii–xiii.

Notes

_____

_____

_____

_____

_____

_____

_____

_____

_____

_____

Solving Equations

Essential question: *How do you solve equations by combining like terms and multiplying expressions?*

COMMON CORE Standards for Mathematical Content

CC.8.EE.7b Solve linear equations with rational number coefficients, including equations whose solutions require expanding expressions using the distributive property and collecting like terms.

Prerequisites

Identifying and combining like terms
Solving equations in one variable

Math Background

Solving equations involves finding the value of a variable that makes the equation a true statement. This is accomplished by isolating the variable on one side of the equation and simplifying the expression on the other side. To solve some equations, you need to combine like terms. This means to add or subtract terms that have the same variable raised to the same exponent. For example, $2x + 3x$ can be simplified as $5x$. Other equations require you to expand an expression using the Distributive Property. For example, $2(x + 3) = 2(x) + 2(3) = 2x + 6$. To solve equations with variables on both sides, use properties of equality to "move" all the constants to one side of the equation and all the variable terms to the other side. Continue until the variable is isolated and the expression on the other side is simplified.

INTRODUCE

Connect to prior learning by asking students to identify like terms such as $5x$, $-3x$, and $2.5x$. Ask students to explain how to use the Distributive Property to show that $2(3 + 4) = 14$. Explain that equations can be used to represent real-world situations. For example, an equation may be used to calculate the cost of a cell phone bill. Constants and variables in equations represent fixed and variable amounts, such as a flat fee per month plus the cost per minute over a certain number of minutes. In this lesson, students will solve equations by combining like terms and using the Distributive Property.

TEACH

1 EXPLORE

Questioning Strategies

- What is the difference between a fixed cost and a variable cost? **The fixed cost does not change. The variable cost depends on the number of trophies.**

- How do you know what value to use for the Club's total cost? **The club spent $97.50 on trophies.**

Differentiated Instruction

Visual and kinesthetic learners may benefit from a hands-on approach to solving the equation in Part D. Have students use algebra tiles to model a similar equation that uses simpler numbers, such as $3 + 2x + 4 + x = 13$. On the left side of an equation mat, place a group of 3 unit-tiles, a group of 2 x-tiles, a group of 4 unit-tiles, and 1 x-tile. On the right side, place 13 unit-tiles. Students can model combining the like terms on the left side before performing operations on both sides of the equation to solve for x.

2 EXPLORE

Questioning Strategies

- What does the variable x represent in this situation? **Carla's number**

- What key words can help you write an equation? **subtract, multiply, quantity, add, result**

- How do you use the Distributive Property to simplify an expression? **Multiply the term outside the parentheses by each term inside the parentheses. Then combine like terms.**

Teaching Strategies

Help students translate the keywords in the problem. For example, *multiply* means multiplication, *quantity* probably means there is an expression inside parentheses, and *result* means the value on the other side of the equal sign. Verify that students write the equation as $4(x - 5) + 7 = 35$.

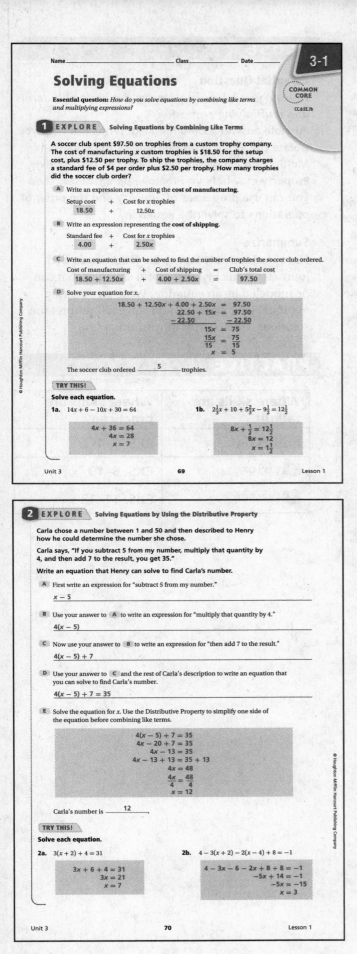

Solving Equations

Essential question: *How do you solve equations by combining like terms and multiplying expressions?*

3-1

COMMON CORE

CC.8.EE.7b

1 EXPLORE Solving Equations by Combining Like Terms

A soccer club spent $97.50 on trophies from a custom trophy company. The cost of manufacturing x custom trophies is $18.50 for the setup cost, plus $12.50 per trophy. To ship the trophies, the company charges a standard fee of $4 per order plus $2.50 per trophy. How many trophies did the soccer club order?

A Write an expression representing the **cost of manufacturing**.

Setup cost + Cost for x trophies
18.50 + 12.50x

B Write an expression representing the **cost of shipping**.

Standard fee + Cost for x trophies
4.00 + 2.50x

C Write an equation that can be solved to find the number of trophies the soccer club ordered.

Cost of manufacturing	+	Cost of shipping	=	Club's total cost
18.50 + 12.50x	+	4.00 + 2.50x	=	97.50

D Solve your equation for x.

$$18.50 + 12.50x + 4.00 + 2.50x = 97.50$$
$$22.50 + 15x = 97.50$$
$$-22.50 \qquad -22.50$$
$$15x = 75$$
$$\frac{15x}{15} = \frac{75}{15}$$
$$x = 5$$

The soccer club ordered ___5___ trophies.

TRY THIS!

Solve each equation.

1a. $14x + 6 - 10x + 30 = 64$

$$4x + 36 = 64$$
$$4x = 28$$
$$x = 7$$

1b. $2\frac{1}{3}x + 10 + 5\frac{2}{3}x - 9\frac{1}{2} = 12\frac{1}{2}$

$$8x + \frac{1}{2} = 12\frac{1}{2}$$
$$8x = 12$$
$$x = 1\frac{1}{2}$$

Unit 3   69   Lesson 1

© Houghton Mifflin Harcourt Publishing Company

2 EXPLORE Solving Equations by Using the Distributive Property

Carla chose a number between 1 and 50 and then described to Henry how he could determine the number she chose.

Carla says, "If you subtract 5 from my number, multiply that quantity by 4, and then add 7 to the result, you get 35."

Write an equation that Henry can solve to find Carla's number.

A First write an expression for "subtract 5 from my number."

$x - 5$

B Use your answer to **A** to write an expression for "multiply that quantity by 4."

$4(x - 5)$

C Now use your answer to **B** to write an expression for "then add 7 to the result."

$4(x - 5) + 7$

D Use your answer to **C** and the rest of Carla's description to write an equation that you can solve to find Carla's number.

$4(x - 5) + 7 = 35$

E Solve the equation for x. Use the Distributive Property to simplify one side of the equation before combining like terms.

$$4(x - 5) + 7 = 35$$
$$4x - 20 + 7 = 35$$
$$4x - 13 = 35$$
$$4x - 13 + 13 = 35 + 13$$
$$4x = 48$$
$$\frac{4x}{4} = \frac{48}{4}$$
$$x = 12$$

Carla's number is ___12___.

TRY THIS!

Solve each equation.

2a. $3(x + 2) + 4 = 31$

$$3x + 6 + 4 = 31$$
$$3x = 21$$
$$x = 7$$

2b. $4 - 3(x + 2) - 2(x - 4) + 8 = -1$

$$4 - 3x - 6 - 2x + 8 + 8 = -1$$
$$-5x + 14 = -1$$
$$-5x = -15$$
$$x = 3$$

© Houghton Mifflin Harcourt Publishing Company

Unit 3   70   Lesson 1

Questioning Strategies

- For each gym, identify the fixed amount and the variable amount. The fixed amount is the flat fee per month for membership. The variable amount is the cost for *x* training sessions.

- What keyword or phrase in the original problem tells you how to set up the equation for Part D? The phrase "cost at the two gyms equal" tells you to write an equation that sets the expressions for total cost at each gym equal to each other.

Avoid Common Errors

Show students that the variable amount (cost for *x* training sessions) depends on the number of training sessions (*x*). The cost for training sessions is greater when the number of training sessions is greater.

MATHEMATICAL PRACTICE **Highlighting the Standards**

This example is an opportunity to address Standard 4 (Model with mathematics). Students are asked to model real-world situations using fixed and variable costs. Students solve an equation to determine how many training sessions Sarah needs to buy to make the total costs at the two gyms equal.

CLOSE

Essential Question

How do you solve equations by combining like terms and multiplying expressions?
Possible answer: Combining like terms can help you isolate the variable on one side of the equation. Multiplying expressions by using the Distributive Property may help you remove parentheses. Then you can use properties of equality and the order of operations to solve the equation.

Summarize

Have students respond to the following in their journals: Think of a real-world situation that can be modeled by an equation. Write an equation to model your situation and solve it. Interpret the solution in the context of your situation.

PRACTICE

Where skills are taught	Where skills are practiced
1 EXPLORE	EXS. 1–4
2 EXPLORE	EXS. 5–10
3 EXPLORE	EXS. 11–13

3 EXPLORE Solving Equations with Variables on Both Sides

At Silver Gym, membership is $25 per month, and personal training sessions are $30 each. At Fit Factor, membership is $65 per month, and personal training sessions are $20 each. In one month, how many personal training sessions would Sarah have to buy to make the total cost at the two gyms equal?

A Write an expression representing the **total monthly cost at Silver Gym**.

Monthly membership	+	Cost for x training sessions
25	+	$30x$

B Write an expression representing the **total monthly cost at Fit Factor**.

Monthly membership	+	Cost for x training sessions
65	+	$20x$

C How can you find the number of personal training sessions in one month that would make the total costs of the gyms equal?

Set the expressions equal to each other and solve for x.

D Write an equation that can be solved to find the number of training sessions in one month that makes the total costs equal.

Total cost at Silver Gym = Total cost at Fit Factor

$$25 + 30x = 65 + 20x$$

E Solve the equation for x. Use inverse operations to get all variable terms on one side of the equation and all constants on the other side.

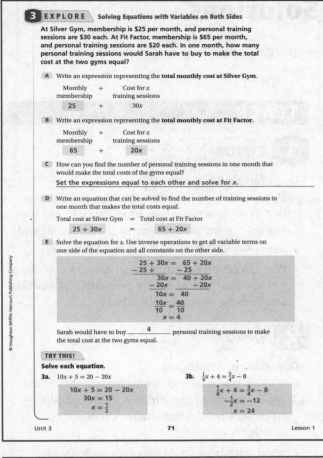

$$
\begin{aligned}
25 + 30x &= 65 + 20x \\
-25 & -25 \\
30x &= 40 + 20x \\
-20x & -20x \\
10x &= 40 \\
\frac{10x}{10} &= \frac{40}{10} \\
x &= 4
\end{aligned}
$$

Sarah would have to buy ____4____ personal training sessions to make the total cost at the two gyms equal.

TRY THIS!

Solve each equation.

3a. $10x + 5 = 20 - 20x$

$$
\begin{aligned}
10x + 5 &= 20 - 20x \\
30x &= 15 \\
x &= \tfrac{1}{2}
\end{aligned}
$$

3b. $\frac{1}{4}x + 4 = \frac{3}{4}x - 8$

$$
\begin{aligned}
\tfrac{1}{4}x + 4 &= \tfrac{3}{4}x - 8 \\
-\tfrac{1}{2}x &= -12 \\
x &= 24
\end{aligned}
$$

PRACTICE

Solve each equation.

1. $3x + 4 + 2x + 5 = 34$

$x = 5$

2. $2.5x - 5 + 3x + 8 = 19.5$

$x = 3$

3. $\frac{1}{2}x + 6 - 2x + \frac{1}{2} = \frac{7}{2}$

$x = 2$

4. $-10x - 3 - 2.5x + 20 = 67$

$x = -4$

5. $2(x + 1) + 4 = 12$

$x = 3$

6. $-3(x + 4) + 15 = -12$

$x = 5$

7. $15 - 3(x - 1) = 12$

$x = 2$

8. $3(x - 2) + 2(x + 1) = -14$

$x = -2$

9. $\frac{1}{2}(x + 8) - 15 = -3$

$x = 16$

10. $2.5(x + 2) + 4.5 + 1.5(x - 3) = 15$

$x = 2.5$

The monthly membership dues and private lesson fees at three tennis clubs are shown in the table.

	Club A	Club B	Club C
Monthly Membership Dues	$25	$55	$15
Private Lesson Fee	$30	$20	$40

11. After how many private lessons in one month is the total monthly cost of Club A equal to the total monthly cost at Club B?

3 lessons

12. After how many private lessons in one month is the total monthly cost of Club A equal to the total monthly cost at Club C?

1 lesson

13. After how many private lessons in one month is the total monthly cost of Club B equal to the total monthly cost at Club C?

2 lessons

Analyzing Solutions

Essential question: How can you give examples of equations with a given number of solutions?

Standards for Mathematical Content

CC.8.EE.7a Give examples of linear equations in one variable with one solution, infinitely many solutions, or no solutions. Show which of these possibilities is the case by successively transforming the given equation into simpler forms, until an equivalent equation of the form $x = a$, $a = a$, or $a = b$ results (where a and b are different numbers).

Prerequisites

Solving multi-step equations

Math Background

Linear equations assume many forms. In this lesson, students work with linear equations in one variable. The standard form of a linear equation in one variable is $ax + b = c$, though not every linear equation is presented in the standard form.

Every linear equation in one variable can be simplified to one of three forms: $x = a$, $a = a$, or $a = b$ (for $a \neq b$). When an equation simplifies to $x = a$, the equation is true only when the variable assumes the value a, and the equation has only one solution. When an equation simplifies to $a = a$, there are infinitely many solutions because this statement is true for any value of the variable. When an equation simplifies to $a = b$ (for $a \neq b$), the equation has no solutions because there is no value of the variable that will make a equal to b.

INTRODUCE

In your everyday life, some questions have exactly one answer: "Who is your homeroom teacher?". Other questions have many right answers: "Who is your friend?". Tell students that in this lesson, they will learn to analyze linear equations to determine whether they have one solution, many solutions, or no solution at all.

TEACH

1 EXPLORE

Questioning Strategies

- How would you begin to simplify the equation in Part A? **Use properties of equality to get the variable terms on one side of the equation and the constant terms on the other side.**

- Why isn't the final equation in Part C in the form $x = a$? **When you used the properties of equality, the variable terms simplified to 0.**

2 EXPLORE

Questioning Strategies

- Why do you start with a false statement? **There are no values of the variable that make the statement true, which means there are no solutions.**

- What statement could you start with if you wanted to write a linear equation that has many solutions? **Any statement in the form $a = a$, such as $2 = 2$.**

MATHEMATICAL PRACTICE — **Highlighting the Standards**

This Lesson is an opportunity to address Standard 7 (Look for and make use of structure). Students should look at the "big picture" as they work. Guide them to see patterns in the processes of simplifying and building equations.

CLOSE

Essential Question

How can you give examples of equations with a given number of solutions?

Equations that simplify to the form $x = a$ have one solution, equations that simplify to the form $a = a$ have many solutions, and equations that simplify to the form $a = b$ have no solution.

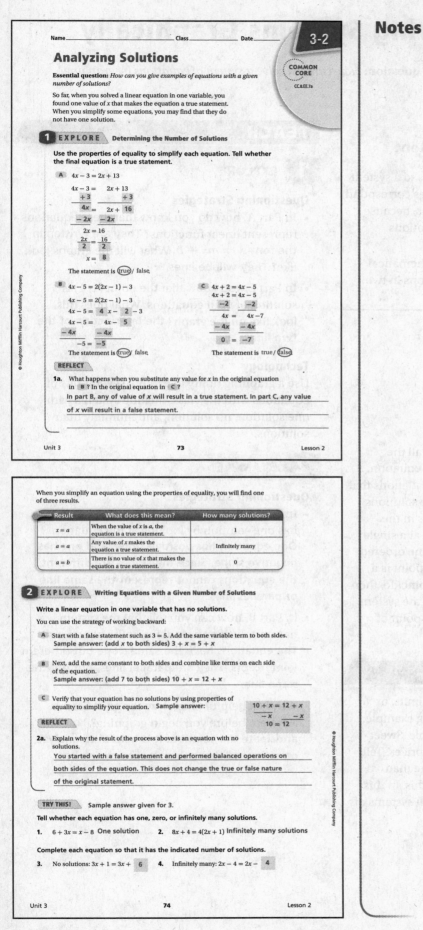

Analyzing Solutions

3-2

COMMON
CORE
CC.8.EE.7a

Essential question: *How can you give examples of equations with a given number of solutions?*

So far, when you solved a linear equation in one variable, you found one value of x that makes the equation a true statement. When you simplify some equations, you may find that they do not have one solution.

1 EXPLORE   Determining the Number of Solutions

Use the properties of equality to simplify each equation. Tell whether the final equation is a true statement.

A $4x - 3 = 2x + 13$

$$\begin{array}{r} 4x - 3 = \quad 2x + 13 \\ \underline{+3} \qquad \underline{+3} \\ 4x \qquad 2x + 16 \\ \underline{-2x} \quad \underline{-2x} \\ 2x = 16 \\ \frac{2x}{2} = \frac{16}{2} \\ x = 8 \end{array}$$

The statement is (true)/ false.

B $4x - 5 = 2(2x - 1) - 3$

$4x - 5 = 2(2x - 1) - 3$

$4x - 5 = \boxed{4} \; x - \boxed{2} - 3$

$4x - 5 = \quad 4x - \boxed{5}$

$\underline{-4x} \qquad \underline{-4x}$

$-5 = -5$

The statement is (true)/ false.

C $4x + 2 = 4x - 5$

$4x + 2 = 4x - 5$

$\underline{-2} \qquad \underline{-2}$

$4x = \quad 4x - 7$

$\underline{-4x} \quad \underline{-4x}$

$0 = -7$

The statement is true / (false).

REFLECT

1a. What happens when you substitute any value for x in the original equation in   B ? In the original equation in   C ?

In part B, any of value of x will result in a true statement. In part C, any value

of x will result in a false statement.

© Houghton Mifflin Harcourt Publishing Company

When you simplify an equation using the properties of equality, you will find one of three results.

Result	What does this mean?	How many solutions?
$x = a$	When the value of x is a, the equation is a true statement.	1
$a = a$	Any value of x makes the equation a true statement.	Infinitely many
$a = b$	There is no value of x that makes the equation a true statement.	0

2 EXPLORE   Writing Equations with a Given Number of Solutions

Write a linear equation in one variable that has no solutions.

You can use the strategy of working backward:

A   Start with a false statement such as $3 = 5$. Add the same variable term to both sides.
Sample answer: (add x to both sides) $3 + x = 5 + x$

B   Next, add the same constant to both sides and combine like terms on each side of the equation.
Sample answer: (add 7 to both sides) $10 + x = 12 + x$

C   Verify that your equation has no solutions by using properties of equality to simplify your equation.   Sample answer:

$$\begin{array}{r} 10 + x = 12 + x \\ \underline{-x} \qquad \underline{-x} \\ 10 = 12 \end{array}$$

REFLECT

2a. Explain why the result of the process above is an equation with no solutions.

You started with a false statement and performed balanced operations on

both sides of the equation. This does not change the true or false nature

of the original statement.

TRY THIS!   Sample answer given for 3.

Tell whether each equation has one, zero, or infinitely many solutions.

1. $6 + 3x = x - 8$ One solution   **2.** $8x + 4 = 4(2x + 1)$ Infinitely many solutions

Complete each equation so that it has the indicated number of solutions.

3.   No solutions: $3x + 1 = 3x + \boxed{6}$ **4.**   Infinitely many: $2x - 4 = 2x - \boxed{4}$

© Houghton Mifflin Harcourt Publishing Company

Notes

Solving Systems Graphically

Essential question: *How can you solve a system of equations by graphing?*

COMMON CORE · **Standards for Mathematical Content**

CC.8.EE.8a Understand that solutions to a system of two linear equations in two variables correspond to points of intersection of their graphs, because points of intersection satisfy both equations simultaneously.

CC.8.EE.8c Solve real-world and mathematical problems leading to two linear equations in two variables.

Vocabulary

system of equations

Prerequisites

Solving equations

Graphing in the coordinate plane

Math Background

The graph of a function is a picture of all the ordered pairs that are solutions of the equation. A system of linear equations is a set of equations that have the same variables. Graphing the solutions of the equations results in a set of lines in the coordinate plane. If the lines intersect at a single point, then that point represents the one ordered pair that satisfies each equation. This point is a solution of the system. If the graphs coincide, then every point on the line is a solution of the system. Systems with no solution will have no point of intersection.

INTRODUCE

Real-life situations can be affected by limits, or constraints. Give students the following example: You have $20 to buy snacks for 10 people. Sweet snacks and salty snacks have different prices. Tell students that they will need to use more than one equation to model situations like this. In this lesson, students will learn how to graph systems of equations to solve problems.

TEACH

1 EXPLORE

Questioning Strategies

- In Part A, how do you know that these equations represent linear functions? **They are written in the form** $y = mx + b$**. What will the graphs look like? They will be lines.**

- In Part E, you know that the point $(1, 1)$ is a solution of both equations. What does this look like on the graph? **the intersection of the two lines**

Technology

Use a graphing utility to explore several sets of equations with the class. Include systems with one solution, no solution, and infinitely many solutions.

2 EXAMPLE

Questioning Strategies

- In Part A, how can you tell that the system has one solution by looking at the equations? **One equation has positive slope, and one has negative slope. Since the slopes are different, the equations cannot represent the same line or parallel lines.**

- In Part B, how can you tell that the system has no solutions by looking at the equations? **The equations have the same slope but different** y**-intercepts. They are parallel lines, but not the same line.**

- Why is it helpful to analyze the equations in a system before you begin graphing? **You can anticipate the solution. It is helpful to analyze equations to recognize algebraic mistakes.**

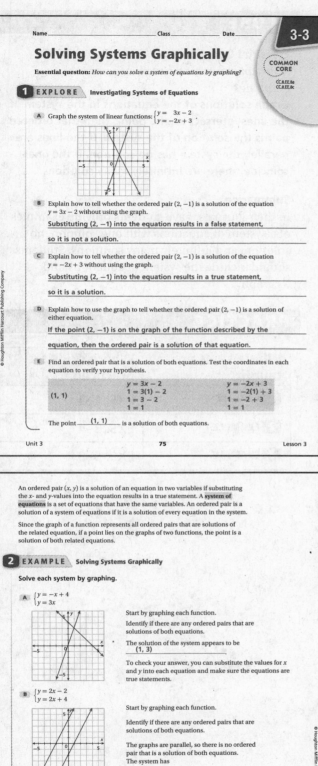

Name _____ Class _____ Date _____

3-3

Solving Systems Graphically

Essential question: *How can you solve a system of equations by graphing?*

COMMON CORE
CC.8.EE.8a
CC.8.EE.8c

1 EXPLORE Investigating Systems of Equations

A Graph the system of linear functions: $\begin{cases} y = 3x - 2 \\ y = -2x + 3 \end{cases}$

B Explain how to tell whether the ordered pair $(2, -1)$ is a solution of the equation $y = 3x - 2$ without using the graph.

Substituting $(2, -1)$ into the equation results in a false statement,

so it is not a solution.

C Explain how to tell whether the ordered pair $(2, -1)$ is a solution of the equation $y = -2x + 3$ without using the graph.

Substituting $(2, -1)$ into the equation results in a true statement,

so it is a solution.

D Explain how to use the graph to tell whether the ordered pair $(2, -1)$ is a solution of either equation.

If the point $(2, -1)$ is on the graph of the function described by the

equation, then the ordered pair is a solution of that equation.

E Find an ordered pair that is a solution of both equations. Test the coordinates in each equation to verify your hypothesis.

$(1, 1)$	$y = 3x - 2$	$y = -2x + 3$
	$1 = 3(1) - 2$	$1 = -2(1) + 3$
	$1 = 3 - 2$	$1 = -2 + 3$
	$1 = 1$	$1 = 1$

The point ___(1, 1)___ is a solution of both equations.

© Houghton Mifflin Harcourt Publishing Company

An ordered pair (x, y) is a solution of an equation in two variables if substituting the x- and y-values into the equation results in a true statement. A **system of equations** is a set of equations that have the same variables. An ordered pair is a solution of a system of equations if it is a solution of every equation in the system.

Since the graph of a function represents all ordered pairs that are solutions of the related equation, if a point lies on the graphs of two functions, the point is a solution of both related equations.

2 EXAMPLE Solving Systems Graphically

Solve each system by graphing.

A $\begin{cases} y = -x + 4 \\ y = 3x \end{cases}$

Start by graphing each function.

Identify if there are any ordered pairs that are solutions of both equations.

The solution of the system appears to be ___(1, 3)___

To check your answer, you can substitute the values for x and y into each equation and make sure the equations are true statements.

B $\begin{cases} y = 2x - 2 \\ y = 2x + 4 \end{cases}$

Start by graphing each function.

Identify if there are any ordered pairs that are solutions of both equations.

The graphs are parallel, so there is no ordered pair that is a solution of both equations. The system has

___no solutions___

C $\begin{cases} y = 3x - 3 \\ y = 3(x - 1) \end{cases}$

Start by graphing each function.

Identify if there are any ordered pairs that are solutions of both equations.

The graphs overlap, so every ordered pair that is a solution of one equation is also a solution of the other equation. The system has

___infinitely many solutions___

© Houghton Mifflin Harcourt Publishing Company

Questioning Strategies

• How do you decide what the variables represent? The variables represent the information you are looking for: how many hot dogs and how many drinks.

• In Part B, why do you rewrite the equations? Slope-intercept form makes it easy to sketch a graph of the solutions.

• How can you use the graph in Part C to tell how many solutions the system has? The lines intersect at one point, so there is one solution.

• In Part D, why is it important to check your solution by substituting the solution into each original equation? You might have made a mistake when sketching the graphs.

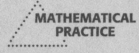

MATHEMATICAL PRACTICE **Highlighting the Standards**

This Example is an opportunity to address Standard 2 (Reason abstractly and quantitatively). Students must reason quantitatively to correctly sketch the graphs described by a system of equations. They must reason abstractly to analyze the graphs and draw conclusions about the solution(s) of the system. Quantitative reasoning is required to write equations that define a system. Abstract reasoning is needed to analyze the solution in order to determine whether or not it makes sense in the context of the problem.

CLOSE

Essential Question

How can you solve a system of equations by graphing?
Graph solutions of the equations in the system. If the lines intersect at one point, then that ordered pair is the solution of the system. If the lines are parallel, the system has no solution. If the lines coincide, there are infinitely many solutions.

Summarize

In their journals, have students provide examples of a system of equations with one solution, no solution, and infinitely many solutions. Students should include the system of equations and its graph.

PRACTICE

Where skills are taught	Where skills are practiced
1 EXPLORE	EXS. 1–2
2 EXAMPLE	EXS. 3–4
3 EXAMPLE	EXS. 5–8

3 EXAMPLE Solving a Real-World Problem by Graphing

Keisha and her friends visit the concession stand at a football game. The stand charges $2 for a hot dog and $1 for a drink. The friends buy a total of 8 items for $11. Tell how many hot dogs and how many drinks they bought.

A Let x represent the number of hot dogs they bought and y represent the number of drinks they bought.

Write an equation representing the **number of items they purchased**.

Number of hot dogs	+	Number of drinks	=	Total items
x	+	y	=	8

Write an equation representing the **money spent on the items**.

Cost of 1 hot dog times number of hot dogs	+	Cost of 1 drink times number of drinks	=	Total cost
$2x$	+	$1y$	=	11

B Write your equations in slope-intercept form.

$y = -x + 8; y = -2x + 11$

C Graph the solutions of both equations.

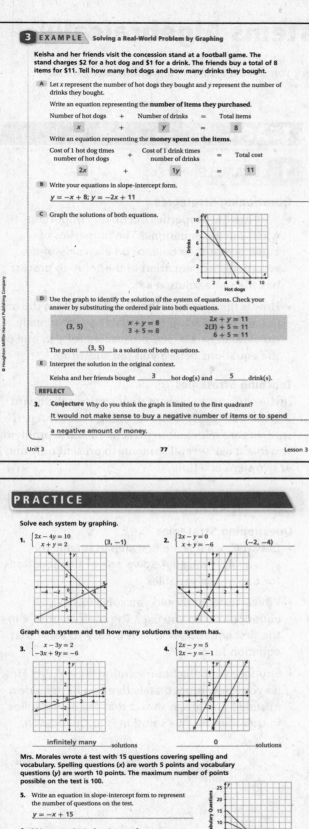

D Use the graph to identify the solution of the system of equations. Check your answer by substituting the ordered pair into both equations.

(3, 5)	$x + y = 8$	$2x + y = 11$
	$3 + 5 = 8$	$2(3) + 5 = 11$
		$6 + 5 = 11$

The point ___(3, 5)___ is a solution of both equations.

E Interpret the solution in the original context.

Keisha and her friends bought ___3___ hot dog(s) and ___5___ drink(s).

REFLECT

3. **Conjecture** Why do you think the graph is limited to the first quadrant?

It would not make sense to buy a negative number of items or to spend

a negative amount of money.

PRACTICE

Solve each system by graphing.

1. $\begin{cases} 2x - 4y = 10 \\ x + y = 2 \end{cases}$ ___(3, −1)___

2. $\begin{cases} 2x - y = 0 \\ x + y = -6 \end{cases}$ ___(−2, −4)___

Graph each system and tell how many solutions the system has.

3. $\begin{cases} x - 3y = 2 \\ -3x + 9y = -6 \end{cases}$

___infinitely many___ solutions

4. $\begin{cases} 2x - y = 5 \\ 2x - y = -1 \end{cases}$

___0___ solutions

Mrs. Morales wrote a test with 15 questions covering spelling and vocabulary. Spelling questions (x) are worth 5 points and vocabulary questions (y) are worth 10 points. The maximum number of points possible on the test is 100.

5. Write an equation in slope-intercept form to represent the number of questions on the test.

$y = -x + 15$

6. Write an equation in slope-intercept form to represent the total points on the test.

$y = -0.5x + 10$

7. Graph the solutions of both equations.

8. Use your graph to tell how many of each question type are on the test.

___10___ spelling questions; ___5___ vocabulary questions

Solving Systems Algebraically

Essential question: *How can you solve a system of equations algebraically?*

COMMON CORE

Standards for Mathematical Content

CC.8.EE.8b Solve systems of two linear equations in two variables algebraically, and estimate solutions by graphing the equations. Solve simple cases by inspection.

CC.8.EE.8c Solve real-world and mathematical problems leading to two linear equations in two variables.

Prerequisites

Solving systems of equations graphically

Slope-intercept form

Math Background

It may be difficult to use a graph to solve equations with very large values or when the solution has non-integer coordinates. Sometimes an approximate solution is sufficient. For instance, when comparing prices from two different companies, a graph might clearly show that when buying fewer than about 30 items, Company A has lower prices than Company B. This may be enough information for you to make a decision. In other situations, an exact solution is needed. In these cases, you will need to solve the system algebraically.

INTRODUCE

Sketch the graph of a system of equations with decimal solutions on the board. For example, graph $2x - y = 6$ and $3x + y = 10$. Invite students to try solving the system using the graphs. Check students' solutions by substituting values for the variables in the equations. Discuss why solving this system graphically is difficult.

TEACH

1 EXAMPLE

Questioning Strategies

• Why are the properties of equality important when solving equations? **The properties of equality maintain balance on each side of the equation. Each equation in the solution process has the same solution set.**

• How is the system in Part B different from the one in Part A? **In Part A, the variable *y* was already isolated. In Part B, you must solve for *y* in one of the equations before you can substitute.**

Teaching Strategies

Invite students to present their work on the board. Ask them to justify their reasoning at each step. If students are reluctant to present an entire problem, you might ask several students to present only one or two steps at a time.

2 EXAMPLE

Questioning Strategies

• In Part C, what is the first step in solving the system algebraically? **Solve one of the equations for one of the variables.**

• Which variable should you solve for? Which equation should you use? **The coefficient of *x* in the first equation is 1, so it is easy to solve that equation for *x*.**

• Suppose your algebraic solution is $\left(-\frac{11}{5}, \frac{24}{5}\right)$. How do you know immediately that you have made a mistake? **The graph shows that the solution lies in Quadrant III. This solution is in Quadrant II.**

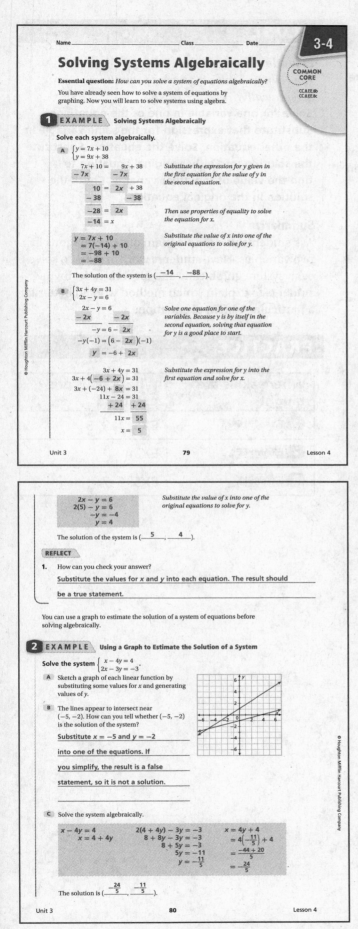

Name_____ Class_____ Date_____

Solving Systems Algebraically

Essential question: *How can you solve a system of equations algebraically?*

You have already seen how to solve a system of equations by graphing. Now you will learn to solve systems using algebra.

1 EXAMPLE Solving Systems Algebraically

Solve each system algebraically.

A $\begin{cases} y = 7x + 10 \\ y = 9x + 38 \end{cases}$

$7x + 10 = 9x + 38$
$\underline{-7x \qquad -7x}$

Substitute the expression for y given in the first equation for the value of y in the second equation.

$10 = 2x + 38$
$\underline{-38 \qquad -38}$

$-28 = 2x$
$-14 = x$

Then use properties of equality to solve the equation for x.

$y = 7x + 10$
$= 7(-14) + 10$
$= -98 + 10$
$= -88$

Substitute the value of x into one of the original equations to solve for y.

The solution of the system is (-14 , -88).

B $\begin{cases} 3x + 4y = 31 \\ 2x - y = 6 \end{cases}$

$2x - y = 6$
$\underline{-2x \qquad -2x}$
$-y = 6 - 2x$
$-y(-1) = (6 - 2x)(-1)$
$y = -6 + 2x$

Solve one equation for one of the variables. Because y is by itself in the second equation, solving that equation for y is a good place to start.

$3x + 4y = 31$
$3x + 4(-6 + 2x) = 31$
$3x + (-24) + 8x = 31$
$11x - 24 = 31$
$\underline{+24 \qquad +24}$
$11x = 55$
$x = 5$

Substitute the expression for y into the first equation and solve for x.

$2x - y = 6$
$2(5) - y = 6$
$-y = -4$
$y = 4$

Substitute the value of x into one of the original equations to solve for y.

The solution of the system is (5 , 4).

REFLECT

1. How can you check your answer?

Substitute the values for x and y into each equation. The result should be a true statement.

You can use a graph to estimate the solution of a system of equations before solving algebraically.

2 EXAMPLE Using a Graph to Estimate the Solution of a System

Solve the system $\begin{cases} x - 4y = 4 \\ 2x - 3y = -3 \end{cases}$.

A Sketch a graph of each linear function by substituting some values for x and generating values of y.

B The lines appear to intersect near $(-5, -2)$. How can you tell whether $(-5, -2)$ is the solution of the system?

Substitute $x = -5$ and $y = -2$ into one of the equations. If you simplify, the result is a false statement, so it is not a solution.

C Solve the system algebraically.

$x - 4y = 4$
$x = 4 + 4y$

$2(4 + 4y) - 3y = -3$
$8 + 8y - 3y = -3$
$8 + 5y = -3$
$5y = -11$
$y = -\frac{11}{5}$

$x = 4y + 4$
$= 4\left(-\frac{11}{5}\right) + 4$
$= \frac{-44 + 20}{5}$
$= -\frac{24}{5}$

The solution is ($-\frac{24}{5}$, $-\frac{11}{5}$).

Questioning Strategies

- How do you find the slope of a line? **Calculate the ratio of the change in *y* to the change in *x*.**

- How do you write an equation in slope-intercept form? **Start with the general form $y = mx + b$. Then substitute the coordinates of a known point for *x* and *y* and the slope for *m*. Solve for *b*. Then return to the general form and substitute for *m* and *b*.**

Avoid Common Errors

Students may calculate the slope for an incorrect combination of points (for example, the slope of the lines connecting A with C and B with D). They should double-check their work. Students can check their work by comparing their calculated slopes to the lines on the graph. The graph shows that one slope is positive and one is negative.

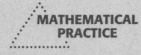

MATHEMATICAL PRACTICE	Highlighting the Standards

This Example is an opportunity to address Standard 5 (Use appropriate tools strategically). Students must choose when to solve a system graphically and when to solve a system algebraically. Students need to think strategically to solve the problem in the most efficient manner. Present several problem-solving situations to students and ask them to determine the best approach to solving the problem. Ask students why they prefer one method over another.

CLOSE

Essential Question

How can you solve a system of equations algebraically?

Solve for one variable in one of the equations. Substitute that expression for the same variable in the other equation. Solve the equation. Substitute the solution into either original equation to find the value of the other variable. Check the solution in the original equations.

Summarize

Ask students to write a system of two equations in two variables. Have students work in pairs to solve each system graphically and algebraically. Invite students to explain which method worked better for a particular system of equations.

PRACTICE

Where skills are taught	Where skills are practiced
1 EXAMPLE	EXS. 1–3, 5
2 EXAMPLE	EX. 4
3 EXAMPLE	EXS. 6–7

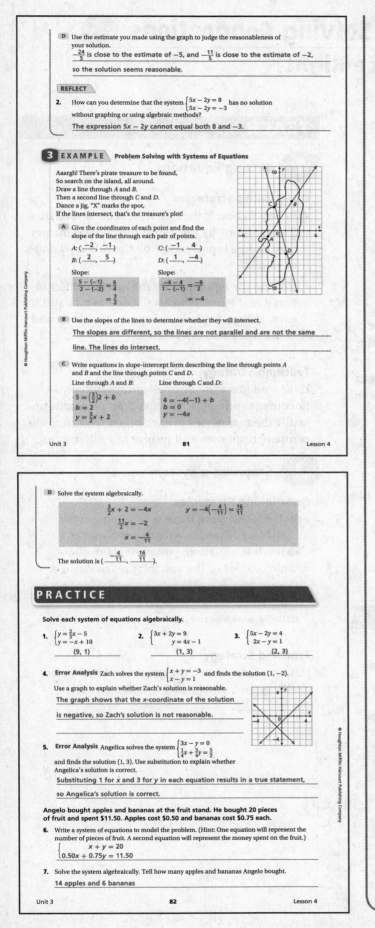

D Use the estimate you made using the graph to judge the reasonableness of your solution.

$-\frac{24}{5}$ is close to the estimate of -5, and $-\frac{11}{5}$ is close to the estimate of -2, so the solution seems reasonable.

REFLECT

2. How can you determine that the system $\begin{cases} 5x - 2y = 8 \\ 5x - 2y = -3 \end{cases}$ has no solution without graphing or using algebraic methods?

The expression $5x - 2y$ cannot equal both 8 and -3.

3 EXAMPLE Problem Solving with Systems of Equations

Aaargh! There's pirate treasure to be found,
So search on the island, all around.
Draw a line through A and B.
Then a second line through C and D.
Dance a jig, "X" marks the spot,
If the lines intersect, that's the treasure's plot!

A Give the coordinates of each point and find the slope of the line through each pair of points.

$A: (\underline{-2}, \underline{-1})$ $C: (\underline{-1}, \underline{4})$

$B: (\underline{2}, \underline{5})$ $D: (\underline{1}, \underline{-4})$

Slope: Slope:

$\dfrac{5-(-1)}{2-(-2)} = \dfrac{6}{4}$ $\dfrac{-4-4}{1-(-1)} = \dfrac{-8}{2}$

$\qquad\qquad = \dfrac{3}{2}$ $\qquad\qquad = -4$

B Use the slopes of the lines to determine whether they will intersect.

The slopes are different, so the lines are not parallel and are not the same line. The lines do intersect.

C Write equations in slope-intercept form describing the line through points A and B and the line through points C and D.

Line through A and B: Line through C and D:

$5 = \left(\dfrac{3}{2}\right)2 + b$ $4 = -4(-1) + b$

$b = 2$ $b = 0$

$y = \dfrac{3}{2}x + 2$ $y = -4x$

D Solve the system algebraically.

$\dfrac{3}{2}x + 2 = -4x$ $y = -4\left(-\dfrac{4}{11}\right) = \dfrac{16}{11}$

$\dfrac{11}{2}x = -2$

$x = -\dfrac{4}{11}$

The solution is $(\underline{-\dfrac{4}{11}}, \underline{\dfrac{16}{11}})$.

PRACTICE

Solve each system of equations algebraically.

1. $\begin{cases} y = \frac{2}{3}x - 5 \\ y = -x + 10 \end{cases}$ 2. $\begin{cases} 3x + 2y = 9 \\ y = 4x - 1 \end{cases}$ 3. $\begin{cases} 5x - 2y = 4 \\ 2x - y = 1 \end{cases}$

   (9, 1)   (1, 3)   (2, 3)

4. **Error Analysis** Zach solves the system $\begin{cases} x + y = -3 \\ x - y = 1 \end{cases}$ and finds the solution $(1, -2)$.

   Use a graph to explain whether Zach's solution is reasonable.

   The graph shows that the x-coordinate of the solution

   is negative, so Zach's solution is not reasonable.

5. **Error Analysis** Angelica solves the system $\begin{cases} 3x - y = 0 \\ \frac{1}{4}x + \frac{3}{4}y = \frac{5}{2} \end{cases}$

   and finds the solution $(1, 3)$. Use substitution to explain whether Angelica's solution is correct.

   Substituting 1 for x and 3 for y in each equation results in a true statement,

   so Angelica's solution is correct.

Angelo bought apples and bananas at the fruit stand. He bought 20 pieces of fruit and spent $11.50. Apples cost $0.50 and bananas cost $0.75 each.

6. Write a system of equations to model the problem. (Hint: One equation will represent the number of pieces of fruit. A second equation will represent the money spent on the fruit.)

   $\begin{cases} x + y = 20 \\ 0.50x + 0.75y = 11.50 \end{cases}$

7. Solve the system algebraically. Tell how many apples and bananas Angelo bought.

   14 apples and 6 bananas

© Houghton Mifflin Harcourt Publishing Company

UNIT 3

Problem Solving Connections
Is the Price Right?

COMMON CORE | Standards for Mathematical Content

CC.8.EE.7a Give examples of linear equations in one variable with one solution, infinitely many solutions, or no solutions. Show which of these possibilities is the case by successively transforming the given equation into simpler forms, until an equivalent equation of the form $x = a$, $a = a$, or $a = b$ results (where a and b are different numbers).

CC.8.EE.7b Solve linear equations with rational number coefficients, including equations whose solutions require expanding expressions using the distributive property and collecting like terms.

CC.8.EE.8a Understand that solutions to a system of two linear equations in two variables correspond to points of intersection of their graphs, because points of intersection satisfy both equations simultaneously.

CC.8.EE.8b Solve systems of two linear equations in two variables algebraically, and estimate solutions by graphing the equations. Solve simple cases by inspection.

CC.8.EE.8c Solve real-world and mathematical problems leading to two linear equations in two variables.

INTRODUCE

When planning a vacation, there are many decisions to make including where to go, how to get there, how to get around once you arrive, and where to stay. Analyzing the situation and your options helps you make the best choices for your family.

TEACH

1 Writing Equations

Questioning Strategies

- In Part A, how is the initial fee represented in the equation? **by the *y*-intercept** How is the per mile charge represented? **by the rate of change, or slope**

- How do the equations for the taxi fare differ in Part B and Part C? **In Part C, you have to add the extra charge for Jackie's friends. The slope and initial charge do not change.**

Teaching Strategy

Have students work in small groups initially. Encourage students to discuss their reasoning and justify their strategies to each other. Ask groups to compare responses and resolve any differences.

2 Graphing a System

Questioning Strategies

- In Part C, why are there restrictions on the variables? **When an equation represents a real-world situation, you must think about which values of the variables make sense in the context. For example, for variables that represent distance, a negative value does not usually make sense.**

Teaching Strategy

Have students sketch the graphs by hand before checking their work with a graphing utility.

Name _____ Class _____ Date _____

Problem Solving Connections

UNIT 3

Is the Price Right? Travelers who arrive at an aiport usually have transportation options for getting to their next destination. Most travelers can choose between taxi or shuttle services to get to their hotels.

COMMON CORE

CC.8.EE.7a,
CC.8.EE.7b,
CC.8.EE.8a,
CC.8.EE.8b,
CC.8.EE.8c

1 Writing Equations

Jackie just arrived at the Orlando International Airport. There are two routes from the airport to Jackie's hotel:

- If the driver uses city streets, the distance to the hotel is 29 miles.
- If the driver takes the expressway, the distance is only 23 miles, but Jackie will pay an additional $2.75 in toll charges.

A The first taxi company Jackie talks to charges an initial fee of $2.00 plus $2.40 for each mile. Write an equation to show the total charge y for traveling x miles.

$y = 2 + 2.4x$

B Calculate the total cost to travel to Jackie's hotel taking each route.

Streets:	Expressway:
$y = 2 + 2.4x$	$y = 2 + 2.4x + 2.75$
$= 2 + 2.4(29)$	$= 4.75 + 2.4(23)$
$= 2 + 69.6$	$= 4.75 + 55.2$
$= 71.6$	$= 59.95$

Which route should Jackie instruct the driver to take? Why?

The expressway; the total cost is less than taking city streets.

C Jackie learns that the taxi can transport up to 4 people to the same destination at the rates given above. There is a $3 charge for each additional person. A shuttle bus company offers transportation to the hotel for $15 per person. Jackie is traveling with 3 friends. Calculate the total cost for Jackie and her friends to take the taxi along the expressway and the shuttle.

Taxi:	Shuttle:
$59.95 + 3(3) = 68.95$	$15 \times 4 = 60$

Should Jackie and her friends choose the taxi or the shuttle? Explain.
The shuttle; the total cost is less for 4 people to take the shuttle.

2 Graphing a System

Chuck and his family are also vacationing in Florida. He researches taxi rates before they leave home. There are 5 people in Chuck's family (including Chuck).

Company 1: $2 initial fee, plus $2.40 per mile for 1 to 2 passengers and $3 per person for each additional person.

Company 2: $3.75 initial fee, plus $2.00 per mile for 1 to 2 passengers and $1.50 per person for each additional person.

Company 3: $3.85 initial fee, plus $2.20 per mile for up to 5 passengers.

A Write equations in slope-intercept form to model each company's fare y for traveling x miles with 5 passengers.

Company 1:	Company 2:	Company 3:
$y = 2 + 2.4x + 3(3)$	$y = 3.75 + 2x + 3(1.5)$	$y = 2.2x + 3.85$
$= 2.4x + 11$	$= 2x + 8.25$	

B Sketch a graph of the system.

C Explain any restrictions that should be placed on the values of x and y.

Both x and y should be restricted to values greater than

or equal to 0 because it would not make sense to drive

a negative number of miles or to pay a negative amount

of money.

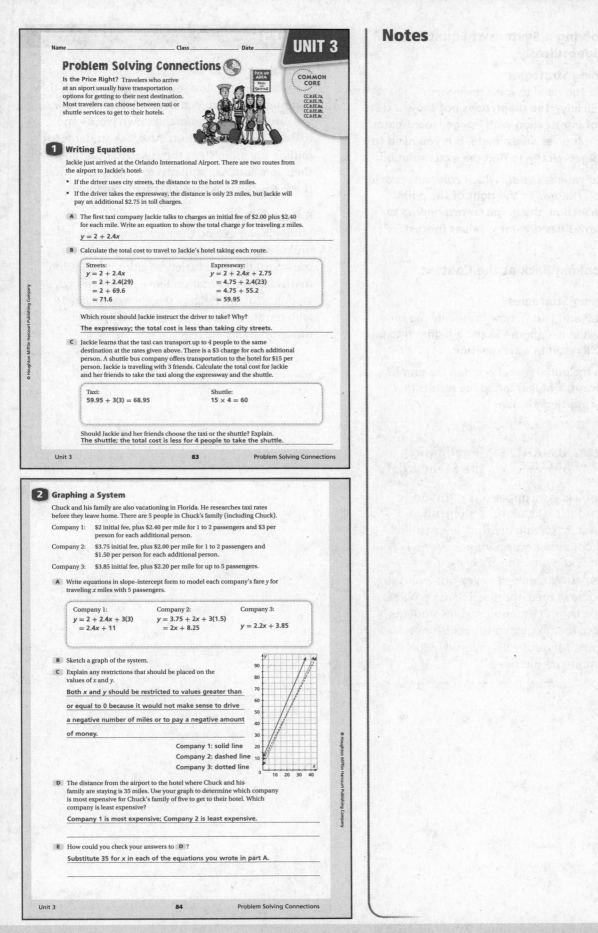

Company 1: solid line
Company 2: dashed line
Company 3: dotted line

D The distance from the airport to the hotel where Chuck and his family are staying is 35 miles. Use your graph to determine which company is most expensive for Chuck's family of five to get to their hotel. Which company is least expensive?

Company 1 is most expensive; Company 2 is least expensive.

E How could you check your answers to **D**?

Substitute 35 for x in each of the equations you wrote in part A.

3 Solving a System of Equations Algebraically

Questioning Strategies

- Why do you need to solve the system algebraically? **The graph does not show a clear point of intersection with integer coordinates. The graph gives an estimate, but you need to solve algebraically to find the exact solution.**

- How do you determine which company provides the better value? **To the right of the point of intersection, the graph corresponding to Company 3 has greater y-values (prices).**

4 Looking Back at the Context

Questioning Strategies

- In Part B and Part C, how is the rate per mile reflected in the graph? **Slope; a higher rate per mile will result in a steeper line.**

- How is the initial fee reflected in the graph? **y-intercept; a higher initial fee results in a greater starting y-value.**

> **MATHEMATICAL PRACTICE** **Highlighting the Standards**
>
> This project is an opportunity to address Standard 1 (Make sense of problems and persevere in solving them). The question posed does not have an immediate answer. In fact, as the situation changes, the mathematical model changes. Students must be flexible in their approach to the problem. Looking back at the context gives students a chance to draw general conclusions and develop reasoning skills that will help them solve future problems.

CLOSE

Journal

Have students write a journal entry in which they summarize the project. Remind them to state the project's problem in their own words and to describe their solution. Also, ask students to outline the main steps they used in order to reach their solution. Ask students to summarize what these conclusions mean to them, personally.

Research Options

Students can extend their learning by doing online research to find costs associated with transportation in a variety of cities. In addition to private transportation like a shuttle or taxi, students can investigate the costs associated with renting a car or the options for public transportation.

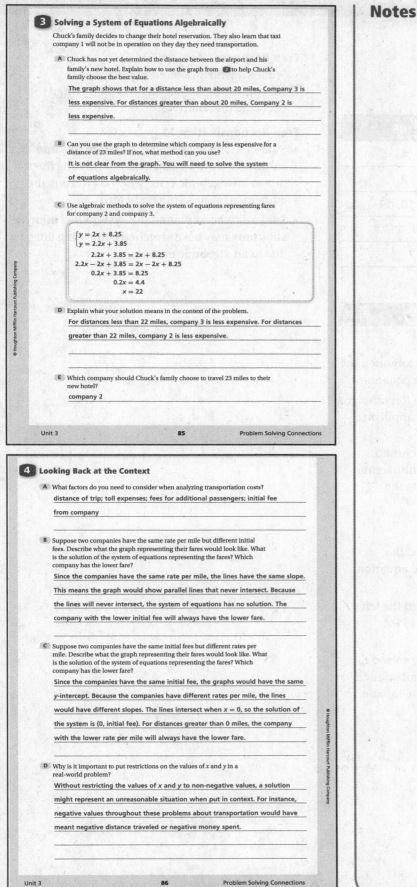

3 Solving a System of Equations Algebraically

Chuck's family decides to change their hotel reservation. They also learn that taxi company 1 will not be in operation on they day they need transportation.

A Chuck has not yet determined the distance between the airport and his family's new hotel. Explain how to use the graph from ❷ to help Chuck's family choose the best value.

The graph shows that for a distance less than about 20 miles, Company 3 is

less expensive. For distances greater than about 20 miles, Company 2 is

less expensive.

B Can you use the graph to determine which company is less expensive for a distance of 23 miles? If not, what method can you use?

It is not clear from the graph. You will need to solve the system

of equations algebraically.

C Use algebraic methods to solve the system of equations representing fares for company 2 and company 3.

$$\begin{cases} y = 2x + 8.25 \\ y = 2.2x + 3.85 \end{cases}$$
$$2.2x + 3.85 = 2x + 8.25$$
$$2.2x - 2x + 3.85 = 2x - 2x + 8.25$$
$$0.2x + 3.85 = 8.25$$
$$0.2x = 4.4$$
$$x = 22$$

D Explain what your solution means in the context of the problem.

For distances less than 22 miles, company 3 is less expensive. For distances

greater than 22 miles, company 2 is less expensive.

E Which company should Chuck's family choose to travel 23 miles to their new hotel?

company 2

4 Looking Back at the Context

A What factors do you need to consider when analyzing transportation costs?

distance of trip; toll expenses; fees for additional passengers; initial fee

from company

B Suppose two companies have the same rate per mile but different initial fees. Describe what the graph representing their fares would look like. What is the solution of the system of equations representing the fares? Which company has the lower fare?

Since the companies have the same rate per mile, the lines have the same slope.

This means the graph would show parallel lines that never intersect. Because

the lines will never intersect, the system of equations has no solution. The

company with the lower initial fee will always have the lower fare.

C Suppose two companies have the same initial fees but different rates per mile. Describe what the graph representing their fares would look like. What is the solution of the system of equations representing the fares? Which company has the lower fare?

Since the companies have the same initial fee, the graphs would have the same

y-intercept. Because the companies have different rates per mile, the lines

would have different slopes. The lines intersect when $x = 0$, so the solution of

the system is (0, initial fee). For distances greater than 0 miles, the company

with the lower rate per mile will always have the lower fare.

D Why is it important to put restrictions on the values of x and y in a real-world problem?

Without restricting the values of x and y to non-negative values, a solution

might represent an unreasonable situation when put in context. For instance,

negative values throughout these problems about transportation would have

meant negative distance traveled or negative money spent.

Notes

COMMON CORE CORRELATION

Standard	Items
CC.8.EE.7a	3, 4
CC.8.EE.7b	1, 2
CC.8.EE.8a	5, 9, 10, 12
CC.8.EE.8b	6, 8, 11
CC.8.EE.8c	7

TEST PREP DOCTOR ⊕

Multiple Choice: Item 2

- Students who answered **F** may have forgotten the negative sign on the right side of the equation.
- Students who answered **H** may have forgotten to use the distributive property when simplifying the equation.
- Students who answered **J** may have chosen the wrong operation (for example, subtraction instead of addition) when simplifying the equation.

Multiple Choice: Item 6

- Students who answered **F** substituted the expression $4x + 3$ for x in the second equation instead of for y.
- Students who answered **H** substituted the left side of the second equation for part of the first equation.
- Students who answered **J** incorrectly solved the second equation for a variable and substituted this incorrect expression into the first equation.

Free Response: Item 10

- Students who answered **yes** may have substituted or simplified incorrectly when checking the solution.

Free Response: Item 11

- Students who answered **the system has one solution** may have sketched intersecting lines due to an algebraic error when converting the equations to slope-intercept form.
- Students who answered **the system has many solutions** may have sketched coinciding lines due to an algebraic error.

Name _____ Class _____ Date _____

MULTIPLE CHOICE

1. Which value of x makes the equation $5(x - 2) - 4 = 6$ true?

   A. 2   C. 4
   B. 3   D. 5

2. Which has the same solution as $2(x + 4) = -7 - 3x$?

   F. $5x = 15$
   G. $-5x = 15$
   H. $-x = 11$
   J. $x = 15$

3. How many solutions does the equation $2(x - 5) = 2x + 3$ have?

   A. 0   C. 2
   B. 1   D. infinitely many

4. How many solutions does the equation $4x + 28 = 4(x + 3) + 16$ have?

   F. 0   H. 2
   G. 1   J. infinitely many

5. Which ordered pair is the solution to the system of equations?

   A. $\left(\frac{3}{5}, \frac{8}{5}\right)$ C. $\left(-\frac{3}{5}, \frac{8}{5}\right)$
   B. $\left(\frac{3}{5}, -\frac{8}{5}\right)$ D. $\left(-\frac{3}{5}, -\frac{8}{5}\right)$

6. Which equation can you use to solve the system of equations shown?
$$\begin{cases} -4x + y = 3 \\ 11x - 5y = 16 \end{cases}$$

   F. $11(4x + 3) - 5y = 16$
   G. $11x - 5(4x + 3) = 16$
   H. $-4(11x - 5y) = 3$
   J. $-4x + 16 - 11x = 3$

7. Students from Thornebrooke Elementary are going on a field trip to an amusement park. Those who have annual passes will pay $10. Other students will pay $35. The school collected $1,375 for 50 students.

   Which system of linear equations models this situation?

   A. $\begin{cases} 10x + 35y = 50 \\ x + y = 1,375 \end{cases}$

   B. $\begin{cases} 10x + 35y = 1,375 \\ x + y = 50 \end{cases}$

   C. $\begin{cases} 10x + y = 50 \\ 35x + y = 1,375 \end{cases}$

   D. $\begin{cases} 10x + y = 1,375 \\ x + 35y = 50 \end{cases}$

8. Which ordered pair is a solution of the system shown?
$$\begin{cases} -4x + 5y = 14 \\ 7x + 3y = -1 \end{cases}$$

   F. $(1, 2)$
   G. $(1, -2)$
   H. $(-1, 2)$
   J. $(-1, -2)$

9. Which graph represents a system of equations with no solution?

   A.

   B.

   C.

   D.

FREE RESPONSE

10. Dani solves the system of equations shown and finds that the solution is $(-2, 7)$. Explain whether Dani is correct.
$$\begin{cases} 7x - y = 7 \\ -3x + 2y = 8 \end{cases}$$

    No; if you substitute –2 for x and 7

    for y in either of the original

    equations, the statement is false.

11. Graph the linear functions. Describe the solution set for the system of equations.
$$\begin{cases} 3x - y = 4 \\ -6x + 2y = 2 \end{cases}$$

    The system has no solution.

12. Solve the system by graphing.
$$\begin{cases} y = -2x + 5 \\ y = 2x + 1 \end{cases}$$

    $(1, 3)$

13. Solve the equation $5(x - 2) + 3 = 7x - 9$.

    $5(x - 2) + 3 = 7x - 9$
    $5x - 10 + 3 = 7x - 9$
    $5x - 7 = 7x - 9$
    $-7 = 2x - 9$
    $2 = 2x$
    $1 = x$

UNIT 4

Geometry: Transformations

Unit Vocabulary

center of dilation	(4-4)
congruent	(4-3)
dilation	(4-4)
image	(4-1)
line of reflection	(4-1)
preimage	(4-1)
reflection	(4-1)
rotation	(4-1)
scale factor	(4-4)
similar	(4-5)
transformation	(4-1)
translation	(4-1)

UNIT 4

UNIT 4

Geometry: Transformations

Unit Focus

In this unit, you will explore mathematical functions that move objects in specified ways in the coordinate plane. A translation slides a figure up or down and left or right without changing its size or shape. A reflection flips a figure of a line to create a mirror image. A rotation turns a figure to have a different orientation. A dilation expands or reduces a figure to have a different size but the same shape.

Unit at a Glance

COMMON CORE

Lesson	Standards for Mathematical Content
4-1 Translations, Reflections, and Rotations	CC.8.G.3
4-2 Properties of Transformations	CC.8.G.1
4-3 Transformations and Congruence	CC.8.G.2
4-4 Dilations	CC.8.G.3
4-5 Transformations and Similarity	CC.8.G.4
Problem Solving Connections	
Test Prep	

UNIT 4

© Houghton Mifflin Harcourt Publishing Company

Unpacking the Common Core State Standards

Use the table to help you understand the Common Core State Standards that are taught in this unit. Refer to the lessons listed after each standard for exploration and practice.

COMMON CORE Standards for Mathematical Content	What It Means For You
CC.8.G.1 Verify experimentally the properties of rotations, reflections, and translations: **a.** Lines are taken to lines, and line segments to line segments of the same length. **b.** Angles are taken to angles of the same measure. **c.** Parallel lines are taken to parallel lines. Lesson 4-2	Translations, reflections, and rotations are called rigid transformations because they do not change the size or shape of a figure. Characteristics such as the length of line segments, angle measures, and parallel lines are unchanged by these three types of transformations.
CC.8.G.2 Understand that a two-dimensional figure is congruent to another if the second can be obtained from the first by a sequence of rotations, reflections, and translations; given two congruent figures, describe a sequence that exhibits the congruence between them. Lesson 4-3	Because size and shape are preserved under translations, reflections, and rotations, the result of these transformations is an exact copy of the original figure. When two figures have the exact same size and shape, they are called congruent figures.
CC.8.G.3 Describe the effect of dilations, translations, rotations, and reflections on two-dimensional figures using coordinates. Lessons 4-1, 4-4	When you apply transformations to figures in the coordinate plane, you can describe the results of the transformation by giving the coordinates of the vertices of the figures. For some of these transformations, it is easy to write a general rule that describes what happens to each coordinate under the transformation.
CC.8.G.4 Understand that a two-dimensional figure is similar to another if the second can be obtained from the first by a sequence of rotations, reflections, translations, and dilations; given two similar two-dimensional figures, describe a sequence that exhibits the similarity between them. Lesson 4-5	A dilation changes the size of a figure but not its shape. When two figures have the same shape but different sizes, they are called similar figures.

Unpacking the Common Core State Standards

This page lists and explains the Standards for Mathematical Content that are addressed in this unit. For information about the Standards for Mathematical Practice, which are integrated throughout the text, see Teacher Edition pages vii–xiii.

Notes

Translation, Reflections, and Rotations

Essential question: *How can you use coordinates to describe the result of a translation, reflection, or rotation?*

⋯ COMMON **Standards for**
⋮ CORE **Mathematical Content**

CC.8.G.3 Describe the effect of dilations, translations, rotations, and reflections on two-dimensional figures using coordinates.

Vocabulary
transformation
pre-image
image
translation
reflection
line of reflection
rotation

Prerequisites
Graphing in the coordinate plane (four quadrants)

Math Background
When a transformation is applied to a geometric figure, the vertices of the original figure are mapped to corresponding vertices in the image. In translations, reflections, and rotations, line segments are also preserved. Suppose point *A* is mapped to point *A′* and *B* is mapped to *B′*. If a line segment connects *A* and *B* in the original figure, then a corresponding line segment connects *A′* and *B′* in the transformed image.

INTRODUCE

Discuss with students some real-world examples of transformations. Translations are often found in tile or textile patterns. The image of a tree on a lake exemplifies a reflection. A pinwheel illustrates rotation. Ask students for other examples of these types of transformations.

TEACH

1 EXPLORE

Questioning Strategies

- How does the size and shape of the image compare with its pre-image? **They are the same size and shape.**

- Did the translation change the orientation of the triangle? **no**

Kinesthetic/Modeling

Clear a large area on the floor and use masking tape to mark off a coordinate grid. Have students stand at different points to represent the vertices of a geometric figure. Students can stretch yarn from person to person to model the sides of the figure. Invite classmates to suggest a translation that the students on the grid can demonstrate. Ask the class to compare the pre-image (initial position) to the image (final position) after the translation.

2 EXPLORE

Questioning Strategies

- How does the size and shape of the image compare to its pre-image? **They are the same size and shape.**

- Did the reflection change the orientation of the triangle? **Yes, the image "flipped" across the axis. The image appears upside down when compared to the original triangle.**

- Compare the locations of the image and the pre-image. **They appear on opposite sides of the *x*-axis. The image appears below the pre-image, but it did not move left or right.**

Name_____ Class_____ Date_____

4-1

COMMON CORE

CC.8.G.3

Translations, Reflections, and Rotations

Essential question: *How can you use coordinates to describe the result of a translation, reflection, or rotation?*

You learned that a function is a rule that assigns exactly one output to each input. A **transformation** is a type of function that describes a change in the position, size, or shape of a figure. The input of a transformation is called the **preimage**, and the output of a transformation is called the **image**.

A **translation** is a transformation that slides a figure along a straight line. The image has the same size and shape as the preimage.

1 EXPLORE Applying Translations

The triangle is the preimage (input). The arrow shows the motion of a translation and how point A is translated to point A'.

A Trace the triangle on a piece of paper. Slide point A of your traced triangle down the arrow to model the translation.

B Sketch the image (output) of the translation.

C Describe the motion modeled by the translation.

Move __7__ units right and __5__ units down.

D Complete the ordered pairs to describe the effect of the translation on point A.

$(1, 11)$ becomes $\left(1 + \boxed{7}, 11 + \boxed{-5}\right) = \left(\boxed{8}, \boxed{6}\right)$

E You can give a general rule for a translation by telling the number of units to move up or down and the number of units to move left or right. Complete the ordered pairs to write a general rule for this transformation.

$(x, y) \rightarrow \left(x + \boxed{7}, y + \boxed{-5}\right)$

TRY THIS!

1. Apply the translation $(x, y) \rightarrow (x - 2, y + 3)$ to the figure shown. Give the coordinates of the vertices of the image. (The image of point A is point A'.)

A': (__0__ , __8__)

B': (__4__ , __8__)

C': (__4__ , __6__)

D': (__0__ , __6__)

© Houghton Mifflin Harcourt Publishing Company

Unit 4   91   Lesson 1

A **reflection** is a transformation that flips a figure across a line called the **line of reflection**. Each point and its image are the same distance from the line of reflection. The image has the same size and shape as the preimage.

2 EXPLORE Applying Reflections

The triangle is the preimage. You will use the x- or y-axis as the line of reflection.

Reflection across the x-axis:

A Trace the triangle and the x- and y-axes on a piece of paper. Fold your paper along the x-axis and trace the image of the triangle on the opposite side of the x-axis.

B Sketch the image of the reflection. Label each vertex of the image. (The image of point E is point E'.)

C Complete the table.

Preimage	(2, 4)	(2, 1)	(5, 1)
Image	(2, −4)	(2, −1)	(5, −1)

D How does reflecting the figure across the x-axis change the x-coordinates? How does it change the y-coordinates?

The x-coordinates do not change. The y-coordinates are opposites.

E Complete the ordered pair to write a general rule for reflection across the x-axis. $(x, y) \rightarrow \left(x, y \times \boxed{-1}\right)$

Reflection across the y-axis:

F Fold your traced image along the y-axis and trace the image of the triangle on the opposite side of the y-axis.

G Sketch the image of the reflection. Label each vertex of the image. (For clarity, label the image of point E as point E''.)

H Complete the table.

Preimage	(2, 4)	(2, 1)	(5, 1)
Image	(−2, 4)	(−2, 1)	(−5, 1)

I How does reflecting the figure across the y-axis change the x-coordinates? How does it change the y-coordinates?

The x-coordinates are opposites. The y-coordinates do not change.

J Complete the ordered pair to write a general rule for reflection across the y-axis. $(x, y) \rightarrow \left(\boxed{x \cdot (-1)}, \boxed{y}\right)$

© Houghton Mifflin Harcourt Publishing Company

Unit 4   92   Lesson 1

- How does the size and shape of the image compare to the pre-image? **They are the same size and shape.**

- Did the rotation change the orientation of the triangle? **Yes, the image "turned" around a point (the origin).**

- Compare the locations of the image and the pre-image. **The vertex at the origin did not move. The other vertices moved in a circular path around the origin.**

MATHEMATICAL PRACTICE   Highlighting the Standards

This Explore provides an opportunity to address Standard 4 (Model with mathematics). Transformations are functions that describe the movement of figures. Students are asked to physically move objects around the coordinate plane to model the transformation of a geometric figure. Then students compare the physical movement to the verbal and algebraic representations of the transformations being discussed. This lesson provides an excellent opportunity to deepen students' understanding of the concept of mathematical modeling.

CLOSE

Essential Question

How can you use coordinates to describe the result of a translation, reflection, or rotation?
Apply the rule of the transformation to the vertices of the original figure. The resulting points are the vertices of the image. To draw the complete image, connect the vertices with sides that correspond to the sides of the original figure.

Summarize

Have students give an example of a translation, a reflection, and a rotation. Students should include the rule and a sketch of the pre-image and image.

PRACTICE

Where skills are taught	Where skills are practiced
1 EXPLORE	EXS. 1, 6, 9
2 EXPLORE	EXS. 2, 4, 5, 7–8
3 EXPLORE	EX. 3

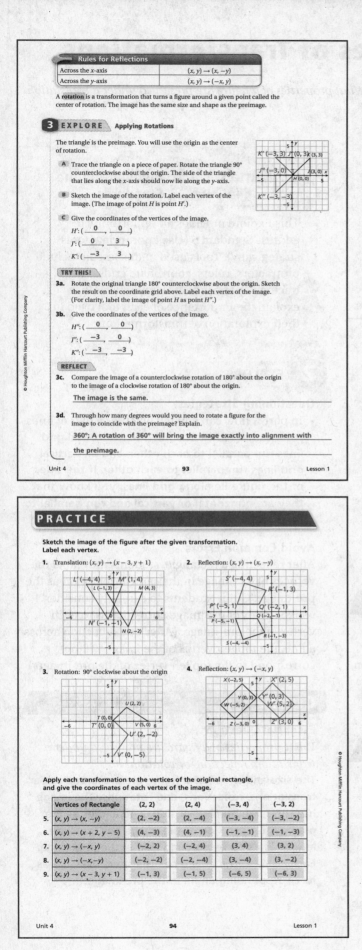

Rules for Reflections	
Across the x-axis	$(x, y) \rightarrow (x, -y)$
Across the y-axis	$(x, y) \rightarrow (-x, y)$

A **rotation** is a transformation that turns a figure around a given point called the center of rotation. The image has the same size and shape as the preimage.

3 EXPLORE Applying Rotations

The triangle is the preimage. You will use the origin as the center of rotation.

A Trace the triangle on a piece of paper. Rotate the triangle 90° counterclockwise about the origin. The side of the triangle that lies along the x-axis should now lie along the y-axis.

B Sketch the image of the rotation. Label each vertex of the image. (The image of point H is point H'.)

C Give the coordinates of the vertices of the image.

H′: (__0__ , __0__)

J′: (__0__ , __3__)

K′: (__−3__ , __3__)

TRY THIS!

3a. Rotate the original triangle 180° counterclockwise about the origin. Sketch the result on the coordinate grid above. Label each vertex of the image. (For clarity, label the image of point H as point H″.)

3b. Give the coordinates of the vertices of the image.

H″: (__0__ , __0__)

J″: (__−3__ , __0__)

K″: (__−3__ , __−3__)

REFLECT

3c. Compare the image of a counterclockwise rotation of 180° about the origin to the image of a clockwise rotation of 180° about the origin.

The image is the same.

3d. Through how many degrees would you need to rotate a figure for the image to coincide with the preimage? Explain.

360°; A rotation of 360° will bring the image exactly into alignment with the preimage.

© Houghton Mifflin Harcourt Publishing Company

PRACTICE

Sketch the image of the figure after the given transformation.
Label each vertex.

1. Translation: $(x, y) \rightarrow (x - 3, y + 1)$

L′ (−4, 4)   M′ (1, 4)
L (−1, 3)   M (4, 3)
N′ (−1, −1)
N (2, −2)

2. Reflection: $(x, y) \rightarrow (x, -y)$

S′ (−4, 4)   R′ (−1, 3)
P′ (−5, 1)   Q′ (−2, 1)
P (−5, −1)   Q (−2, −1)
R (−1, −3)
S (−4, −4)

3. Rotation: 90° clockwise about the origin

U (2, 2)
T (0, 0)
T′ (0, 0)   V (5, 0)
U′ (2, −2)
V′ (0, −5)

4. Reflection: $(x, y) \rightarrow (-x, y)$

X (−2, 5)   X′ (2, 5)
Y (0, 3)   Y′ (0, 3)
W (−5, 2)   W′ (5, 2)
Z (−3, 0)   Z′ (3, 0)

Apply each transformation to the vertices of the original rectangle, and give the coordinates of each vertex of the image.

Vertices of Rectangle	(2, 2)	(2, 4)	(−3, 4)	(−3, 2)
5. $(x, y) \rightarrow (x, -y)$	(2, −2)	(2, −4)	(−3, −4)	(−3, −2)
6. $(x, y) \rightarrow (x + 2, y − 5)$	(4, −3)	(4, −1)	(−1, −1)	(−1, −3)
7. $(x, y) \rightarrow (-x, y)$	(−2, 2)	(−2, 4)	(3, 4)	(3, 2)
8. $(x, y) \rightarrow (-x, -y)$	(−2, −2)	(−2, −4)	(3, −4)	(3, −2)
9. $(x, y) \rightarrow (x − 3, y + 1)$	(−1, 3)	(−1, 5)	(−6, 5)	(−6, 3)

© Houghton Mifflin Harcourt Publishing Company

Properties of Transformations

Essential question: *What properties of a figure are preserved under a translation, reflection, or rotation?*

COMMON CORE Standards for Mathematical Content

CC.8.G.1 Verify experimentally the properties of rotations, reflections, and translations.

CC.8.G.1.a Lines are taken to lines, and line segments to line segments of the same length.

CC.8.G.1.b Angles are taken to angles of the same measure.

CC.8.G.1.c Parallel lines are taken to parallel lines.

Prerequisites

Translations, reflections, and rotations

Math Background

It is important for students to understand how transformations act on geometric figures. When a translation, reflection, or rotation is applied to a figure, that figure does not change in size or shape. Translations, reflections, and rotations are sometimes called rigid transformations because segment lengths and angle measurements are preserved under the transformation. Encourage students to use the mathematical vocabulary of translation, reflection, and rotation instead of the more familiar terms of slide, flip, and turn.

INTRODUCE

Ask students whether they think the length of line segments changes when a figure is translated, reflected, or rotated. Tell students that in this lesson, they will investigate what happens to line segments and angles under translations, reflections, and rotations.

TEACH

1 EXPLORE

Questioning Strategies

• In part D, what is another way to measure $\overline{AD}$? **Count grid squares along the segment.**

• In part E, the figures are very small. How could you make the angles easier to measure? **Extend the rays for each angle until they are long enough to extend past the edge of the protractor.**

MATHEMATICAL PRACTICE **Highlighting the Standards**

This Explore provides an opportunity to address Standard 5 (Use appropriate tools strategically). Tools used in this lesson include protractors, rulers, coordinate grids, and tracing paper. Students should be able to explain the importance of each tool used in their exploration of transformations.

2 EXPLORE

Questioning Strategies

• In part F, how can you tell whether a pair of lines runs parallel to each other? **All horizontal grid lines run parallel to each other, and all vertical grid lines run parallel to each other. If the sides of the figure lie along grid lines, you know that they are horizontal or vertical and run parallel to other horizontal or vertical line segments.**

Avoid Common Errors

After reflecting a rectangle, students may label the vertices of the image in the same orientation as the pre-image. Guide students to carefully consider which vertex of the image corresponds to each vertex of the pre-image. (After one reflection across a line, the top left vertex of the image will not correspond to the top left vertex of the pre-image.)

CLOSE

Essential Question

What properties of a figure are preserved under a translation, reflection, or rotation?
The size and shape of a figure are preserved under translations, reflections, and rotations. The image has the same number of sides and angles as the pre-image. Each side of the image has the same length as its corresponding side in the pre-image. Each angle in the image has the same measure as its corresponding angle in the pre-image.

4-2

Properties of Transformations

Name _____ Class _____ Date _____

Essential question: *What properties of a figure are preserved under a translation, reflection, or rotation?*

1 EXPLORE   Properties of Translations

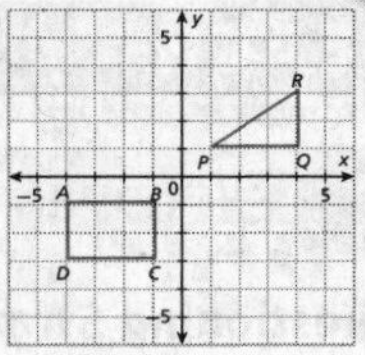

A   Trace the rectangle and triangle on a piece of paper. Then cut out your traced figures.

B   Place your copy of the rectangle on top of the rectangle in the figure. Then translate the rectangle by sliding your copy 6 units to the right and 1 unit down. Draw the new location of the rectangle on the coordinate plane and label the vertices A', B', C', and D'.

C   Place your copy of the triangle on top of the triangle in the figure. Then translate the triangle by sliding your copy 5 units to the left and 2 units up. Draw the new location of the triangle on the coordinate plane and label the vertices P', Q', and R'.

D   Use a ruler to measure line segments $\overline{AD}$ and $\overline{PR}$. Then, measure $\overline{A'D'}$ and $\overline{P'R'}$. What do you notice?

The translation does not change the length of the line segment.

E   Use a protractor to measure $\angle C$ and $\angle R$. Then, measure $\angle C'$ and $\angle R'$. What do you notice?

The translation does not change the angle measures.

F   Count the pairs of parallel lines in rectangle $ABCD$. Count the pairs of parallel lines in rectangle $A'B'C'D'$. What do you notice?

The translation does not change the orientation of segments such as

parallel lines.

REFLECT

1a.   Use your results from **D**, **E**, and **F** to write a conjecture about translations.

Translations preserve the shape and size of a figure.

2 EXPLORE   Properties of Reflections

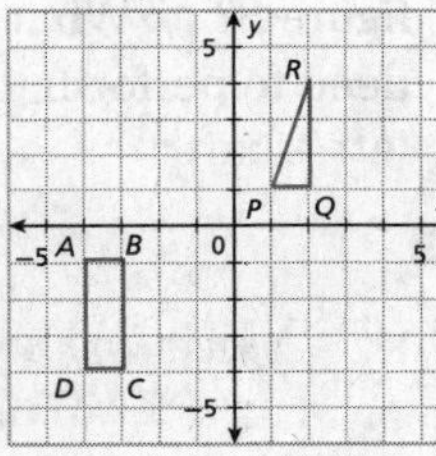

A   Trace the rectangle and triangle on a piece of paper. Then, cut out your traced figures.

B   Place your copy of the rectangle on top of the rectangle in the figure. Then reflect the rectangle across the x-axis by flipping your copy across the x-axis. Draw the new location of the rectangle on the coordinate plane and label the vertices A', B', C', and D'.

C   Place your copy of the triangle on top of the triangle in the figure. Then reflect the triangle across the y-axis by flipping your copy across the y-axis. Draw the new location of the triangle on the coordinate plane and label the vertices P', Q', and R'.

D   Use a ruler to measure line segments $\overline{BC}$ and $\overline{PR}$. Then, measure $\overline{B'C'}$ and $\overline{P'R'}$. What do you notice?

The reflection does not change the length of the line segment.

E   Use a protractor to measure $\angle D$ and $\angle P$. Then, measure $\angle D'$ and $\angle P'$. What do you notice?

The reflection does not change the angle measures.

F   Count the pairs of parallel lines in rectangle $ABCD$. Count the pairs of parallel lines in rectangle $A'B'C'D'$. What do you notice?

The reflection does not change parallel lines.

REFLECT

2a.   Use your results from **D**, **E**, and **F** to write a conjecture about reflections.

Reflections preserve the shape and size of a figure.

TRY THIS!

2b.   Rotate your copy of the triangle from **A** 180° around the origin and draw the new location of the triangle. Make measurements and observations to help you state a conjecture about rotations.

The rotation maps line segments to line segments of equal length

and angles to angles with equal measure. Rotations preserve the

shape and size of a figure.

Transformations and Congruence

Essential question: What is the connection between transformations and figures that have the same shape and size?

COMMON CORE Standards for Mathematical Content

CC.8.G.2 Understand that a two-dimensional figure is congruent to another if the second can be obtained from the first by a sequence of rotations, reflections, and translations; given two congruent figures, describe a sequence that exhibits the congruence between them.

Vocabulary
congruent

Prerequisites
Translations, reflections, and rotations

Math Background
Two-dimensional geometric figures are congruent if they have the same size and shape. This means that they have the same number of sides, the corresponding sides have equal lengths, and corresponding angles have equal measures. Congruent figures may have different locations or orientations.

If there exists a sequence of translations, reflections, and/or rotations that will transform one figure into the other, the two figures are congruent. Note that dilations are not included in this list of transformations. While dilations preserve the shape of a figure, they do not preserve the size when the scale factor does not equal one.

INTRODUCE

Show students two geometric figures in the coordinate plane. The figures should be congruent, but have different orientations. Ask students how they could verify that the two figures are congruent. Tell students that in this lesson, they will learn how to use transformations to determine whether two shapes are identical in shape and size.

TEACH

1 EXPLORE

Questioning Strategies
- Compare the original figure to the image after the transformation in part A in terms of shape, size, location, and orientation. The figures have the same shape and size. The image has a different location and is flipped upside down compared to the pre-image.

- What type of transformation occurs in part B? translation

2 EXAMPLE

Questioning Strategies
- How does figure *A* differ from figure *B*? One is a mirror image of the other.

- Which type of transformation results in a mirror image? reflection

- Will reflecting figure *A* across the *y*-axis result in figure *B*? no What other transformation do you need to perform to result in figure *B*? Translate left 1 unit.

MATHEMATICAL PRACTICE **Highlighting the Standards**

This Example provides an opportunity to address Standard 6 (Attend to precision). It is important that students pay close attention to the coordinates of the vertices as they apply transformations and graph the results. Students must apply each transformation carefully and precisely to obtain the desired outcome.

CLOSE

Essential Question

What is the connection between transformations and figures that have the same shape and size?
If two figures have the same shape and size (are congruent), then there exists a sequence of translations, reflections, and/or rotations that transforms one into the other.

Name_____ Class_____ Date_____

Transformations and Congruence

Essential question: *What is the connection between transformations and figures that have the same shape and size?*

1 EXPLORE — Combining Transformations

Apply the indicated series of transformations to the triangle. Each transformation is applied to the image of the previous translation, not the original figure. Label each image with the letter of the transformation applied.

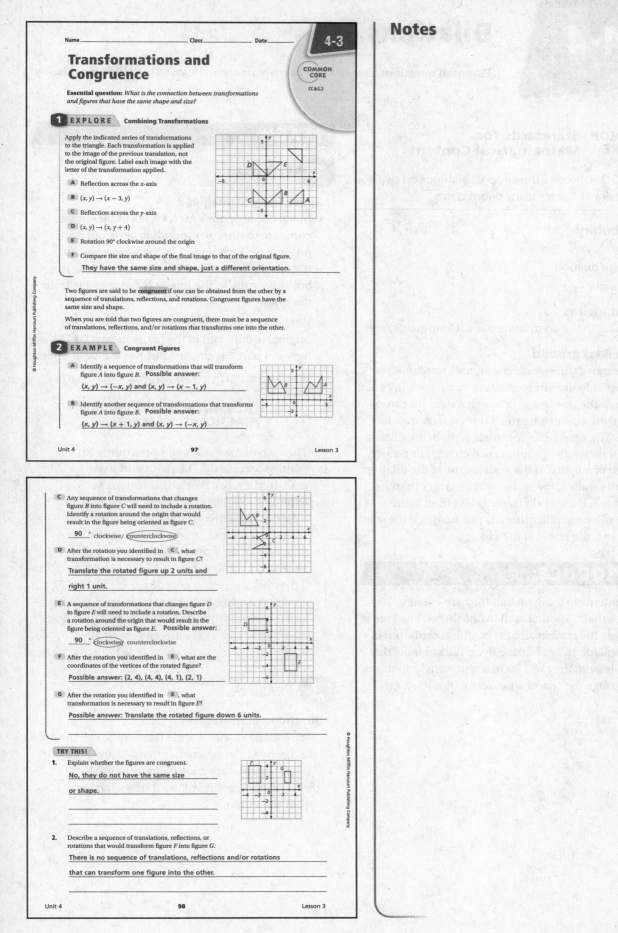

A Reflection across the *x*-axis

B $(x, y) \rightarrow (x - 3, y)$

C Reflection across the *y*-axis

D $(x, y) \rightarrow (x, y + 4)$

E Rotation 90° clockwise around the origin

F Compare the size and shape of the final image to that of the original figure.

__They have the same size and shape, just a different orientation.__

Two figures are said to be **congruent** if one can be obtained from the other by a sequence of translations, reflections, and rotations. Congruent figures have the same size and shape.

When you are told that two figures are congruent, there must be a sequence of translations, reflections, and/or rotations that transforms one into the other.

2 EXAMPLE — Congruent Figures

A Identify a sequence of transformations that will transform figure *A* into figure *B*. **Possible answer:**

__$(x, y) \rightarrow (-x, y)$ and $(x, y) \rightarrow (x - 1, y)$__

B Identify another sequence of transformations that transforms figure *A* into figure *B*. **Possible answer:**

__$(x, y) \rightarrow (x + 1, y)$ and $(x, y) \rightarrow (-x, y)$__

Unit 4   97   Lesson 3

C Any sequence of transformations that changes figure *B* into figure *C* will need to include a rotation. Identify a rotation around the origin that would result in the figure being oriented as figure *C*.

__90__ ° clickwise/ (counterclockwise)

D After the rotation you identified in (C), what transformation is necessary to result in figure *C*?

__Translate the rotated figure up 2 units and__

__right 1 unit.__

E A sequence of transformations that changes figure *D* to figure *E* will need to include a rotation. Describe a rotation around the origin that would result in the figure being oriented as figure *E*. **Possible answer:**

__90__ ° (clockwise) counterclockwise

F After the rotation you identified in E, what are the coordinates of the vertices of the rotated figure?

__Possible answer: (2, 4), (4, 4), (4, 1), (2, 1)__

G After the rotation you identified in E, what transformation is necessary to result in figure *E*?

__Possible answer: Translate the rotated figure down 6 units.__

TRY THIS!

1. Explain whether the figures are congruent.

__No, they do not have the same size__

__or shape.__

2. Describe a sequence of translations, reflections, or rotations that would transform figure *F* into figure *G*.

__There is no sequence of translations, reflections and/or rotations__

__that can transform one figure into the other.__

Unit 4   98   Lesson 3

Unit 4   **98**   Lesson 3

Dilations

Essential question: *How can you use coordinates to describe the result of a dilation?*

COMMON CORE **Standards for Mathematical Content**

CC.8.G.3 Describe the effect of dilations on two-dimensional figures using coordinates.

Vocabulary
dilation
center of dilation
scale factor

Prerequisites
Graphing in the coordinate plane (four quadrants)

Math Background
Unlike translations, reflections, and rotations, the image of a figure after a dilation can have a different size than the pre-image. Though a dilation can change the size of a figure, it does not change its shape. The image of a rectangle after being dilated is still a rectangle. Dilations can enlarge or reduce the size of a figure. If the scale factor of the dilation is greater than 1, the image will be larger than its pre-image. If the scale factor is less than 1, the image will be smaller than its pre-image. If the scale factor is 1, the size will not change.

INTRODUCE

Ask students to imagine that they are creating a logo for their new dog-walking business. The logo is drawn as the correct size for business cards, but is too small for an advertising flyer. Tell students that in this lesson, they will learn about transformations that change the size of a figure, but not its shape.

TEACH

1 EXPLORE

Questioning Strategies
• In part D, how does each vertex in the image compare to the corresponding vertex in the pre-image? **Each vertex in the image lies on the same axis as the vertex in the pre-image, but the vertex in the image is twice as far from the origin.**

• How does the figure in part F compare to the original square and to the figure in part C? **The figure in part F is smaller, but has the same shape.**

MATHEMATICAL PRACTICE **Highlighting the Standards**

This Explore provides an opportunity to address Standard 7 (Look for and make use of structure). Working through the Explore should lead students to see that the relationship between the coordinates of the vertices of the pre-image and image under a dilation can be written symbolically as $(x, y) \rightarrow (kx, ky)$. Students should also notice that if they multiply each coordinate by a number greater than 1 ($k > 1$), the figure gets bigger, and if they multiply by a positive number less than 1 ($0 < k < 1$), the figure gets smaller.

---

2 EXAMPLE

Questioning Strategies
• For a dilation with a scale factor of 3, will the image be larger or smaller than its pre-image? Why? **Larger; each coordinate is multiplied by 3, so each point will be 3 times farther from the origin.**

Name _____ Class _____ Date _____

4-4

Dilations

COMMON CORE

CC.8.G.3

Essential question: *How can you use coordinates to describe the result of a dilation?*

A **dilation** is a transformation that changes the size, but not the shape, of a geometric figure. The center of the figure is known as the **center of dilation**. When dilating in the coordinate plane, the center of dilation is usually the origin.

1 EXPLORE Applying Dilations

The square is the preimage (input). The center of dilation is the origin.

A List the coordinates of the vertices of the square.

A: (__0__ , __2__) C: (__0__ , __-2__)

B: (__2__ , __0__) D: (__-2__ , __0__)

B Multiply each coordinate by 2. List the resulting ordered pairs.

A': (__0__ , __4__) C': (__0__ , __-4__)

B': (__4__ , __0__) D': (__-4__ , __0__)

C Sketch the image of the dilation. Label each vertex of the image.

D How does multiplying the coordinates of the preimage by 2 affect the image?

__The figures have the same shape, but different sizes. The image is twice__

__the size of the preimage.__

E Multiply each coordinate from the preimage by $\frac{1}{2}$. List the resulting ordered pairs.

A'': (__0__ , __1__) C'': (__0__ , __-1__)

B'': (__1__ , __0__) D'': (__-1__ , __0__)

F Sketch the image of the dilation. Label each vertex of the image.

G How does multiplying the coordinates of the preimage by $\frac{1}{2}$ affect the image?

__The figures have the same shape, but different sizes. The image is half__

__the size of the preimage.__

A **scale factor** describes how much larger or smaller the image of a dilation is than the preimage.

Rule for Dilation

For a dilation centered at the origin with scale factor k, the image of point $P(x, y)$ is found by multiplying each coordinate by k.

$$(x, y) \rightarrow (kx, ky)$$

- If $k > 1$, then the image is larger than the preimage.
- If $0 < k < 1$, then the image is smaller than the preimage.

2 EXAMPLE Enlargements

The figure is the preimage. The center of dilation is the origin.

A List the coordinates of the vertices of the preimage in the first column of the table.

Preimage	Image
(2, 2)	(6, 6)
(2, −1)	(6, −3)
(1, −1)	(3, −3)
(1, −2)	(3, −6)
(−2, −2)	(−6, −6)
(−2, 1)	(−6, 3)
(−1, 1)	(−3, 3)
(−1, 2)	(−3, 6)

B What is the scale factor for the dilation $(x, y) \rightarrow (3x, 3y)$? __3__

C Apply the dilation to the preimage and write the coordinates of the vertices of the image in the second column of the table.

D Sketch the image under the dilation on the coordinate grid.

REFLECT

2a. How does the dilation affect the length of line segments?

__Each line segment in the image is three times longer than the__

__corresponding line segment in the preimage.__

2b. How does the dilation affect angle measures?

__The dilation does not change the angle measures.__

Questioning Strategies

- After plotting the points in the image, what is the next step in sketching the image? **Reference the pre-image and connect the corresponding vertices in the image.**

- How can you check that your sketch is correct? **The image should have the same shape and relative dimensions as the initial figure. It should be half the size of the pre-image.**

Teaching Strategies

Divide students into two groups. The groups will take turns providing each other with a figure drawn in the coordinate plane and a rule for its dilation. The other group must tell whether the dilation is an enlargement or a reduction and draw the image of the figure.

CLOSE

Essential Question

How can you use coordinates to describe the result of a dilation?

Apply the rule of the dilation to the vertices of the original figure. The resulting points are the vertices of the image. To draw the complete image, connect the vertices with the sides that correspond to the sides of the original figure.

Summarize

Have students draw a graphic organizer like the one shown in their journals. Students should tell whether an image under each type of transformation has the same size and shape as the original figure.

Translation	Reflection
shape size	shape size
Rotation	**Dilation**
shape size	shape

PRACTICE

Where skills are taught	Where skills are practiced
1 EXPLORE	EX. 1
2 EXAMPLE	EX. 2
3 EXAMPLE	EXS. 3, 4, 5

3 EXAMPLE Reductions

The arrow is the preimage. The center of dilation is the origin.

A. List the coordinates of the vertices of the preimage in the first column of the table.

Preimage	Image
(4, 2)	(2, 1)
(0, 5)	(0, 2.5)
(−4, 2)	(−2, 1)
(−2, 2)	(−1, 1)
(−2, −4)	(−1, −2)
(2, −4)	(1, −2)
(2, 2)	(1, 1)

B. What is the scale factor for the dilation $(x, y) \rightarrow (\frac{1}{2}x, \frac{1}{2}y)$? ___$\frac{1}{2}$___

C. Apply the dilation to the preimage and write the coordinates of the vertices of the image in the second column of the table.

D. Sketch the image under the dilation on the coordinate grid.

REFLECT

3a. How does the dilation affect the length of line segments?

Each line segment in the image is half as long as the corresponding line segment in the preimage.

3b. How would a dilation with scale factor 1 affect the preimage?

There would be no change. The image would be the same size and shape as the preimage.

TRY THIS!

3c. Identify the scale factor of the dilation shown.

scale factor = $\frac{1}{3}$

PRACTICE

1. The square is the preimage. The center of dilation is the origin. Write the coordinates of the vertices of the preimage in the first column of the table. Then apply the dilation $(x, y) \rightarrow (\frac{3}{2}x, \frac{3}{2}y)$ and write the coordinates of the vertices of the image in the second column. Sketch the image of the figure under the dilation.

Preimage	Image
(2, 0)	(3, 0)
(0, 2)	(0, 3)
(−2, 0)	(−3, 0)
(0, −2)	(0, −3)

Sketch the image of the figure under the given dilation.

2. $(x, y) \rightarrow (2x, 2y)$

3. $(x, y) \rightarrow (\frac{2}{3}x, \frac{2}{3}y)$

Identify the scale factor of the dilation shown.

4. scale factor = $\frac{1}{4}$

5. scale factor = $\frac{1}{2}$

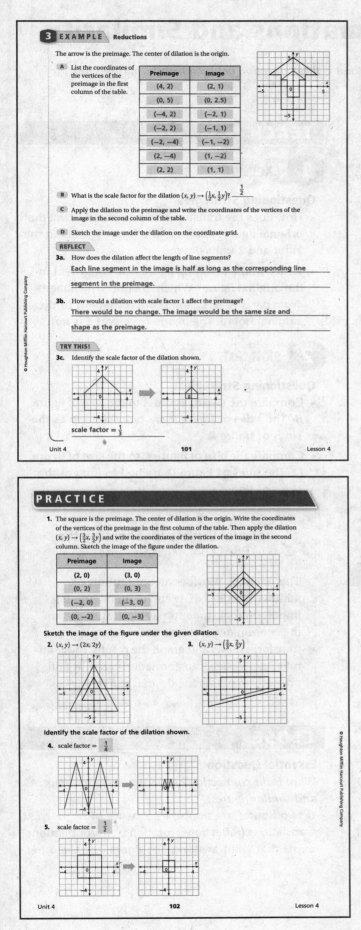

Notes

Transformations and Similarity

Essential question: What is the connection between transformations and similar figures?

COMMON **Standards for**
CORE **Mathematical Content**

CC.8.G.4 Understand that a two-dimensional figure is similar to another if the second figure can be obtained from the first by a sequence of rotations, reflections, translations, and dilations; given two similar two-dimensional figures, describe a sequence that exhibits the similarity between them.

Vocabulary
similar

Prerequisites
Translations, reflections, rotations, and dilations

Math Background
Two-dimensional geometric figures are similar if they have the same shape. In similar figures, corresponding angles have the same measure, but corresponding sides may have unequal lengths. The lengths of corresponding sides of similar figures are proportional, however.

Two figures are similar if a sequence of translations, reflections, rotations, and dilations can transform one figure into the other.

INTRODUCE

If two figures are congruent, then there exists a sequence of transformations (translations, reflections, and rotations) that translates one figure into the other. Perhaps you noticed that dilations were not included in the list of possible transformations. In this lesson, we will learn about sequences of transformations that include dilations.

TEACH

1 EXPLORE

Questioning Strategies
- How does the transformation in part A affect the original figure? **It moves the figure 7 units to the right and 2 units down.**
- Which of the resulting figures are congruent to the original figure? Which are not? **The images from parts A, B, C, and D are congruent to the original figure. The image from part E is not.**

2 EXAMPLE

Questioning Strategies
- Compare the size of figure *A* to the size of figure *B*. **The sides of figure *B* are twice as long as the sides of figure *A*.**
- Compare the size of figure *C* to the size of figure *D*. **The sides of figure *D* are half as long as the sides of figure *C*.**

MATHEMATICAL **Highlighting the**
PRACTICE **Standards**

This Example provides an opportunity to address Standard 6 (Attend to precision). It is important that students pay close attention to the coordinates of the vertices as they apply transformations and graph the results. Students must apply each transformation carefully and precisely to obtain the desired outcome.

CLOSE

Essential Question
What is the connection between transformations and similar figures?
If two figures are similar, a sequence of translations, reflections, rotations, and/or dilations exists that will transform one figure into the other.

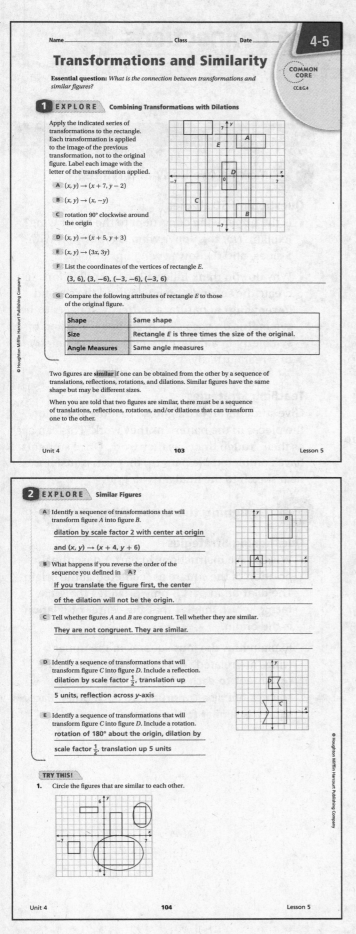

Name _____ **Class** _____ **Date** _____

Transformations and Similarity

COMMON
CORE
CC.8.G.4

Essential question: _What is the connection between transformations and similar figures?_

1 EXPLORE Combining Transformations with Dilations

Apply the indicated series of transformations to the rectangle. Each transformation is applied to the image of the previous transformation, not to the original figure. Label each image with the letter of the transformation applied.

A $(x, y) \rightarrow (x + 7, y - 2)$

B $(x, y) \rightarrow (x, -y)$

C rotation 90° clockwise around the origin

D $(x, y) \rightarrow (x + 5, y + 3)$

E $(x, y) \rightarrow (3x, 3y)$

F List the coordinates of the vertices of rectangle E.

(3, 6), (3, −6), (−3, −6), (−3, 6)

G Compare the following attributes of rectangle E to those of the original figure.

Shape	Same shape
Size	Rectangle E is three times the size of the original.
Angle Measures	Same angle measures

Two figures are **similar** if one can be obtained from the other by a sequence of translations, reflections, rotations, and dilations. Similar figures have the same shape but may be different sizes.

When you are told that two figures are similar, there must be a sequence of translations, reflections, rotations, and/or dilations that can transform one to the other.

Unit 4   **103**   Lesson 5

2 EXPLORE Similar Figures

A Identify a sequence of transformations that will transform figure A into figure B.

dilation by scale factor 2 with center at origin

and $(x, y) \rightarrow (x + 4, y + 6)$

B What happens if you reverse the order of the sequence you defined in **A**?

If you translate the figure first, the center

of the dilation will not be the origin.

C Tell whether figures A and B are congruent. Tell whether they are similar.

They are not congruent. They are similar.

D Identify a sequence of transformations that will transform figure C into figure D. Include a reflection.

dilation by scale factor $\frac{1}{2}$, translation up

5 units, reflection across y-axis

E Identify a sequence of transformations that will transform figure C into figure D. Include a rotation.

rotation of 180° about the origin, dilation by

scale factor $\frac{1}{2}$, translation up 5 units

TRY THIS!

1. Circle the figures that are similar to each other.

Unit 4   **104**   Lesson 5

UNIT 4

Problem Solving Connections
Stitch Perfect

COMMON CORE Standards for Mathematical Content

CC.8.G.1 Verify experimentally the properties of rotations, reflections, and translations: (a) Lines are taken to lines, and line segments to line segments of the same length. (b) Angles are taken to angles of the same measure. (c) Parallel lines are taken to parallel lines.

CC.8.G.2 Understand that a two-dimensional figure is congruent to another if the second figure can be obtained from the first by a sequence of rotations, reflections, and translations; given two congruent figures, describe a sequence that exhibits the congruence between them.

CC.8.G.3 Describe the effect of dilations, translations, rotations, and reflections on two-dimensional figures using coordinates.

CC.8.G.4 Understand that a two-dimensional figure is similar to another if the second figure can be obtained from the first by a sequence of rotations, reflections, translations, and dilations; given two similar two-dimensional figures, describe a sequence that exhibits the similarity between them.

INTRODUCE

Mathematical modeling is the process of using numbers, algebra, geometry, or other mathematical disciplines to describe and analyze the real world. Transformations are a powerful modeling tool that can be used to describe objects from real life, including nature and art. In this lesson, you will combine nature, art, and mathematics to create a cross-stitch pattern using transformations.

TEACH

1 Making the Body and Wings

Questioning Strategies

- Is the upper wing congruent to the lower wing? Explain. No; the upper wing is a polygon with 5 sides, and the lower wing has 6 sides.

- Why do you think Ellie would use reflections to create the second upper wing and the second lower wing? In nature, a butterfly appears to be symmetric on each side of its body. The line of symmetry in a reflection mimics the symmetry of a real butterfly.

Teaching Strategies

Give students an extra grid so that they can plot the pieces of the pattern as they work. This can act as their "rough draft" as they work. Once students have completed the pattern, they can transfer a neat sketch to the final answer grid.

2 Designing the Upper-Wing Pattern

Questioning Strategies

- Why do the instructions in part A describe the position of the square as "centered at the origin"? The dilation in part B only provides the scale factor, which implies that the center of dilation is the origin.

- Explain how the four squares in the upper wings are related. The two larger squares are congruent to each other. The two smaller squares are also congruent to each other. Each square is similar to the others.

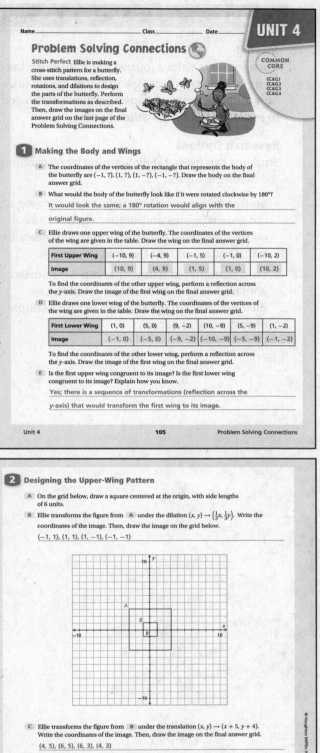

Problem Solving Connections 🌐

COMMON CORE
CC.8.G.1
CC.8.G.2
CC.8.G.3
CC.8.G.4

UNIT 4

Name_____ Class_____ Date_____

Stitch Perfect Ellie is making a cross-stitch pattern for a butterfly. She uses translations, reflection, rotations, and dilations to design the parts of the butterfly. Perform the transformations as described. Then, draw the images on the final answer grid on the last page of the Problem Solving Connections.

1 Making the Body and Wings

A The coordinates of the vertices of the rectangle that represents the body of the butterfly are $(-1, 7)$, $(1, 7)$, $(1, -7)$, $(-1, -7)$. Draw the body on the final answer grid.

B What would the body of the butterfly look like if it were rotated clockwise by 180°?

It would look the same; a 180° rotation would align with the

original figure.

C Ellie draws one upper wing of the butterfly. The coordinates of the vertices of the wing are given in the table. Draw the wing on the final answer grid.

First Upper Wing	(−10, 9)	(−4, 9)	(−1, 5)	(−1, 0)	(−10, 2)
Image	(10, 9)	(4, 9)	(1, 5)	(1, 0)	(10, 2)

To find the coordinates of the other upper wing, perform a reflection across the y-axis. Draw the image of the first wing on the final answer grid.

D Ellie draws one lower wing of the butterfly. The coordinates of the vertices of the wing are given in the table. Draw the wing on the final answer grid.

First Lower Wing	(1, 0)	(5, 0)	(9, −2)	(10, −9)	(5, −9)	(1, −2)
Image	(−1, 0)	(−5, 0)	(−9, −2)	(−10, −9)	(−5, −9)	(−1, −2)

To find the coordinates of the other lower wing, perform a reflection across the y-axis. Draw the image of the first wing on the final answer grid.

E Is the first upper wing congruent to its image? Is the first lower wing congruent to its image? Explain how you know.

Yes; there is a sequence of transformations (reflection across the

y-axis) that would transform the first wing to its image.

2 Designing the Upper-Wing Pattern

A On the grid below, draw a square centered at the origin, with side lengths of 6 units.

B Ellie transforms the figure from A under the dilation $(x, y) \rightarrow \left(\frac{1}{3}x, \frac{1}{3}y\right)$. Write the coordinates of the image. Then, draw the image on the grid below.

$(-1, 1)$, $(1, 1)$, $(1, -1)$, $(-1, -1)$

C Ellie transforms the figure from B under the translation $(x, y) \rightarrow (x + 5, y + 4)$. Write the coordinates of the image. Then, draw the image on the final answer grid.

$(4, 5)$, $(6, 5)$, $(6, 3)$, $(4, 3)$

D Ellie transforms the figure from C by reflecting it across the y-axis. Write the coordinates of the image. Then, draw the image on the final answer grid.

$(-4, 5)$, $(-6, 5)$, $(-6, 3)$, $(-4, 3)$

E On the final answer grid, there is a black square. Ellie reflects the square across the y-axis. Write the coordinates of the image. Then, draw the image on the final answer grid.

$(-9, 8)$, $(-6, 8)$, $(-6, 5)$, $(-9, 5)$

3 Designing the Lower-Wing Pattern

Questioning Strategies

• Explain how the four triangles in the lower wings are related. **All the triangles are congruent. Each one was created from the original figure using a sequence of translations, reflections, and rotations.**

• How can you double-check your algebraic work? **If a figure is out of place in the design on the final answer grid, you know that you have made an error.**

4 Final Answer Grid

Questioning Strategies

• What is the difference between two figures being congruent and two figures being similar? **Both congruent figures and similar figures are characterized by the same shape and congruent corresponding angle measures. In congruent figures, corresponding side lengths are congruent. While in similar figures, corresponding side lengths are proportional.**

> **MATHEMATICAL PRACTICE Highlighting the Standards**
>
> This Project provides an opportunity to address Standard 4 (Model with mathematics). As students work through the lesson, they should discover the structure behind the final image. This will lead to an understanding of how mathematics can be used to describe, or model, real-life objects.

CLOSE

Journal

Have students write a journal entry in which they summarize the project. Ask students to explain how different types of transformations were used to make the final cross-stitch pattern.

Research Options

Students can extend their learning by researching the following topics:

• Study other cross-stitch patterns to discover congruent figures and similar figures. Draw a coordinate plane over the pattern and describe transformations that result in the design.

• Find examples in nature that can be modeled with translations, reflections, rotations, or dilations. Encourage students to find examples of symmetry in nature.

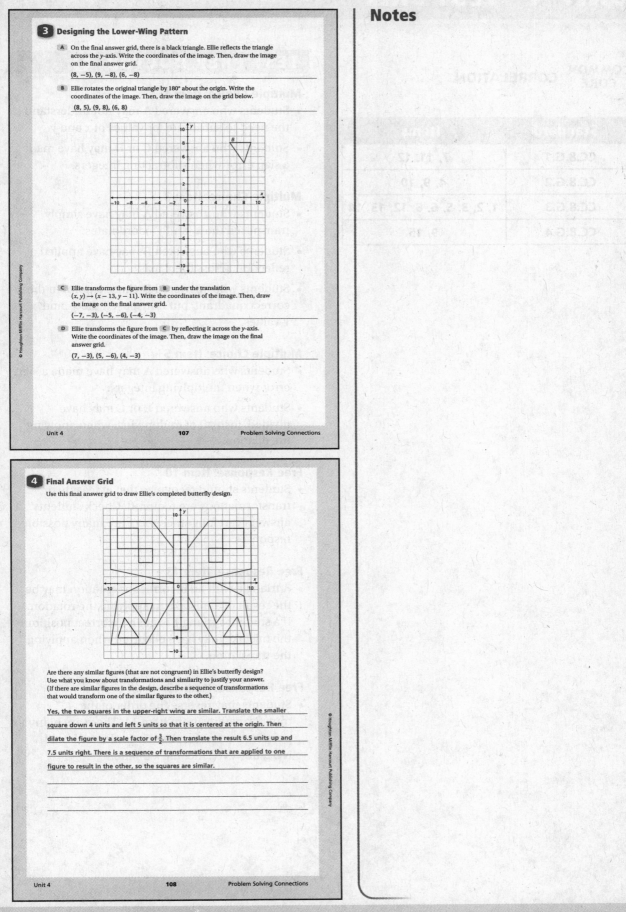

3 Designing the Lower-Wing Pattern

A On the final answer grid, there is a black triangle. Ellie reflects the triangle across the y-axis. Write the coordinates of the image. Then, draw the image on the final answer grid.

(8, −5), (9, −8), (6, −8)

B Ellie rotates the original triangle by 180° about the origin. Write the coordinates of the image. Then, draw the image on the grid below.

(8, 5), (9, 8), (6, 8)

C Ellie transforms the figure from **B** under the translation $(x, y) \rightarrow (x − 13, y − 11)$. Write the coordinates of the image. Then, draw the image on the final answer grid.

(−7, −3), (−5, −6), (−4, −3)

D Ellie transforms the figure from **C** by reflecting it across the y-axis. Write the coordinates of the image. Then, draw the image on the final answer grid.

(7, −3), (5, −6), (4, −3)

© Houghton Mifflin Harcourt Publishing Company

4 Final Answer Grid

Use this final answer grid to draw Ellie's completed butterfly design.

Are there any similar figures (that are not congruent) in Ellie's butterfly design? Use what you know about transformations and similarity to justify your answer. (If there are similar figures in the design, describe a sequence of transformations that would transform one of the similar figures to the other.)

Yes, the two squares in the upper-right wing are similar. Translate the smaller square down 4 units and left 5 units so that it is centered at the origin. Then dilate the figure by a scale factor of $\frac{3}{2}$. Then translate the result 6.5 units up and 7.5 units right. There is a sequence of transformations that are applied to one figure to result in the other, so the squares are similar.

© Houghton Mifflin Harcourt Publishing Company

CORRELATION

Standard	Items
CC.8.G.1	7, 11, 12
CC.8.G.2	4, 9, 10
CC.8.G.3	1, 2, 3, 5, 6, 8, 12, 13, 14
CC.8.G.4	9, 15

TEST PREP DOCTOR ✚

Multiple Choice: Item 1

- Students who answered **A** may not understand the need to substitute for values of x and y.
- Students who answered **C** or **D** may have made a sign error when subtracting integers.

Multiple Choice: Item 3

- Students who answered **A** may have simply transposed the x- and y-coordinates.
- Students who answered **B** may have applied a reflection across the x-axis.
- Students who answered **D** chose a point in the correct quadrant, but transposed the x- and y-values.

Multiple Choice: Item 5

- Students who answered **A** may have made a sign error when multiplying integers.
- Students who answered **B** or **C** may have divided, instead of multiplying, when applying the dilation.

Free Response: Item 10

- Students should recognize that at least two transformations are required. Check students' answers carefully since there are many possible responses.

Free Response: Item 13

- A triangle with an incorrect orientation may be the result of a mistake in applying the rotation. If a student's triangle is in an incorrect position, the mistake may have occurred when applying the translation.

Free Response: Item 15

- Students may reverse the order of the transformations from Item 14. There are many possible correct responses. Students should NOT, however, include a dilation.

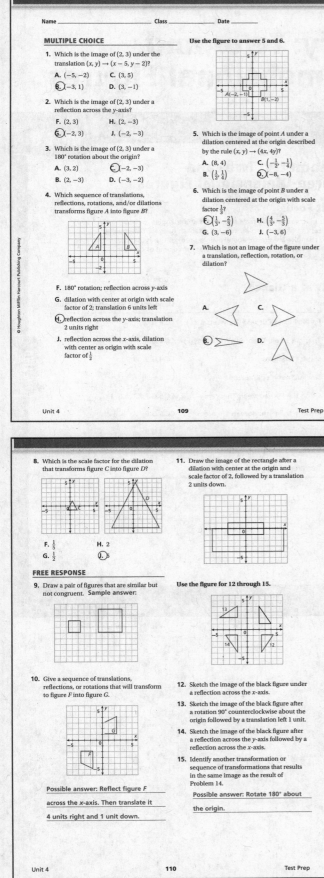

UNIT 4 TEST PREP

Name _____ Class _____ Date _____

MULTIPLE CHOICE

1. Which is the image of $(2, 3)$ under the translation $(x, y) \rightarrow (x - 5, y - 2)$?

   A. $(-5, -2)$ C. $(3, 5)$

   B. $(-3, 1)$ D. $(3, -1)$

2. Which is the image of $(2, 3)$ under a reflection across the y-axis?

   F. $(2, 3)$ H. $(2, -3)$

   G. $(-2, 3)$ J. $(-2, -3)$

3. Which is the image of $(2, 3)$ under a 180° rotation about the origin?

   A. $(3, 2)$ C. $(-2, -3)$

   B. $(2, -3)$ D. $(-3, -2)$

4. Which sequence of translations, reflections, rotations, and/or dilations transforms figure A into figure B?

   F. 180° rotation; reflection across y-axis

   G. dilation with center at origin with scale factor of 2; translation 6 units left

   H. reflection across the y-axis; translation 2 units right

   J. reflection across the x-axis, dilation with center as origin with scale factor of $\frac{1}{2}$

Use the figure to answer 5 and 6.

$A(-2, -1)$ $B(1, -2)$

5. Which is the image of point A under a dilation centered at the origin described by the rule $(x, y) \rightarrow (4x, 4y)$?

   A. $(8, 4)$ C. $\left(-\frac{1}{2}, -\frac{1}{4}\right)$

   B. $\left(\frac{1}{2}, \frac{1}{4}\right)$ D. $(-8, -4)$

6. Which is the image of point B under a dilation centered at the origin with scale factor $\frac{1}{3}$?

   F. $\left(\frac{1}{3}, -\frac{2}{3}\right)$ H. $\left(\frac{4}{3}, -\frac{5}{3}\right)$

   G. $(3, -6)$ J. $(-3, 6)$

7. Which is not an image of the figure under a translation, reflection, rotation, or dilation?

   A.   C.

   B.   D.

© Houghton Mifflin Harcourt Publishing Company

---

8. Which is the scale factor for the dilation that transforms figure C into figure D?

   F. $\frac{1}{5}$ H. 2

   G. $\frac{1}{2}$ J. 5

FREE RESPONSE

9. Draw a pair of figures that are similar but not congruent. **Sample answer:**

10. Give a sequence of translations, reflections, or rotations that will transform to figure F into figure G.

   Possible answer: Reflect figure F

   across the x-axis. Then translate it

   4 units right and 1 unit down.

11. Draw the image of the rectangle after a dilation with center at the origin and scale factor of 2, followed by a translation 2 units down.

Use the figure for 12 through 15.

12. Sketch the image of the black figure under a reflection across the x-axis.

13. Sketch the image of the black figure after a rotation 90° counterclockwise about the origin followed by a translation left 1 unit.

14. Sketch the image of the black figure after a reflection across the y-axis followed by a reflection across the x-axis.

15. Identify another transformation or sequence of transformations that results in the same image as the result of Problem 14.

   Possible answer: Rotate 180° about

   the origin.

© Houghton Mifflin Harcourt Publishing Company

UNIT 5

Geometry: Two- and Three-Dimensional Figures

Unit Vocabulary

alternate exterior
angles   (5-1)

alternate interior
angles   (5-1)

corresponding
angles   (5-1)

exterior angles   (5-1)

hypotenuse   (5-5)

interior angles   (5-2)

leg   (5-5)

remote interior
angles   (5-2)

same-side interior
angles   (5-1)

transversal   (5-1)

UNIT 5

Geometry: Two- and Three-Dimensional Figures

Unit Focus

In this unit, you will use facts about lines and triangles to determine the sizes of unknown angles. You will establish rules for determining if two triangles are similar, and explain a proof of the Pythagorean Theorem. You will also learn the formulas for volume of cylinders, cones, and spheres.

Unit at a Glance

COMMON CORE

UNIT 5

Unit 5   **111**   Geometry: Two- and Three-Dimensional Figures

---

Unpacking the Common Core State Standards

Use the table to help you understand the Common Core State Standards that are taught in this unit. Refer to the lessons listed after each standard for exploration and practice.

COMMON CORE Standards for Mathematical Content	What It Means For You
CC.8.EE.6 Use similar triangles to explain why the slope *m* is the same between any two distinct points on a non-vertical line in the coordinate plane. Lesson 5-4	Given similar triangles, you will explain why the slope is the same between any two points.
CC.8.G.5 Use informal arguments to establish facts about the angle sum and exterior angle of triangles, about the angles created when parallel lines are cut by a transversal, and the angle-angle criterion for similarity of triangles. Lessons 5-1, 5-2, 5-3	You will learn about the special angle relationships formed when parallel lines are intersected by a third line called a transversal. You will learn that the sum of the angle measures in a triangle is the same for all triangles. You will learn one way to determine whether two triangles are similar.
CC.8.G.6 Explain a proof of the Pythagorean Theorem and its converse. Lesson 5-6	You will use an area model to prove the Pythagorean Theorem. You will also explore whether the converse (opposite) of the Pythagorean Theorem is true.
CC.8.G.7 Apply the Pythagorean Theorem to determine unknown side lengths in right triangles in real-world and mathematical problems in two and three dimensions. Lesson 5-5	You will use the Pythagorean Theorem to find the lengths of sides in a right triangle.
CC.8.G.8 Apply the Pythagorean Theorem to find the distance between two points in a coordinate system. Lesson 5-5	You will use the Pythagorean Theorem to find the hypotenuse of a right triangle in the coordinate plane.
CC.8.G.9 Know the formulas for the volumes of cones, cylinders, and spheres, and use them to solve real-world and mathematical problems. Lesson 5-7	You will learn the formulas for volume of a cylinder, cone, and sphere.

UNIT 5

© Houghton Mifflin Harcourt Publishing Company

Unpacking the Common Core State Standards

This page lists and explains the Standards for Mathematical Content that are addressed in this unit. For information about the Standards for Mathematical Practice, which are integrated throughout the text, see Teacher Edition pages vii–xiii.

UNIT 5

Notes

_____

_____

_____

_____

_____

_____

_____

_____

_____

_____

_____

Parallel Lines Cut by a Transversal

Essential question: *What can you conclude about the angles formed by parallel lines that are cut by a transversal?*

COMMON CORE Standards for Mathematical Content

CC.8.G.5 Use informal arguments to establish facts about the angle sum and exterior angle of triangles, about the angles created when parallel lines are cut by a transversal, and the angle-angle criterion for similarity of triangles.

Vocabulary

transversal

corresponding angles

alternate interior angles

alternate exterior angles

same-side interior angles

Prerequisites

Parallel lines

Translations

Solving equations

Math Background

If t is a line that intersects lines ℓ_1 and ℓ_2 then t is a transversal. In this lesson, students discover the angle relationships that result from a transversal intersecting two parallel lines. They learn that when a transversal intersects parallel lines, corresponding angles are congruent, alternate interior angles are congruent, alternate exterior angles are congruent, and same-side interior angles are supplementary. Knowing these angle relationships allows students to solve for missing angle measures in a diagram.

INTRODUCE

Angles and angle measurement are key ideas throughout geometry. Students know the definition of an angle, have measured angles, and have explored special angle pairs. In this lesson, students will continue this work by exploring special angle relationships that are created by one line intersecting two parallel lines.

TEACH

1 EXPLORE

Questioning Strategies

• In part C, is it important that your diagram look exactly like the image shown? **No; but it is important that the relationships among the lines are accurate.**

• How many pairs of corresponding angles are there? Explain how you know. **4; the intersection of the transversal with one of the parallel lines creates four angles. Each of these angles is half of a corresponding pair.**

Differentiated Instruction

Allow students to work in small groups. Each group should draw a pair of parallel lines and a transversal. Guide groups to work independently and then share their conjectures.

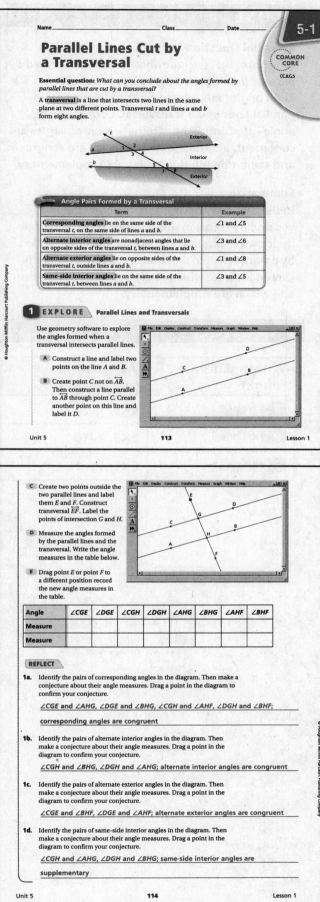

Questioning Strategies

- Along what line do you translate ∠2? **line *t***
- After the translation, which angle does ∠2 align with? **∠2 aligns with ∠6.**

3 **EXAMPLE**

- In part A, what are the measures of the other numbered angles? **$m\angle 1 = m\angle 8 = 55°$; $m\angle 2 = m\angle 3 = m\angle 6 = m\angle 7 = 125°$**
- In part B, if you are given the measure of one angle ($m\angle SVW$), can you determine the measure of the other angles? **Yes; you can use the relationships among the remaining angles to find each measure.**

⋰ **MATHEMATICAL PRACTICE** **Highlighting the Standards**

This Lesson is an opportunity to address Standard 7 (Look for and make use of structure). Students should recognize the clear structure created by the intersection of parallel lines by a transversal. By understanding the relationships among the angles created, students will be able to solve a variety of problems.

CLOSE

Essential Question

What can you conclude about the angles formed by parallel lines that are cut by a transversal?
Eight angles are created by the intersection of parallel lines and a transversal. Corresponding angles are congruent, alternate interior angles are congruent, alternate exterior angles are congruent, and same-side interior angles are supplementary.

Summarize

In their journal, have students define the five vocabulary terms in this lesson. Have them draw their own diagram with parallel lines intersected by a transversal to illustrate each term. Students should indicate which angle pairs are congruent and which are supplementary.

PRACTICE

Where skills are taught	Where skills are practiced
1 EXPLORE	EXS. 1–10
2 EXPLORE	EXS. 1–10
3 EXPLORE	EXS. 11–16

You can use your knowledge of transformations to informally justify the angle relationships formed by parallel lines and a transversal.

2 EXPLORE Justifying Angle Relationships

Lines *a* and *b* are parallel. (The blue arrows on the diagram indicate parallel lines.)

A Trace line *a* and line *t* on a piece of paper. Label ∠1. Translate your traced angle down so that line *a* aligns with line *b* and line *t* aligns with itself. Which angle does ∠1 align with? __∠5__

B Because there is a translation that transforms ∠1 to __∠5__, ∠1 and __∠5__ are congruent.

TRY THIS!

2. Name a pair of alternate interior angles. What transformation(s) could you use to show that that those angles are congruent?

Sample answer: ∠3 and ∠6; **rotate ∠3 about the intersection point of line *a* and**

line *t*, then translate along line *t* to align with ∠6

3 EXAMPLE Finding Unknown Angle Measures

Find each angle measure.

A m∠5 when m∠4 = 55°

∠4 is congruent to ∠5 because they are
__alternate interior angles__

m∠5 = __55__ °

B m∠SVW

∠SVW is __supplementary__ to ∠YVW because they are a linear pair.

∠SVW + ∠YVW = 180°

$4x° +$ __8x__ ° = 180°

__12__ *x* = 180°

$\dfrac{\text{12}\ x}{\text{12}} = \dfrac{180}{12}$

x = __15__

∠SVW = ∠8x° = $\left(8 \cdot \text{15}\right)° =$ __120__ °

PRACTICE

Use the figure for 1–4.

1. Name a pair of corresponding angles.
Sample answer: **∠1 and ∠5**

2. Name a pair of alternate exterior angles.
Sample answer: **∠2 and ∠7**

3. Name the relationship between ∠3 and ∠6.
alternate interior angles

4. Name the relationship between ∠4 and ∠6.
same-side interior angles

For parallel lines intersected by a transversal, tell whether each type of angle pair is congruent or supplementary.

5. alternate interior angles
congruent

6. linear pair
supplementary

7. corresponding angles
congruent

8. same-side interior angles
supplementary

9. vertical angles
congruent

10. alternate exterior angles
congruent

Find each angle measure.

11. m∠2 when m∠1 = 30°
150°

12. m∠6 when m∠1 = 30°
150°

13. m∠7 when m∠3 = 150°
150°

14. m∠EGB
100°

15. m∠AGH
100°

16. m∠DHF
80°

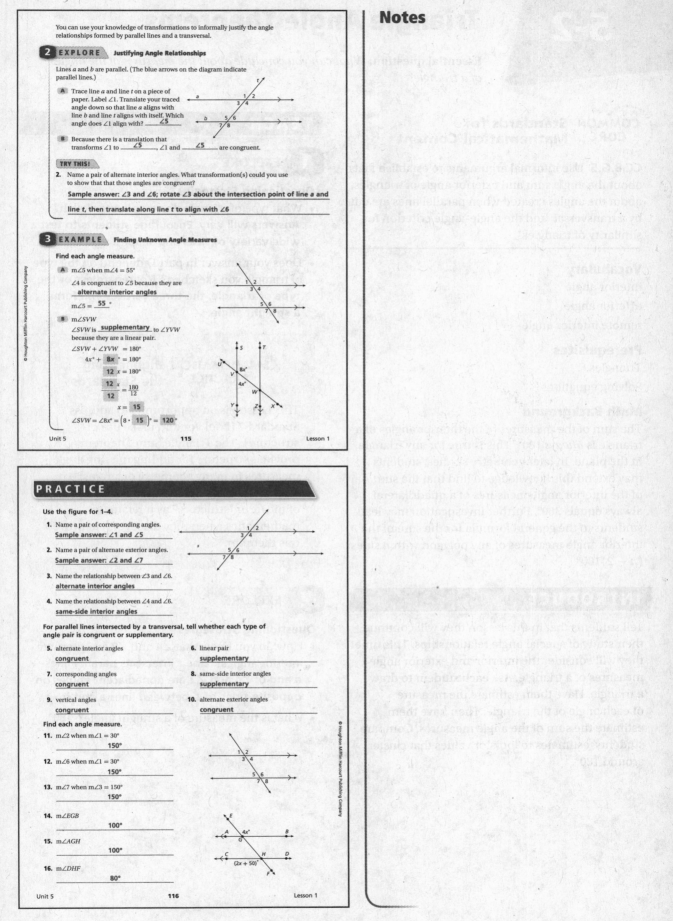

Notes

© Houghton Mifflin Harcourt Publishing Company

Triangle Angle Theorems

Essential question: *What can you conclude about the measures of the angles of a triangle?*

COMMON CORE **Standards for Mathematical Content**

CC.8.G.5 Use informal arguments to establish facts about the angle sum and exterior angle of triangles, about the angles created when parallel lines are cut by a transversal, and the angle-angle criterion for similarity of triangles.

Vocabulary

interior angle

exterior angle

remote interior angle

Prerequisites

Triangles

Solving equations

Math Background

The sum of the measures of the interior angles of a triangle is *always* 180°. This is true for any triangle in the plane. In later geometry studies, students may extend this knowledge to find that the sum of the interior angle measures of a quadrilateral always equals 360°. Further investigation may lead students to the general formula for the sum of the interior angle measures of any polygon with *n* sides: $(n - 2)180°$

INTRODUCE

Tell students that in this lesson they will continue their study of special angle relationships. This time they will consider the interior and exterior angle measures of a triangle. Ask each student to draw a triangle. Have them estimate the measure of each angle of the triangle. Then have them estimate the sum of the angle measures. Compare students' estimates to look for values that cluster around 180°.

TEACH

1 EXPLORE

Questioning Strategies

- What type of triangle do you plan to sketch? **Answers will vary. Encourage students to test a wide variety of sizes and shapes.**

- Does your answer in part D depend on the type of triangle you sketched? **No; regardless of the type of triangle, the three vertices will form a straight angle.**

> **MATHEMATICAL PRACTICE** **Highlighting the Standards**
>
> This Lesson is an opportunity to address Standard 7 (Look for and make use of structure). The Triangle Sum Theorem provides structure for finding missing angle measures in many geometry diagrams. Students will strengthen their understanding of the term "structure" as it relates to mathematics when they discover and prove this theorem.

2 EXPLORE

Questioning Strategies

- How do you know that ∠4 and ∠2 are alternate interior angles? **Line *t* intersects parallel lines *a* and *b*; ∠4 and ∠2 are nonadjacent angles on opposite sides of *t*, between lines *a* and *b*.**

- What is the measure of a straight angle? **180°**

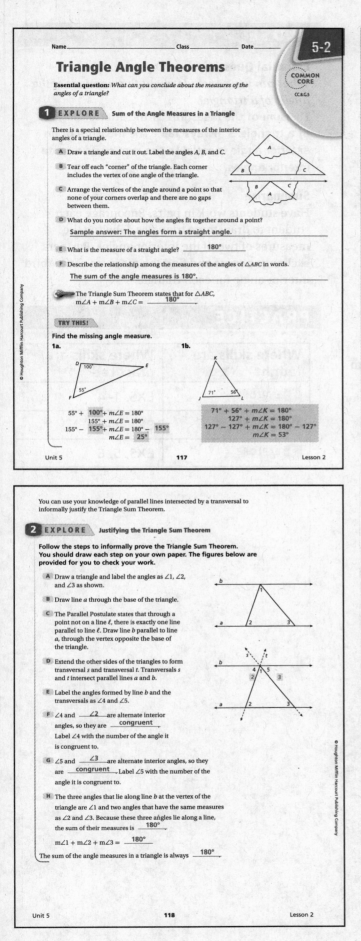

Name_____ Class_____ Date_____

5-2

Triangle Angle Theorems

COMMON CORE
CC&G.5

Essential question: *What can you conclude about the measures of the angles of a triangle?*

1 EXPLORE Sum of the Angle Measures in a Triangle

There is a special relationship between the measures of the interior angles of a triangle.

A Draw a triangle and cut it out. Label the angles A, B, and C.

B Tear off each "corner" of the triangle. Each corner includes the vertex of one angle of the triangle.

C Arrange the vertices of the angle around a point so that none of your corners overlap and there are no gaps between them.

D What do you notice about how the angles fit together around a point?

Sample answer: The angles form a straight angle.

E What is the measure of a straight angle?   **180°**

F Describe the relationship among the measures of the angles of △ABC in words.

The sum of the angle measures is 180°.

The Triangle Sum Theorem states that for △ABC,
$m\angle A + m\angle B + m\angle C =$ ___**180°**___

TRY THIS!

Find the missing angle measure.

1a.

$55° + 100° + m\angle E = 180°$
$155° + m\angle E = 180°$
$155° - 155° + m\angle E = 180° -$ **155°**
$m\angle E =$ **25°**

1b.

$71° + 56° + m\angle K = 180°$
$127° + m\angle K = 180°$
$127° - 127° + m\angle K = 180° - 127°$
$m\angle K = 53°$

© Houghton Mifflin Harcourt Publishing Company

You can use your knowledge of parallel lines intersected by a transversal to informally justify the Triangle Sum Theorem.

2 EXPLORE Justifying the Triangle Sum Theorem

Follow the steps to informally prove the Triangle Sum Theorem. You should draw each step on your own paper. The figures below are provided for you to check your work.

A Draw a triangle and label the angles as ∠1, ∠2, and ∠3 as shown.

B Draw line *a* through the base of the triangle.

C The Parallel Postulate states that through a point not on a line ℓ, there is exactly one line parallel to line ℓ. Draw line *b* parallel to line *a*, through the vertex opposite the base of the triangle.

D Extend the other sides of the triangles to form transversal *s* and transversal *t*. Transversals *s* and *t* intersect parallel lines *a* and *b*.

E Label the angles formed by line *b* and the transversals as ∠4 and ∠5.

F ∠4 and __∠2__ are alternate interior angles, so they are __congruent__.
Label ∠4 with the number of the angle it is congruent to.

G ∠5 and __∠3__ are alternate interior angles, so they are __congruent__. Label ∠5 with the number of the angle it is congruent to.

H The three angles that lie along line *b* at the vertex of the triangle are ∠1 and two angles that have the same measures as ∠2 and ∠3. Because these three angles lie along a line, the sum of their measures is __180°__.

$m\angle 1 + m\angle 2 + m\angle 3 =$ ___**180°**___

The sum of the angle measures in a triangle is always ___**180°**___

© Houghton Mifflin Harcourt Publishing Company

Questioning Strategies

- Suppose m∠1 = 80° and m∠4 = 140°. How can you determine the measures of ∠2 and ∠3? ∠4 and ∠3 form a linear pair, so they are supplementary: m∠4 + m∠3 = 140° + m∠3 = 180°, so m∠3 = 40°; m∠1 + m∠2 + m∠3 = 80° + m∠2 + 40° = 180°, so m∠2 = 60°.

- Look at the triangle and exterior angles in Reflect 3a. Do you see any special relationship among the exterior angles of the triangle? **When two angles are exterior angles at the same vertex, they are congruent. They form vertical angles.**

Teaching Strategies

Before beginning the Practice problems, invite students to sketch triangles on the board and practice finding the measures of all interior and exterior angles. Work through at least one problem which gives measures for two angles and at least one problem that provides algebraic expressions for the angle measures.

CLOSE

Essential Question

What can you conclude about the measures of the angles of a triangle?
The sum of the measures of the interior angles of a triangle is always 180°. The measure of an exterior angle is equal to the sum of its remote interior angles.

Summarize

Have students work in pairs. Encourage each student to draw three triangles, labeling the measures of two of the interior angles. Partners exchange papers and find the measure of the third interior angle for each triangle.

PRACTICE

Where skills are taught	Where skills are practiced
1 EXPLORE	EXS. 1–4
2 EXPLORE	EXS. 1–4
3 EXPLORE	EXS. 5, 6

An **interior angle** of a triangle is formed by two sides of the triangle. An **exterior angle** of a triangle is formed by one side of the triangle and the extension of an adjacent side. Each exterior angle has two *remote interior angles*. A **remote interior angle** is an interior angle that is not adjacent to the exterior angle.

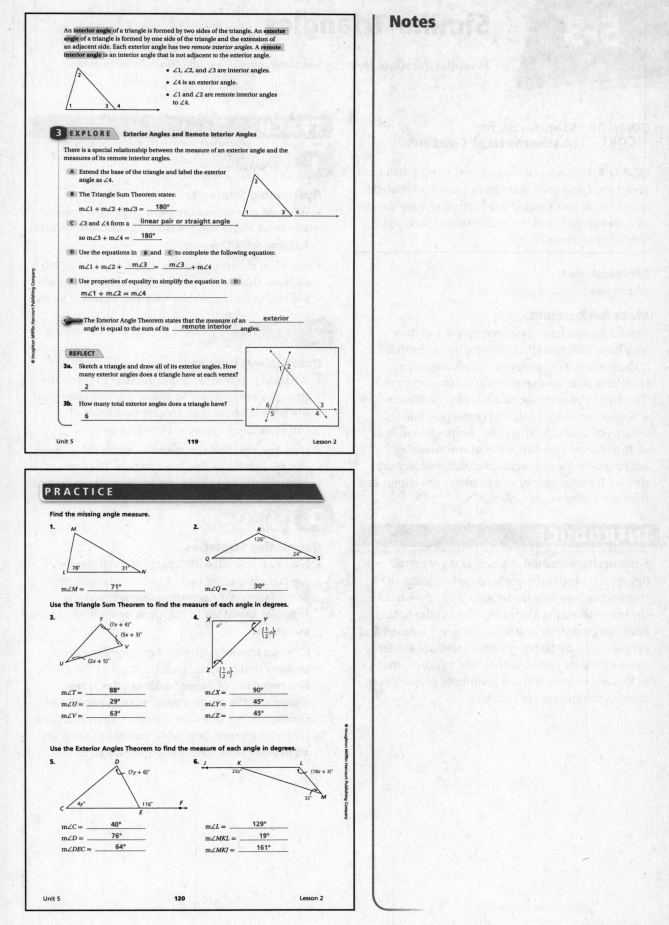

- ∠1, ∠2, and ∠3 are interior angles.
- ∠4 is an exterior angle.
- ∠1 and ∠2 are remote interior angles to ∠4.

3 EXPLORE   Exterior Angles and Remote Interior Angles

There is a special relationship between the measure of an exterior angle and the measures of its remote interior angles.

A Extend the base of the triangle and label the exterior angle as ∠4.

B The Triangle Sum Theorem states:

$$m\angle 1 + m\angle 2 + m\angle 3 = \underline{180°}$$

C ∠3 and ∠4 form a ___linear pair or straight angle___

so $m\angle 3 + m\angle 4 = \underline{180°}$

D Use the equations in **B** and **C** to complete the following equation:

$$m\angle 1 + m\angle 2 + \underline{m\angle 3} = \underline{m\angle 3} + m\angle 4$$

E Use properties of equality to simplify the equation in **D**:

$$\underline{m\angle 1 + m\angle 2 = m\angle 4}$$

🔑 The Exterior Angle Theorem states that the measure of an ___exterior___ angle is equal to the sum of its ___remote interior___ angles.

REFLECT

3a. Sketch a triangle and draw all of its exterior angles. How many exterior angles does a triangle have at each vertex?

___2___

3b. How many total exterior angles does a triangle have?

___6___

PRACTICE

Find the missing angle measure.

1.

$m\angle M = \underline{71°}$

2.

$m\angle Q = \underline{30°}$

Use the Triangle Sum Theorem to find the measure of each angle in degrees.

3.

$(7x + 4)°$
$(5x + 3)°$
$(2x + 5)°$

$m\angle T = \underline{88°}$
$m\angle U = \underline{29°}$
$m\angle V = \underline{63°}$

4.

$n°$
$\left(\frac{1}{2}n\right)°$
$\left(\frac{1}{2}n\right)°$

$m\angle X = \underline{90°}$
$m\angle Y = \underline{45°}$
$m\angle Z = \underline{45°}$

Use the Exterior Angles Theorem to find the measure of each angle in degrees.

5.

$(7y + 6)°$
$4y°$
$116°$

$m\angle C = \underline{40°}$
$m\angle D = \underline{76°}$
$m\angle DEC = \underline{64°}$

6.

$23z°$
$(18z + 3)°$
$32°$

$m\angle L = \underline{129°}$
$m\angle MKL = \underline{19°}$
$m\angle MKJ = \underline{161°}$

Similar Triangles

Essential question: *How can you determine when two triangles are similar?*

COMMON CORE **Standards for Mathematical Content**

CC.8.G.5 Use informal arguments to establish facts about the angle sum and exterior angle of triangles, about the angles created when parallel lines are cut by a transversal, and the angle-angle criterion for similarity of triangles.

Prerequisites

Writing and solving proportions

Math Background

Similar figures have the same shape, but they may have different sizes. Two figures are similar if there exists a sequence of transformations including dilation that transforms one figure onto the other. The corresponding angles of similar triangles are congruent, and corresponding side lengths of similar triangles are proportional. If all three corresponding sides of two triangles are proportional in length, then the triangles are similar. If two angles of two triangles are congruent, then the triangles are similar.

INTRODUCE

Students have learned that any two geometric figures are similar if there is some sequence of transformations that transforms one figure onto the other. Students also know that similar triangles have congruent corresponding angle measures and proportional corresponding side lengths. Review these concepts with students, and tell them that in this lesson they will use geometric properties to show that triangles are similar.

TEACH

1 EXPLORE

Questioning Strategies

- What do you expect the third angle to measure? **The third angle will measure 75° because of the Triangle Sum Theorem.**

- Are all of the triangles drawn the same size? **No, all have the same three angle measures and all are the same shape, but they are different sizes.**

2 EXAMPLE

Questioning Strategies

- What do you need to show in order to prove the triangles are similar? **To prove the two triangles are similar, show that at least two pairs of corresponding angles are congruent.**

- How can you find the measure of the third angle in a triangle? **Use the Triangle Sum Theorem to subtract the two given angle measures from 180°.**

3 EXAMPLE

Questioning Strategies

- How can you tell which parts of the triangles are corresponding parts from the given names of the triangles? **Corresponding parts of the triangles are listed in the same order in similarity statements.**

- Can you use two pairs of corresponding sides to show that two triangles are similar? Explain. **No, two pairs of corresponding sides is not enough. If the angle measures between the two corresponding sides are different, then the third pair of corresponding sides would not form an equivalent ratio with the other two pairs.**

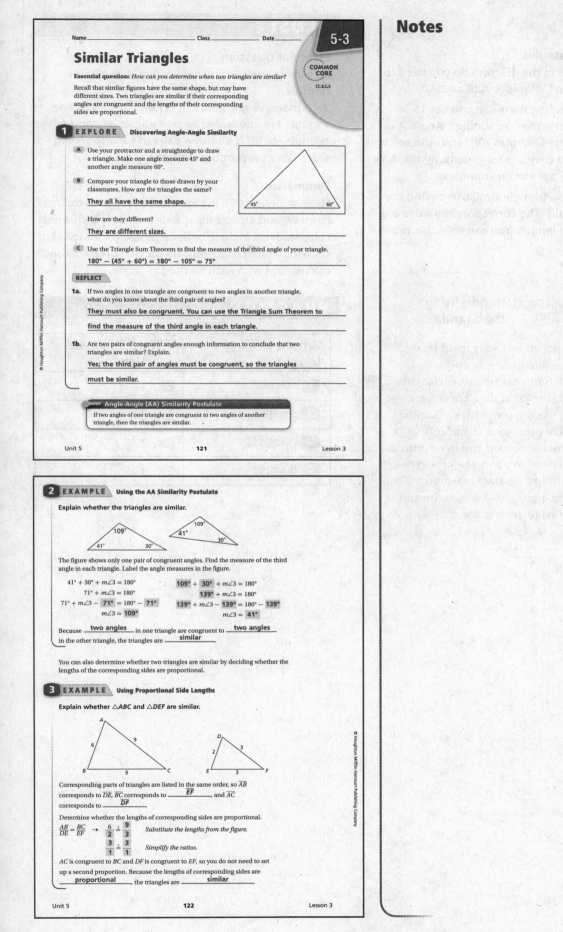

Similar Triangles

Essential question: *How can you determine when two triangles are similar?*

Recall that similar figures have the same shape, but may have different sizes. Two triangles are similar if their corresponding angles are congruent and the lengths of their corresponding sides are proportional.

1 EXPLORE Discovering Angle-Angle Similarity

A Use your protractor and a straightedge to draw a triangle. Make one angle measure 45° and another angle measure 60°.

B Compare your triangle to those drawn by your classmates. How are the triangles the same?

They all have the same shape.

How are they different?

They are different sizes.

C Use the Triangle Sum Theorem to find the measure of the third angle of your triangle.

180° − (45° + 60°) = 180° − 105° = 75°

REFLECT

1a. If two angles in one triangle are congruent to two angles in another triangle, what do you know about the third pair of angles?

They must also be congruent. You can use the Triangle Sum Theorem to

find the measure of the third angle in each triangle.

1b. Are two pairs of congruent angles enough information to conclude that two triangles are similar? Explain.

Yes; the third pair of angles must be congruent, so the triangles

must be similar.

> **Angle-Angle (AA) Similarity Postulate**
> If two angles of one triangle are congruent to two angles of another triangle, then the triangles are similar.

2 EXAMPLE Using the AA Similarity Postulate

Explain whether the triangles are similar.

The figure shows only one pair of congruent angles. Find the measure of the third angle in each triangle. Label the angle measures in the figure.

$41° + 30° + m\angle 3 = 180°$

$71° + m\angle 3 = 180°$

$71° + m\angle 3 - \boxed{71°} = 180° - \boxed{71°}$

$m\angle 3 = \boxed{109°}$

$\boxed{109°} + \boxed{30°} + m\angle 3 = 180°$

$139° + m\angle 3 = 180°$

$139° + m\angle 3 - \boxed{139°} = 180° - \boxed{139°}$

$m\angle 3 = \boxed{41°}$

Because ___two angles___ in one triangle are congruent to ___two angles___ in the other triangle, the triangles are ___similar___.

You can also determine whether two triangles are similar by deciding whether the lengths of the corresponding sides are proportional.

3 EXAMPLE Using Proportional Side Lengths

Explain whether △ABC and △DEF are similar.

Corresponding parts of triangles are listed in the same order, so $\overline{AB}$ corresponds to $\overline{DE}$, $\overline{BC}$ corresponds to ___$\overline{EF}$___, and $\overline{AC}$ corresponds to ___$\overline{DF}$___

Determine whether the lengths of corresponding sides are proportional.

$\dfrac{AB}{DE} = \dfrac{BC}{EF} \rightarrow \dfrac{6}{2} \stackrel{?}{=} \dfrac{9}{3}$ *Substitute the lengths from the figure.*

$\dfrac{3}{1} \stackrel{?}{=} \dfrac{3}{1}$ *Simplify the ratios.*

AC is congruent to *BC* and *DF* is congruent to *EF*, so you do not need to set up a second proportion. Because the lengths of corresponding sides are ___proportional___, the triangles are ___similar___

Questioning Strategies

- Which triangles in the diagram do you need to show are similar? triangles *ABC* and *ADE*

- What corresponding parts can you use to show that the triangles are similar? Angle *A* is congruent to itself. Angles *ABC* and *ADE* are both right angles, so they are congruent. By the AA postulate, they are similar triangles.

- How can you use triangle similarity to find the height of the ball? The corresponding sides are proportional in length. You can then use ratios to find *h*.

MATHEMATICAL PRACTICE Highlighting the Standards

This Lesson is an opportunity to address Standard 2 (Reason abstractly and quantitatively). Students examine triangles to find ways to show that they are similar. Then students use the properties of similar triangles to solve problems. In order to interpret information given and determine the information needed to apply the properties, students have to use abstract reasoning. Then students reason quantitatively to write and solve proportions to answer the question.

CLOSE

Essential Question

How can you determine when two triangles are similar?

Two triangles are similar if (1) two angles of one triangle are congruent to two angles of another triangle, or (2) if all three pairs of corresponding sides have proportional lengths.

Summarize

Have students write the essential question in their journals, and answer the question in their own words. Have students include both methods (AA and SSS) of showing similar triangles, and provide diagrams and calculations with each method.

PRACTICE

Where skills are taught	Where skills are practiced
1 EXPLORE	EX. 1
2 EXAMPLE	EX. 2
3 EXAMPLE	EX. 2
4 EXAMPLE	EX. 3

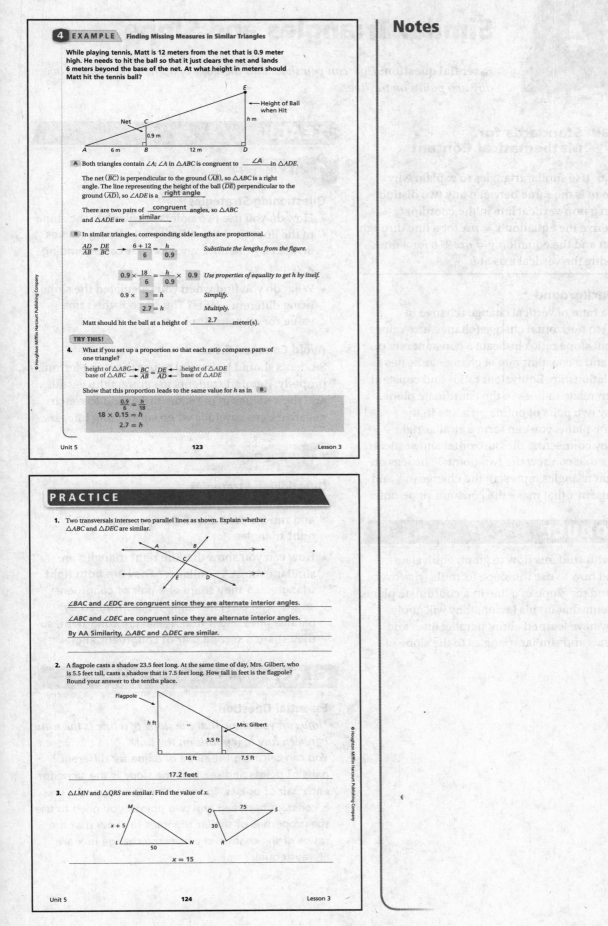

4 EXAMPLE Finding Missing Measures in Similar Triangles

While playing tennis, Matt is 12 meters from the net that is 0.9 meter high. He needs to hit the ball so that it just clears the net and lands 6 meters beyond the base of the net. At what height in meters should Matt hit the tennis ball?

A Both triangles contain ∠A; ∠A in △ABC is congruent to ___∠A___ in △ADE.

The net ($\overline{BC}$) is perpendicular to the ground ($\overline{AB}$), so △ABC is a right angle. The line representing the height of the ball ($\overline{DE}$) perpendicular to the ground ($\overline{AD}$), so ∠ADE is a ___right angle___.

There are two pairs of ___congruent___ angles, so △ABC and △ADE are ___similar___.

B In similar triangles, corresponding side lengths are proportional.

$$\frac{AD}{AB} = \frac{DE}{BC} \rightarrow \frac{6+12}{6} = \frac{h}{0.9}$$ *Substitute the lengths from the figure.*

$$0.9 \times \frac{18}{6} = \frac{h}{0.9} \times 0.9$$ *Use properties of equality to get h by itself.*

$$0.9 \times 3 = h$$ *Simplify.*

$$2.7 = h$$ *Multiply.*

Matt should hit the ball at a height of ___2.7___ meter(s).

TRY THIS!

4. What if you set up a proportion so that each ratio compares parts of one triangle?

$$\frac{\text{height of } \triangle ABC}{\text{base of } \triangle ABC} \rightarrow \frac{BC}{AB} = \frac{DE}{AD} \leftarrow \frac{\text{height of } \triangle ADE}{\text{base of } \triangle ADE}$$

Show that this proportion leads to the same value for h as in **B**.

$$\frac{0.9}{6} = \frac{h}{18}$$
$$18 \times 0.15 = h$$
$$2.7 = h$$

PRACTICE

1. Two transversals intersect two parallel lines as shown. Explain whether △ABC and △DEC are similar.

∠BAC and ∠EDC are congruent since they are alternate interior angles.

∠ABC and ∠DEC are congruent since they are alternate interior angles.

By AA Similarity, △ABC and △DEC are similar.

2. A flagpole casts a shadow 23.5 feet long. At the same time of day, Mrs. Gilbert, who is 5.5 feet tall, casts a shadow that is 7.5 feet long. How tall in feet is the flagpole? Round your answer to the tenths place.

17.2 feet

3. △LMN and △QRS are similar. Find the value of x.

x = 15

Similar Triangles and Slope

Essential question: *How can you show that the slope of a line is the same between any two points on the line?*

COMMON CORE **Standards for Mathematical Content**

CC.8.EE.6 Use similar triangles to explain why the slope m is the same between any two distinct points on a non-vertical line in the coordinate plane; derive the equation $y = mx$ for a line through the origin and the equation $y = mx + b$ for a line intercepting the vertical axis at b.

Math Background

Slope is a ratio of vertical change (change in y-values) to horizontal change (change in x-values). Equivalent slope ratios indicate a constant rate of change, and a constant rate of change indicates a linear relationship. Equivalent ratios and constant rates both relate to lines in the coordinate plane. Using any two pairs of points on a line in the coordinate plane, you can form a similar right triangle by connecting the horizontal and vertical segments that connect the two points. The legs of these right triangles represent the change in y and the change in x that make the constant slope ratio.

INTRODUCE

Review with students how to graph equivalent ratios and how to use the slope formula (rise over run) to find the slope of a line in a coordinate plane. Tell students that in this lesson, they will apply what they have learned about parallel lines and transversals and similar triangles to the slope of a line.

TEACH

1 EXPLORE

Questioning Strategies
- How do you use two points to calculate the slope of the line? Find the difference in their y-values divided by the difference in their corresponding x-values.

- What do you find when you calculated the slope using different points? The slope is the same value for all pairs of points.

Avoid Common Errors

Students should be careful to use the slope formula properly. Remind students to subtract the y-values and the x-values in the same order, and to watch negative signs carefully when subtracting integers.

2 EXPLORE

Questioning Strategies
- What shapes do you form by drawing the rise and run for the indicated slopes in part B? right triangles

- How can you show that the right triangles are similar using AA Similarity? They are both right triangles, so they share one pair of congruent angles. The corresponding angles formed by parallel lines and a transversal are congruent, so they share a second pair of congruent angles

CLOSE

Essential Question

How can you show that the slope of a line is the same between any two points on the line?
You can calculate the slope of a line for different pairs of points and see that the slope is the same for each pair of points. To show that the slope of a line is constant between *any* two points, you need to use the properties of similar triangles to show that the ratios of the change in y over the change in x are always equal.

5-4

Similar Triangles and Slope

Essential question: *How can you show that the slope of a line is the same between any two points on the line?*

COMMON CORE

CC.8.EE.6

1 EXPLORE   Investigating Slope

The graph shows the linear function $y = -\frac{2}{3}x + 4$.

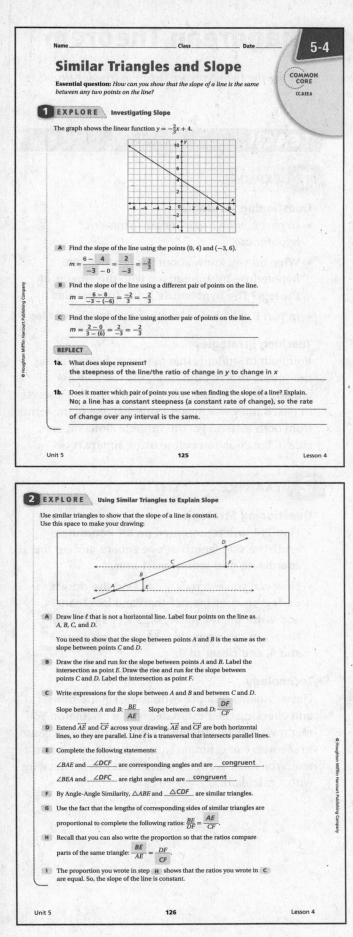

A Find the slope of the line using the points $(0, 4)$ and $(-3, 6)$.

$$m = \frac{6 - 4}{-3 - 0} = \frac{2}{-3} = -\frac{2}{3}$$

B Find the slope of the line using a different pair of points on the line.

$$m = \frac{6 - 8}{-3 - (-6)} = \frac{-2}{3} = -\frac{2}{3}$$

C Find the slope of the line using another pair of points on the line.

$$m = \frac{2 - 0}{3 - (6)} = \frac{2}{-3} = -\frac{2}{3}$$

REFLECT

1a. What does slope represent?

the steepness of the line/the ratio of change in y to change in x

1b. Does it matter which pair of points you use when finding the slope of a line? Explain.

No; a line has a constant steepness (a constant rate of change), so the rate

of change over any interval is the same.

© Houghton Mifflin Harcourt Publishing Company

---

2 EXPLORE   Using Similar Triangles to Explain Slope

Use similar triangles to show that the slope of a line is constant.
Use this space to make your drawing:

A Draw line ℓ that is not a horizontal line. Label four points on the line as A, B, C, and D.

You need to show that the slope between points A and B is the same as the slope between points C and D.

B Draw the rise and run for the slope between points A and B. Label the intersection as point E. Draw the rise and run for the slope between points C and D. Label the intersection as point F.

C Write expressions for the slope between A and B and between C and D.

Slope between A and B: $\dfrac{BE}{AE}$ Slope between C and D: $\dfrac{DF}{CF}$

D Extend $\overleftrightarrow{AE}$ and $\overleftrightarrow{CF}$ across your drawing. $\overleftrightarrow{AE}$ and $\overleftrightarrow{CF}$ are both horizontal lines, so they are parallel. Line ℓ is a transversal that intersects parallel lines.

E Complete the following statements:

$\angle BAE$ and $\angle DCF$ are corresponding angles and are congruent .

$\angle BEA$ and $\angle DFC$ are right angles and are congruent .

F By Angle-Angle Similarity, $\triangle ABE$ and $\triangle CDF$ are similar triangles.

G Use the fact that the lengths of corresponding sides of similar triangles are proportional to complete the following ratios: $\dfrac{BE}{DF} = \dfrac{AE}{CF}$.

H Recall that you can also write the proportion so that the ratios compare parts of the same triangle: $\dfrac{BE}{AE} = \dfrac{DF}{CF}$.

I The proportion you wrote in step **H** shows that the ratios you wrote in **C** are equal. So, the slope of the line is constant.

© Houghton Mifflin Harcourt Publishing Company

Using the Pythagorean Theorem

Essential question: *How can you use the Pythagorean Theorem to solve problems?*

Standards for Mathematical Content

CC.8.G.7 Apply the Pythagorean Theorem to determine unknown side lengths in right triangles in real-world and mathematical problems in two and three dimensions.

CC.8.G.8 Apply the Pythagorean Theorem to find the distance between two points in a coordinate system.

Vocabulary

legs

hypotenuse

Prerequisites

Properties of right triangles

Simplifying square roots

Math Background

The Pythagorean Theorem states that in a right triangle with legs a and b and hypotenuse c, the relationship between side lengths is:

$$a^2 + b^2 = c^2$$

Using the Pythagorean Theorem, you can find the length of any side of a right triangle when given the length of the two other sides. Students will substitute values in the Pythagorean Theorem and solve for the unknown length. The relationship can also be rewritten as follows:

$$c = \sqrt{a^2 + b^2} \quad \text{or} \quad b = \sqrt{c^2 - a^2} \quad \text{or} \quad a = \sqrt{c^2 - b^2}$$

INTRODUCE

Review with students the properties of a right triangle, including the Pythagorean Theorem. Allow students to practice using the Pythagorean Theorem with lengths of a right triangle to practice working with square roots. Tell students that in this lesson, they will use this relationship between sides of a right triangle to solve real-world problems.

TEACH

1 EXPLORE

Questioning Strategies

- In part A, which side length is missing? **hypotenuse**

- What do you know about the length of the hypotenuse in comparison with the lengths of the legs? **The hypotenuse is the longest side.**

- In part B, which side length is missing? **longer leg**

Teaching Strategies

Point out to students that in part A, before taking the square root of both sides, the variable c is already alone on one side of the equation. However in part B, they will need to subtract one of the terms from both sides to get the variable alone on one side of the equation before using square roots.

2 EXAMPLE

Questioning Strategies

- How is 1 unit represented on the coordinate grid? **The side length of one square grid on the coordinate grid represents 1 unit.**

- How can you estimate $\sqrt{34}$? **Find the closest perfect squares greater than and less than 34, and write the inequality $\sqrt{25} < \sqrt{34} < \sqrt{36}$. Now you can estimate $\sqrt{34}$ to be between 5 and 6, and closer to 6.**

Technology

Have students practice estimating square roots and checking their estimates with a calculator. You might want to let students play a contest-style game to see who can estimate square roots to the nearest tenth the most accurately and most often, checking with a calculator.

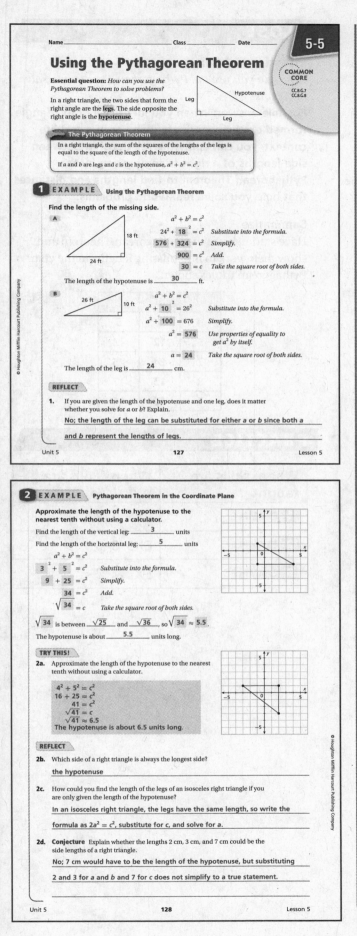

Using the Pythagorean Theorem

Essential question: *How can you use the Pythagorean Theorem to solve problems?*

In a right triangle, the two sides that form the right angle are the **legs**. The side opposite the right angle is the **hypotenuse**.

COMMON CORE
CC.8.G.7
CC.8.G.8

The Pythagorean Theorem

In a right triangle, the sum of the squares of the lengths of the legs is equal to the square of the length of the hypotenuse.

If a and b are legs and c is the hypotenuse, $a^2 + b^2 = c^2$.

1 EXAMPLE — Using the Pythagorean Theorem

Find the length of the missing side.

A

18 ft
24 ft

$$a^2 + b^2 = c^2$$
$$24^2 + 18^2 = c^2 \quad \textit{Substitute into the formula.}$$
$$576 + 324 = c^2 \quad \textit{Simplify.}$$
$$900 = c^2 \quad \textit{Add.}$$
$$30 = c \quad \textit{Take the square root of both sides.}$$

The length of the hypotenuse is ___30___ ft.

B

26 ft
10 ft

$$a^2 + b^2 = c^2$$
$$a^2 + 10^2 = 26^2 \quad \textit{Substitute into the formula.}$$
$$a^2 + 100 = 676 \quad \textit{Simplify.}$$
$$a^2 = 576 \quad \textit{Use properties of equality to get } a^2 \textit{ by itself.}$$
$$a = 24 \quad \textit{Take the square root of both sides.}$$

The length of the leg is ___24___ cm.

REFLECT

1. If you are given the length of the hypotenuse and one leg, does it matter whether you solve for a or b? Explain.

   No; the length of the leg can be substituted for either a or b since both a

   and b represent the lengths of legs.

2 EXAMPLE — Pythagorean Theorem in the Coordinate Plane

Approximate the length of the hypotenuse to the nearest tenth without using a calculator.

Find the length of the vertical leg: ___3___ units

Find the length of the horizontal leg: ___5___ units

$$a^2 + b^2 = c^2$$
$$3^2 + 5^2 = c^2 \quad \textit{Substitute into the formula.}$$
$$9 + 25 = c^2 \quad \textit{Simplify.}$$
$$34 = c^2 \quad \textit{Add.}$$
$$\sqrt{34} = c \quad \textit{Take the square root of both sides.}$$

$\sqrt{34}$ is between ___$\sqrt{25}$___ and ___$\sqrt{36}$___, so $\sqrt{34} \approx$ ___5.5___.

The hypotenuse is about ___5.5___ units long.

TRY THIS!

2a. Approximate the length of the hypotenuse to the nearest tenth without using a calculator.

$$4^2 + 5^2 = c^2$$
$$16 + 25 = c^2$$
$$41 = c^2$$
$$\sqrt{41} = c$$
$$\sqrt{41} \approx 6.5$$
The hypotenuse is about 6.5 units long.

REFLECT

2b. Which side of a right triangle is always the longest side?

the hypotenuse

2c. How could you find the length of the legs of an isosceles right triangle if you are only given the length of the hypotenuse?

In an isosceles right triangle, the legs have the same length, so write the

formula as $2a^2 = c^2$, substitute for c, and solve for a.

2d. Conjecture Explain whether the lengths 2 cm, 3 cm, and 7 cm could be the side lengths of a right triangle.

No; 7 cm would have to be the length of the hypotenuse, but substituting

2 and 3 for a and b and 7 for c does not simplify to a true statement.

Questioning Strategies

- How do you find the diagonal length along the bottom of the box? **Use the length and width of the bottom rectangle as the lengths of the legs, and the diagonal as the hypotenuse.**

- How can you find the diagonal length from a bottom corner to the opposite top corner? **Use the diagonal length along the bottom box as the length of the longer leg and the height as the other leg.**

Teaching Strategies

Have students practice identifying the legs and hypotenuse of a right triangle in various positions in different settings. You may include right triangles in a variety of orientations drawn on the board and right triangles found in three-dimensional figures, such as prisms.

```
     MATHEMATICAL   Highlighting
        PRACTICE    the Standards
```

This example is an opportunity to address Standard 2 (Reason abstractly and quantitatively). Students must reason abstractly to identify right triangles in three-dimensional figures in a real-world setting, such as in a box. Students reason quantitatively when they apply the Pythagorean Theorem and solve equations to find lengths within a box in order to answer real-world questions.

CLOSE

Essential Question

How can you use the Pythagorean Theorem to solve problems?

Possible answer: When you identify a right triangle formed on the coordinate plane or in a real-life context, you can apply the relationship between side lengths of a right triangle given by the Pythagorean Theorem to find lengths and distances that help you solve real-world problems.

Summarize

Have students use the Pythagorean Theorem and show their work to find missing lengths in the chart of Pythagorean triples shown.

a	b	c
3	4	5
5	12	13
7	24	25
8	15	17
9	40	41

PRACTICE

Where skills are taught	Where skills are practiced
1 EXAMPLE	EXS. 1–2
2 EXAMPLE	EXS. 3–6
3 EXAMPLE	EX. 7

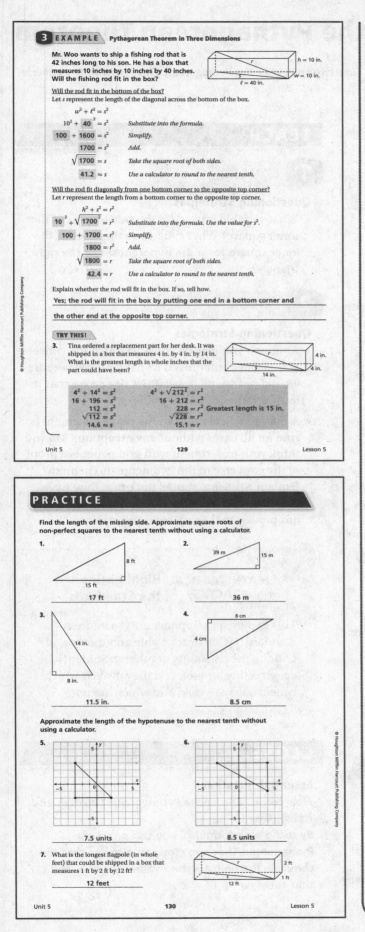

3 EXAMPLE Pythagorean Theorem in Three Dimensions

Mr. Woo wants to ship a fishing rod that is 42 inches long to his son. He has a box that measures 10 inches by 10 inches by 40 inches. Will the fishing rod fit in the box?

Will the rod fit in the bottom of the box?
Let s represent the length of the diagonal across the bottom of the box.

$$w^2 + \ell^2 = s^2$$

$10^2 + 40^2 = s^2$	Substitute into the formula.
$100 + 1600 = s^2$	Simplify.
$1700 = s^2$	Add.
$\sqrt{1700} = s$	Take the square root of both sides.
$41.2 \approx s$	Use a calculator to round to the nearest tenth.

Will the rod fit diagonally from one bottom corner to the opposite top corner?
Let r represent the length from a bottom corner to the opposite top corner.

$$h^2 + s^2 = r^2$$

$10^2 + \sqrt{1700}^2 = r^2$	Substitute into the formula. Use the value for s^2.
$100 + 1700 = r^2$	Simplify.
$1800 = r^2$	Add.
$\sqrt{1800} = r$	Take the square root of both sides.
$42.4 \approx r$	Use a calculator to round to the nearest tenth.

Explain whether the rod will fit in the box. If so, tell how.

Yes; the rod will fit in the box by putting one end in a bottom corner and

the other end at the opposite top corner.

TRY THIS!

3. Tina ordered a replacement part for her desk. It was shipped in a box that measures 4 in. by 4 in. by 14 in. What is the greatest length in whole inches that the part could have been?

$4^2 + 14^2 = s^2$	$4^2 + \sqrt{212}^2 = r^2$
$16 + 196 = s^2$	$16 + 212 = r^2$
$112 = s^2$	$228 = r^2$ Greatest length is 15 in.
$\sqrt{112} = s^2$	$\sqrt{228} = r^2$
$14.6 \approx s$	$15.1 \approx r$

PRACTICE

Find the length of the missing side. Approximate square roots of non-perfect squares to the nearest tenth without using a calculator.

1.

8 ft
15 ft

17 ft

2.

39 m
15 m

36 m

3.

14 in.
8 in.

11.5 in.

4.

8 cm
4 cm

8.5 cm

Approximate the length of the hypotenuse to the nearest tenth without using a calculator.

5.

7.5 units

6.

8.5 units

7. What is the longest flagpole (in whole feet) that could be shipped in a box that measures 1 ft by 2 ft by 12 ft?

2 ft
12 ft
1 ft

12 feet

Proving the Pythagorean Theorem

Essential question: *How can you prove the Pythagorean Theorem and its converse?*

COMMON **Standards for**
CORE **Mathematical Content**

CC.8.G.6 Explain a proof of the Pythagorean Theorem and its converse.

Prerequisites

Pythagorean Theorem

Math Background

The proof of the Pythagorean Theorem in this lesson is a hands-on approach and does not require knowledge of algebra. You can also use algebra to prove the Pythagorean Theorem as follows:

The area of the large square is $(a + b)^2$.
The area of each triangle is $\frac{1}{2}ab$.

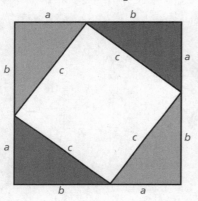

To find the area of the inner square, subtract the area of the four triangles from the area of the larger square:

$$(a + b)^2 - 4\left(\frac{1}{2}ab\right)$$
$$=a^2 + 2ab + b^2 - 2ab$$
$$=a^2 + b^2$$

Therefore, $c^2 = a^2 + b^2$.

INTRODUCE

In this lesson, you will develop a proof of the Pythagorean Theorem, which states: "If a triangle is a right triangle, then $a^2 + b^2 = c^2$." You will also consider the converse of the Pythagorean Theorem, which states "If $a^2 + b^2 = c^2$, then the triangle is a right triangle," and determine whether the converse is true.

TEACH

1 EXPLORE

Questioning Strategies

• What variable is used for the side lengths of the inner square? Why? *c*; because the sides of the inner square form the hypotenuses of the right triangles.

2 EXPLORE

Questioning Strategies

• Although you may be convinced that the converse is true, have you proved it? Explain. No, because we did not try all possibilities nor prove that it must be true for all possibilities.

• A mathematical proof shows that a statement is true for all cases without any exceptions. Do you think your experiment with grid paper is a proof of the converse of the Pythagorean Theorem? Explain. Students should note that they have only shown that a few cases are true and have not proven that there are no exceptions.

MATHEMATICAL **Highlighting**
PRACTICE **the Standards**

This Explore is an opportunity to address Standard 3 (Construct viable arguments and critique the reasoning of others). Students are constructing a proof, and they discuss which conclusions are valid and which are not.

CLOSE

Essential Question

How can you prove the Pythagorean Theorem and its converse?
By using area formulas, you can prove the Pythagorean Theorem. You can also see that the converse is true by testing values for *a*, *b*, and *c* that satisfy $a^2 + b^2 = c^2$.

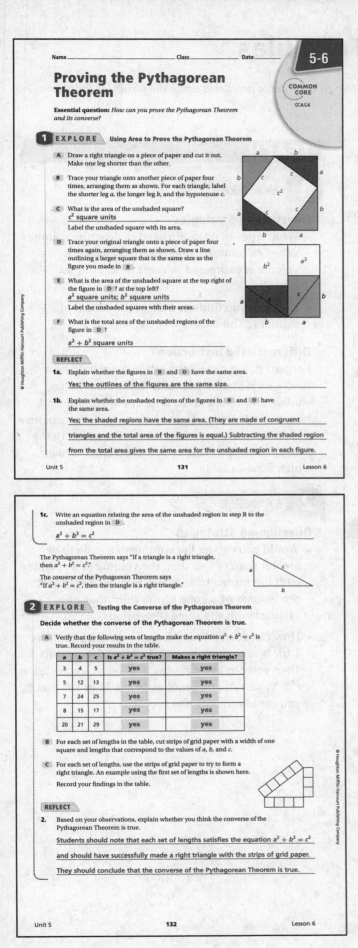

Proving the Pythagorean Theorem

Essential question: *How can you prove the Pythagorean Theorem and its converse?*

COMMON CORE
CC.8.G.6

1 EXPLORE Using Area to Prove the Pythagorean Theorem

A Draw a right triangle on a piece of paper and cut it out. Make one leg shorter than the other.

B Trace your triangle onto another piece of paper four times, arranging them as shown. For each triangle, label the shorter leg a, the longer leg b, and the hypotenuse c.

C What is the area of the unshaded square?
c^2 square units

Label the unshaded square with its area.

D Trace your original triangle onto a piece of paper four times again, arranging them as shown. Draw a line outlining a larger square that is the same size as the figure you made in **B**.

E What is the area of the unshaded square at the top right of the figure in **D**? at the top left?
a^2 square units; b^2 square units

Label the unshaded squares with their areas.

F What is the total area of the unshaded regions of the figure in **D**?
$a^2 + b^2$ square units

REFLECT

1a. Explain whether the figures in **B** and **D** have the same area.

Yes; the outlines of the figures are the same size.

1b. Explain whether the unshaded regions of the figures in **B** and **D** have the same area.

Yes; the shaded regions have the same area. (They are made of congruent

triangles and the total area of the figures is equal.) Subtracting the shaded region

from the total area gives the same area for the unshaded region in each figure.

1c. Write an equation relating the area of the unshaded region in step B to the unshaded region in **D**.

$a^2 + b^2 = c^2$

The Pythagorean Theorem says "If a triangle is a right triangle, then $a^2 + b^2 = c^2$."

The *converse* of the Pythagorean Theorem says "If $a^2 + b^2 = c^2$, then the triangle is a right triangle."

2 EXPLORE Testing the Converse of the Pythagorean Theorem

Decide whether the converse of the Pythagorean Theorem is true.

A Verify that the following sets of lengths make the equation $a^2 + b^2 = c^2$ is true. Record your results in the table.

a	b	c	Is $a^2 + b^2 = c^2$ true?	Makes a right triangle?
3	4	5	yes	yes
5	12	13	yes	yes
7	24	25	yes	yes
8	15	17	yes	yes
20	21	29	yes	yes

B For each set of lengths in the table, cut strips of grid paper with a width of one square and lengths that correspond to the values of a, b, and c.

C For each set of lengths, use the strips of grid paper to try to form a right triangle. An example using the first set of lengths is shown here.

Record your findings in the table.

REFLECT

2. Based on your observations, explain whether you think the converse of the Pythagorean Theorem is true.

Students should note that each set of lengths satisfies the equation $a^2 + b^2 = c^2$

and should have successfully made a right triangle with the strips of grid paper.

They should conclude that the converse of the Pythagorean Theorem is true.

Volume Formulas

Essential question: *How can you solve problems using the formulas for volume?*

········
COMMON Standards for
CORE Mathematical Content
········

CC.8.G.9 Know the formulas for the volumes of cones, cylinders, and spheres and use them to solve real-world and mathematical problems.

Prerequisites
Circumference and area of a circle

Math Background
Students have worked with three dimensions (volume and surface area of prisms and pyramids) and with circles in two dimensions (area and circumference). The volume of a cylinder is found using the same general formula for volume of a prism: $V = Bh$, where the base area is the area of a circle instead of the area of a polygon. The volume of a cone is found using the same general formula for volume of a pyramid: $V = \frac{1}{3}Bh$, where the base area for a cone is the area of a circle instead of a polygon.

INTRODUCE

Have students give their own definition of volume. Ask them to give examples of items/products that use measures of volume. For example: gallons of milk, juice, soda, mulch, oil, gasoline, and so on. Tell students that in this lesson, they will apply volume formulas for three-dimensional figures including cylinders, cones, and spheres.

TEACH

1 EXPLORE

Questioning Strategies
- What types of units are used to describe volume? **When calculated using length dimensions, volume is expressed in cubic units such as m^3 or in^3.**
- How can you find the area of the base B of a cylinder? **The base is a circle: $A = \pi r^2$.**

Differentiated Instruction
For part A, have students estimate their answer before working the problem. Estimating helps students understand the concept of volume and how it is calculated. It also helps students recognize their own mistakes, when they make them. Using 3 for π in this problem, you can estimate 270 in^3, which is reasonable.

2 EXAMPLE

Questioning Strategies
- Would you expect the volume of a cone to be greater than or less than the volume of a cylinder with the same dimensions? Explain. **Less than; the volume of a cone is one-third that of a cylinder with the same dimensions.**
- How can you estimate the volume of a cone? **Use 3 for π and multiply with $\frac{1}{3}$ to find the product 1. Then you can estimate the volume of a cone using r^2h. In part A, you could estimate 32 in^3. In part B, you could estimate 144 ft^3.**

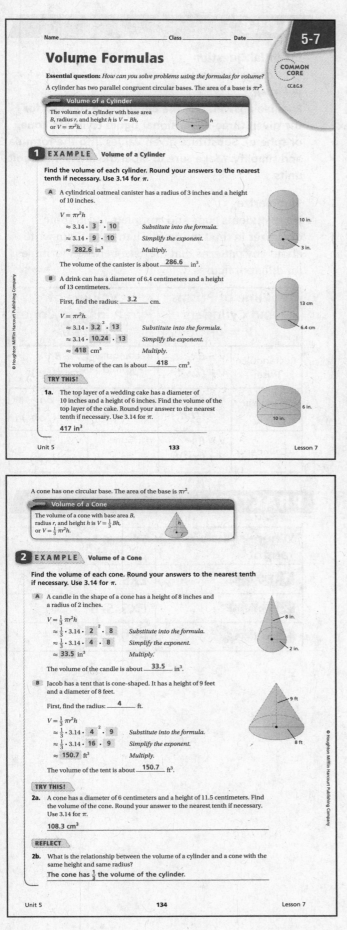

Volume Formulas

Name _____ **Class** _____ **Date** _____

5-7

COMMON CORE
CC.8.G.9

Essential question: *How can you solve problems using the formulas for volume?*

A cylinder has two parallel congruent circular bases. The area of a base is πr^2.

Volume of a Cylinder

The volume of a cylinder with base area
B, radius r, and height h is $V = Bh$,
or $V = \pi r^2 h$.

1 EXAMPLE Volume of a Cylinder

Find the volume of each cylinder. Round your answers to the nearest
tenth if necessary. Use 3.14 for π.

A A cylindrical oatmeal canister has a radius of 3 inches and a height of
10 inches.

$V = \pi r^2 h$

$\approx 3.14 \cdot 3^2 \cdot 10$ *Substitute into the formula.*

$\approx 3.14 \cdot 9 \cdot 10$ *Simplify the exponent.*

≈ 282.6 in³   *Multiply.*

The volume of the canister is about __282.6__ in³.

10 in.
3 in.

B A drink can has a diameter of 6.4 centimeters and a height
of 13 centimeters.

First, find the radius: __3.2__ cm.

$V = \pi r^2 h$

$\approx 3.14 \cdot 3.2^2 \cdot 13$ *Substitute into the formula.*

$\approx 3.14 \cdot 10.24 \cdot 13$ *Simplify the exponent.*

≈ 418 cm³   *Multiply.*

The volume of the can is about __418__ cm³.

13 cm
6.4 cm

TRY THIS!

1a. The top layer of a wedding cake has a diameter of
10 inches and a height of 6 inches. Find the volume of the
top layer of the cake. Round your answer to the nearest
tenth if necessary. Use 3.14 for π.

__417__ in³

6 in.
10 in.

© Houghton Mifflin Harcourt Publishing Company

A cone has one circular base. The area of the base is πr^2.

Volume of a Cone

The volume of a cone with base area B,
radius r, and height h is $V = \frac{1}{3} Bh$,
or $V = \frac{1}{3} \pi r^2 h$.

2 EXAMPLE Volume of a Cone

Find the volume of each cone. Round your answers to the nearest tenth
if necessary. Use 3.14 for π.

A A candle in the shape of a cone has a height of 8 inches and
a radius of 2 inches.

$V = \frac{1}{3} \pi r^2 h$

$\approx \frac{1}{3} \cdot 3.14 \cdot 2^2 \cdot 8$ *Substitute into the formula.*

$\approx \frac{1}{3} \cdot 3.14 \cdot 4 \cdot 8$ *Simplify the exponent.*

≈ 33.5 in³   *Multiply.*

The volume of the candle is about __33.5__ in³.

8 in.
2 in.

B Jacob has a tent that is cone-shaped. It has a height of 9 feet
and a diameter of 8 feet.

First, find the radius: __4__ ft.

$V = \frac{1}{3} \pi r^2 h$

$\approx \frac{1}{3} \cdot 3.14 \cdot 4^2 \cdot 9$ *Substitute into the formula.*

$\approx \frac{1}{3} \cdot 3.14 \cdot 16 \cdot 9$ *Simplify the exponent.*

≈ 150.7 ft³   *Multiply.*

The volume of the tent is about __150.7__ ft³.

9 ft
8 ft

TRY THIS!

2a. A cone has a diameter of 6 centimeters and a height of 11.5 centimeters. Find
the volume of the cone. Round your answer to the nearest tenth if necessary.
Use 3.14 for π.

__108.3__ cm³

REFLECT

2b. What is the relationship between the volume of a cylinder and a cone with the
same height and same radius?

The cone has $\frac{1}{3}$ the volume of the cylinder.

© Houghton Mifflin Harcourt Publishing Company

Questioning Strategies

- What information do you need in order to find the volume of a sphere? **the length of the radius**

- Why is the radius length cubed when finding the volume of a sphere and squared when finding the area of a circle? **Area is a two-dimensional measurement; volume is a three-dimensional measurement.**

- How can you estimate the volume of a sphere? **Use 3 for π and multiply with $\frac{1}{3}$ to find the product 1. Then you can estimate the volume of a sphere using $4r^3$. In part A, you could estimate the volume to be $4 \cdot 2^3$ or 32 cm^3.**

MATHEMATICAL PRACTICE **Highlighting the Standards**

This Example is an opportunity to address Standard 2 (Reason abstractly and quantitatively). Students begin by using the Pythagorean Theorem to solve simple right triangles. They progress to solving right triangles on a coordinate grid, and then finally apply the Pythagorean Theorem to a problem-solving situation.

CLOSE

Essential Question

How can you solve problems using the formulas for volume?

Possible answer: Use the appropriate formula for the given three-dimensional figure (cylinder, cone, or sphere). Substitute given values into the formula and simplify. Make sure to label the answer in cubic units.

Summarize

Have students copy and complete the graphic organizer in their journals. Then have them write about any patterns that they see between formulas for different figures.

Volume of Prisms and Cylinders $V = Bh$		Volume of Pyramids and Cones $V = \frac{1}{3}Bh$	
Rectangular Prism	$V = Bh$ $V = (\ell w)h$	Rectangular Pyramid	$V = Bh$ $V = \frac{1}{3}(\ell w)h$
Triangular Prism	$V = Bh$ $V = (\frac{1}{2}bh_\triangle)h$	Triangular Pyramid	$V = \frac{1}{3}Bh$ $V = \frac{1}{3}(\frac{1}{2}bh_\triangle)h$
Cylinder	$V = Bh$ $V = (\pi r^2)h$	Cone	$V = \frac{1}{3}Bh$ $V = \frac{1}{3}(\pi r^2)h$

PRACTICE

Where skills are taught	Where skills are practiced
1 EXAMPLE	EXS. 1–4, 9
2 EXAMPLE	EXS. 5–6
3 EXAMPLE	EXS. 7–9

All the points in a sphere are the same distance from the center of the sphere.

Volume of a Sphere

The volume of a sphere with radius r is $V = \frac{4}{3}\pi r^3$.

3 EXAMPLE   Volume of a Sphere

Find the volume of each sphere. Round your answers to the nearest tenth if necessary. Use 3.14 for π.

A The radius of a golf ball is 2.1 centimeters.

$V = \frac{4}{3}\pi r^3$

$\approx \frac{4}{3} \cdot 3.14 \cdot \boxed{2.1}^3$ *Substitute into the formula.*

$\approx \frac{4}{3} \cdot 3.14 \cdot \boxed{9.26}$ *Simplify the exponent.*

$\approx \boxed{38.8}$ cm³   *Multiply.*

The volume of a golf ball is about ___38.8___ cm³.

B The diameter of a tennis ball is 7 centimeters.

First, find the radius: ___3.5___ cm.

$V = \frac{4}{3}\pi r^3$

$\approx \frac{4}{3} \cdot 3.14 \cdot \boxed{3.5}^3$ *Substitute into the formula.*

$\approx \frac{4}{3} \cdot 3.14 \cdot \boxed{42.9}$ *Simplify the exponent.*

$\approx \boxed{179.6}$ cm³   *Multiply.*

The volume of the tent is about ___179.6___ cm³.

TRY THIS!

3a. A baseball has a diameter of 2.9 inches. Find the volume of the baseball. Round your answer to the nearest tenth if necessary. Use 3.14 for π.

___12.8 in³___

REFLECT

3b. A hemisphere is half of a sphere. Explain how you would find the volume of a hemisphere.

___Find the volume of a sphere with the same radius as the___

___hemisphere, then divide the result by 2.___

PRACTICE

Find the volume of each figure. Round your answers to the nearest tenth if necessary. Use 3.14 for π.

1.
13 ft, 10 ft

___4,082 ft³___

2.
12 ft, 4 ft

___602.9 ft³___

3. A cylinder has a radius of 4 centimeters and height of 40 centimeters.

___2,009.6 cm³___

4. A cylinder has a radius of 8 meters and height of 4 meters.

___803.8 m³___

5.
7 ft, 6 ft

___65.9 ft³___

6.
100 in., 33 in.

___113,982 in³___

7. A sphere has a radius of 3.1 meters.

___124.72 m³___

8. A sphere has a diameter of 18 inches.

___3,052.08 in³___

9. A farmer stores corn in a silo that is in the shape of a cylinder with a hemisphere on top. The diameter of the silo is 30 feet, and the total height of the silo is 60 feet.

60 ft, 30 ft

a. Find the radius of the hemisphere. ___15 ft___

b. Find the height of the cylinder. ___45 ft___

c. Find the volume of the cylinder. ___31,792.5 ft³___

d. Find the volume of the hemisphere. ___7,065 ft³___

e. Find the volume of the silo. ___38,857.5 ft³___

© Houghton Mifflin Harcourt Publishing Company

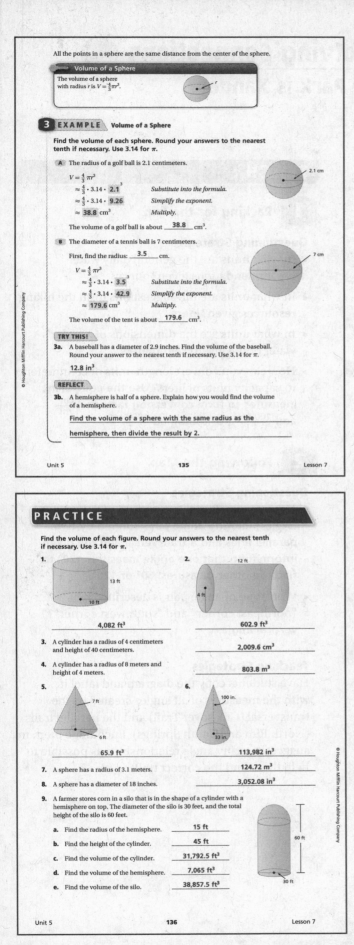

Problem Solving Connections
Where in the Park is Xander?

COMMON CORE Standards for Mathematical Content

CC.8.EE.6 Use similar triangles to explain why the slope m is the same between any two distinct points on a non-vertical line in the coordinate plane; derive the equation $y = mx$ for a line through the origin and the equation $y = mx + b$ for a line intercepting the vertical axis at b.

CC.8.G.5 Use informal arguments to establish facts about the angle sum and exterior angle of triangles, about the angles created when parallel lines are cut by a transversal, and the angle-angle criterion for similarity of triangles.

CC.8.G.6 Explain a proof of the Pythagorean theorem and its converse.

CC.8.G.7 Apply the Pythagorean theorem to determine unknown side lengths in right triangles in real-world and mathematical problems in two and three dimensions.

CC.8.G.8 Apply the Pythagorean theorem to find the distance between two points in a coordinate system.

CC.8.G.9 Know the formulas for the volumes of cones, cylinders, and spheres and use them to solve real-world and mathematical problems.

INTRODUCE

Discuss with students what it would be like to get lost in the woods. Ask students if they believe that geometry could really help them find the way again. Tell students that in this exploration, you will look at ways that geometric formulas and properties can be useful—even in the great outdoors!

TEACH

1 Packing for the Trip

Questioning Strategies

- In what units are the general daily water recommendations given? ounces

- In what units are the suggestions from the hiking resources given? liters

- In what units are the dimensions of Xander's water bottle given? centimeters

- How can you convert length units of centimeters to capacity units of liters? Use the equivalent measures to form conversion factors: $\frac{1 \text{ cm}^3}{1 \text{ mL}}$ and $\frac{1000 \text{ mL}}{1 \text{ L}}$, or combined $\frac{1000 \text{ cm}^3}{1 \text{ L}}$.

2 Following the Map

Questioning Strategies

- How can you find the measures of the other angles? Identify angle pairs formed by two parallel lines and a transversal and the given information that one angle measures 120° to find the other measures: 60° or 120°.

- What type of angle pair is described by "northeast corner" and "southwest corner"? vertical angles

Teaching Strategies

Have students copy the diagram and label it with the measures of all angles created by the transversal (Crossover Trail) and the parallel trails (North Rim and South Springs). Encourage them to suggest as many angle relationships as possible to help them find the correct trail.

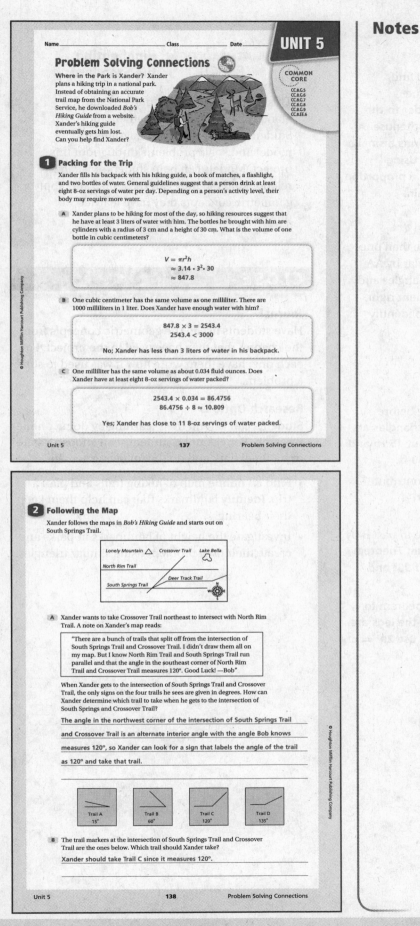

Name_____ Class_____ Date_____

Problem Solving Connections

UNIT 5

COMMON CORE
CC.8.G.5
CC.8.G.6
CC.8.G.7
CC.8.G.8
CC.8.G.9
CC.8.EE.6

Where in the Park is Xander? Xander plans a hiking trip in a national park. Instead of obtaining an accurate trail map from the National Park Service, he downloaded *Bob's Hiking Guide* from a website. Xander's hiking guide eventually gets him lost. Can you help find Xander?

1 Packing for the Trip

Xander fills his backpack with his hiking guide, a book of matches, a flashlight, and two bottles of water. General guidelines suggest that a person drink at least eight 8-oz servings of water per day. Depending on a person's activity level, their body may require more water.

A Xander plans to be hiking for most of the day, so hiking resources suggest that he have at least 3 liters of water with him. The bottles he brought with him are cylinders with a radius of 3 cm and a height of 30 cm. What is the volume of one bottle in cubic centimeters?

$$V = \pi r^2 h$$
$$\approx 3.14 \cdot 3^2 \cdot 30$$
$$\approx 847.8$$

B One cubic centimeter has the same volume as one milliliter. There are 1000 milliliters in 1 liter. Does Xander have enough water with him?

$$847.8 \times 3 = 2543.4$$
$$2543.4 < 3000$$

No; Xander has less than 3 liters of water in his backpack.

C One milliliter has the same volume as about 0.034 fluid ounces. Does Xander have at least eight 8-oz servings of water packed?

$$2543.4 \times 0.034 = 86.4756$$
$$86.4756 \div 8 \approx 10.809$$

Yes; Xander has close to 11 8-oz servings of water packed.

Unit 5   137   Problem Solving Connections

2 Following the Map

Xander follows the maps in *Bob's Hiking Guide* and starts out on South Springs Trail.

Lonely Mountain △   Crossover Trail   Lake Bella

North Rim Trail

South Springs Trail   Deer Track Trail

A Xander wants to take Crossover Trail northeast to intersect with North Rim Trail. A note on Xander's map reads:

"There are a bunch of trails that split off from the intersection of South Springs Trail and Crossover Trail. I didn't draw them all on my map. But I know North Rim Trail and South Springs Trail run parallel and that the angle in the southeast corner of North Rim Trail and Crossover Trail measures 120°. Good Luck! —Bob"

When Xander gets to the intersection of South Springs Trail and Crossover Trail, the only signs on the four trails he sees are given in degrees. How can Xander determine which trail to take when he gets to the intersection of South Springs and Crossover Trail?

The angle in the northwest corner of the intersection of South Springs Trail

and Crossover Trail is an alternate interior angle with the angle Bob knows

measures 120°, so Xander can look for a sign that labels the angle of the trail

as 120° and take that trail.

Trail A
15°

Trail B
60°

Trail C
120°

Trail D
135°

B The trail markers at the intersection of South Springs Trail and Crossover Trail are the ones below. Which trail should Xander take?

Xander should take Trail C since it measures 120°.

Unit 5   138   Problem Solving Connections

3 Finding a Landmark

Questioning Strategies

- How can you use similar triangles to find Xander's distance from the base of the mountain? **A line of sight from Xander to the top of the mountain will be the hypotenuse. A 15-ft tree 50 ft in front of Xander forms a smaller right triangle with the line of sight. Using properties of similar triangles, solve a proportion to find the height of Lonely Mountain.**

Teaching Strategies

Point out to students that there is more than one way to show that the triangles are similar by AA Similarity: (1) use the congruent right angles and the shared angle, or (2) use the congruent right angles and the parallel vertical sides to identify corresponding angles.

4 Finding Xander

Questioning Strategies

- What information does Xander have before making the 911 call? **He knows the triangles are similar; the height of the tree is about 15 ft; and his distance from the tree is about 50 ft.**

- What information does the ranger contribute? **The ranger knows that the mountain is 3000 ft high.**

- How can you use classify the triangle in part B by angle measures? **Use the Triangle Sum Theorem to find the missing angle measure of 90° and classify the triangle as right.**

- How can you use the Pythagorean theorem to find the lengths of the legs? **Because the legs are the same length and $a = b$, you can use $2a^2 = c^2$ or $2b^2 = c^2$.**

┌─ MATHEMATICAL
│ PRACTICE **Highlighting the Standards**

This project is an opportunity to address Standard 4 (Model with mathematics). Students draw geometric diagrams to model and solve problems throughout this project. Models can help students visualize relationships so they can recognize and apply geometric concepts they have learned in this unit.

CLOSE

Journal

Have students list all the geometric concepts from the chapter that they have used in the project. For each one, have them write how it was used to solve a problem.

Research Options

Students can extend their learning by doing online research. For example, students can choose a state or national park and do the following activities:

- Find an online map of hiking trails and plan a trip. Identify landmarks that can help them keep their bearings.

- Investigate the height of landmarks in parks and create their own problem using similar triangles.

3 **Finding a Landmark**

Xander makes a mistake and takes the trail marked 60°. After hiking for a while, he realizes that he is lost and his cell phone battery is almost dead.

A Xander stands 50 feet in front of a young tree and looks up across the top of the tree to the top of a mountain in the distance. Xander estimates the height of the tree as 15 feet. Draw a diagram involving similar triangles that shows the relationship between the tree and the mountain from Xander's perspective.

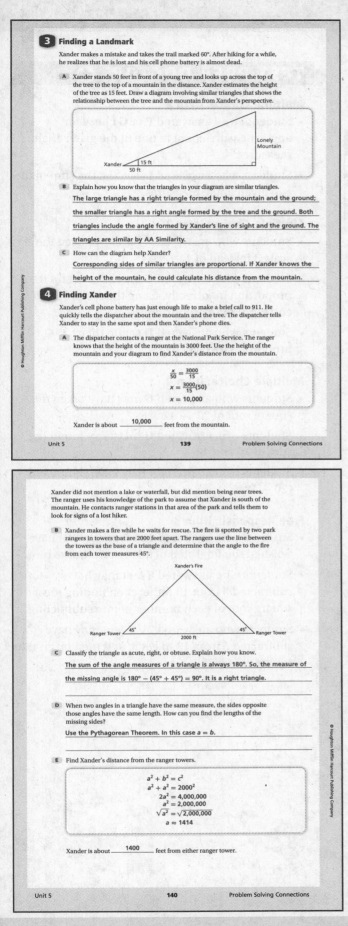

B Explain how you know that the triangles in your diagram are similar triangles.

The large triangle has a right triangle formed by the mountain and the ground; the smaller triangle has a right angle formed by the tree and the ground. Both triangles include the angle formed by Xander's line of sight and the ground. The triangles are similar by AA Similarity.

C How can the diagram help Xander?

Corresponding sides of similar triangles are proportional. If Xander knows the height of the mountain, he could calculate his distance from the mountain.

4 **Finding Xander**

Xander's cell phone battery has just enough life to make a brief call to 911. He quickly tells the dispatcher about the mountain and the tree. The dispatcher tells Xander to stay in the same spot and then Xander's phone dies.

A The dispatcher contacts a ranger at the National Park Service. The ranger knows that the height of the mountain is 3000 feet. Use the height of the mountain and your diagram to find Xander's distance from the mountain.

$$\frac{x}{50} = \frac{3000}{15}$$
$$x = \frac{3000}{15}(50)$$
$$x = 10{,}000$$

Xander is about ____10,000____ feet from the mountain.

Xander did not mention a lake or waterfall, but did mention being near trees. The ranger uses his knowledge of the park to assume that Xander is south of the mountain. He contacts ranger stations in that area of the park and tells them to look for signs of a lost hiker.

B Xander makes a fire while he waits for rescue. The fire is spotted by two park rangers in towers that are 2000 feet apart. The rangers use the line between the towers as the base of a triangle and determine that the angle to the fire from each tower measures 45°.

Xander's Fire

Ranger Tower 45°   45° Ranger Tower
2000 ft

C Classify the triangle as acute, right, or obtuse. Explain how you know.

The sum of the angle measures of a triangle is always 180°. So, the measure of the missing angle is 180° − (45° + 45°) = 90°. It is a right triangle.

D When two angles in a triangle have the same measure, the sides opposite those angles have the same length. How can you find the lengths of the missing sides?

Use the Pythagorean Theorem. In this case $a = b$.

E Find Xander's distance from the ranger towers.

$$a^2 + b^2 = c^2$$
$$a^2 + a^2 = 2000^2$$
$$2a^2 = 4{,}000{,}000$$
$$a^2 = 2{,}000{,}000$$
$$\sqrt{a^2} = \sqrt{2{,}000{,}000}$$
$$a \approx 1414$$

Xander is about ____1400____ feet from either ranger tower.

COMMON CORE **CORRELATION**

Standard	Items
CC.8.G.5	1–3, 10–11
CC.8.G.7	4–5, 8
CC.8.G.9	6–7, 9, 12

TEST PREP DOCTOR ✚

Multiple Choice: Item 2

- Students who answered **F** or **G** chose an angle measure equal to one of the given angle measures.
- Students who answered **J** selected the sum of the two given angle measures.

Multiple Choice: Item 3

- Students who answered **A** may have used the scale 3 instead of 4.
- Students who answered **C** may have set up their proportion incorrectly, using the reciprocal of a corresponding proportion.
- Students who answered **D** set up their proportion incorrectly.

Multiple Choice: Item 4

- Students who answered **G** may have taken the square root of $20^2 + 12^2$.
- Students who answered **H** may have found the sum of 20 and 12.
- Students who answered **J** may have subtracted $(20 - 12)^2$.

Free Response: Item 8

- Students who answered **144 feet** may not have finished the final step of taking the square root.
- Students who answered **8 feet** may have subtracted 5 from 13 rather than finding the square root of each number before subtracting.
- Students who answered $2\sqrt{2}$ **feet** may have subtracted 5 from 13 to get 8, and then taken the square root of 8.

Name _____ Class _____ Date _____

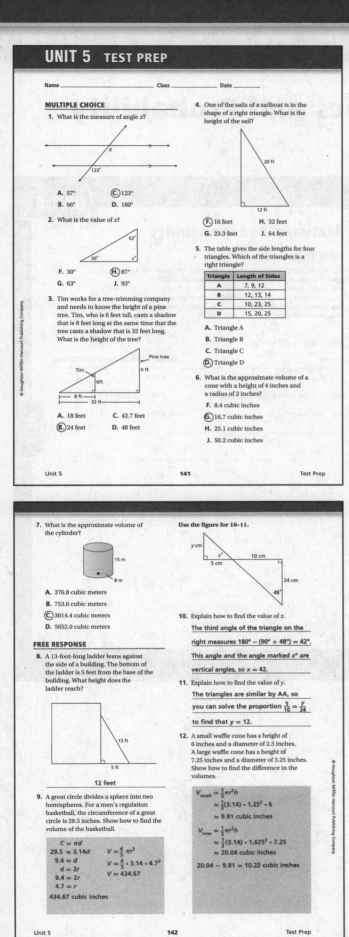

MULTIPLE CHOICE

1. What is the measure of angle x?

123°

A. 57°   **C.** 123°
B. 66°   **D.** 180°

2. What is the value of x?

63°
30° $x°$

F. 30°   **H.** 87°
G. 63°   **J.** 93°

3. Tim works for a tree-trimming company and needs to know the height of a pine tree. Tim, who is 6 feet tall, casts a shadow that is 8 feet long at the same time that the tree casts a shadow that is 32 feet long. What is the height of the tree?

Pine tree
h ft
Tim
6ft
8 ft
32 ft

A. 18 feet   **C.** 42.7 feet
B. 24 feet   **D.** 48 feet

4. One of the sails of a sailboat is in the shape of a right triangle. What is the height of the sail?

20 ft
12 ft

F. 16 feet   **H.** 32 feet
G. 23.3 feet   **J.** 64 feet

5. The table gives the side lengths for four triangles. Which of the triangles is a right triangle?

Triangle	Length of Sides
A	7, 9, 12
B	12, 13, 14
C	10, 23, 25
D	15, 20, 25

A. Triangle A
B. Triangle B
C. Triangle C
D. Triangle D

6. What is the approximate volume of a cone with a height of 4 inches and a radius of 2 inches?

F. 8.4 cubic inches
G. 16.7 cubic inches
H. 25.1 cubic inches
J. 50.2 cubic inches

7. What is the approximate volume of the cylinder?

15 m
8 m

A. 376.8 cubic meters
B. 753.6 cubic meters
C. 3014.4 cubic meters
D. 5652.0 cubic meters

FREE RESPONSE

8. A 13-foot-long ladder leans against the side of a building. The bottom of the ladder is 5 feet from the base of the building. What height does the ladder reach?

13 ft
5 ft

_____
12 feet

9. A great circle divides a sphere into two hemispheres. For a men's regulation basketball, the circumference of a great circle is 29.5 inches. Show how to find the volume of the basketball.

$C = \pi d$
$29.5 \approx 3.14d$ $V = \frac{4}{3}\pi r^3$
$9.4 \approx d$
$d = 2r$ $V \approx \frac{4}{3} \cdot 3.14 \cdot 4.7^3$
$9.4 = 2r$ $V \approx 434.67$
$4.7 \approx r$
434.67 cubic inches

Use the figure for 10–11.

y cm
$x°$ 10 cm
5 cm
24 cm
48°

10. Explain how to find the value of x.

The third angle of the triangle on the right measures $180° - (90° + 48°) = 42°$. This angle and the angle marked $x°$ are vertical angles, so $x = 42$.

11. Explain how to find the value of y.

The triangles are similar by AA, so you can solve the proportion $\frac{5}{10} = \frac{y}{24}$ to find that $y = 12$.

12. A small waffle cone has a height of 6 inches and a diameter of 2.5 inches. A large waffle cone has a height of 7.25 inches and a diameter of 3.25 inches. Show how to find the difference in the volumes.

$V_{small} = \frac{1}{3}\pi r^2 h$
$\approx \frac{1}{3}(3.14) \cdot 1.25^2 \cdot 6$
≈ 9.81 cubic inches
$V_{large} = \frac{1}{3}\pi r^2 h$
$\approx \frac{1}{3}(3.14) \cdot 1.625^2 \cdot 7.25$
≈ 20.04 cubic inches
$20.04 - 9.81 \approx 10.23$ cubic inches

UNIT 6

Statistics and Probability

Unit Vocabulary

bivariate data (6-1)

cluster (6-1)

frequency (6-3)

outlier (6-1)

relative
frequency (6-3)

scatter plot (6-1)

trend line (6-2)

two-way table (6-3)

UNIT 6

Statistics and Probability

Unit Focus

You have worked with one-variable statistics, and now you will expand your statistics skills to bivariate, or two-variable, statistics. You will use scatter plots to analyze the relationship, or association, between two quantities and be able to recognize outliers and clusters. You will use two-way tables to find relative frequencies and determine if there is an association between two variables.

Unit at a Glance

COMMON CORE

Lesson	Standards for Mathematical Content
6-1 Scatter Plots and Association	CC.8.SP.1
6-2 Scatter Plots and Predictions	CC.8.SP.2, CC.8.SP.3
6-3 Two-Way Tables	CC.8.SP.4
Problem Solving Connections	
Test Prep	

Unpacking the Common Core State Standards

Use the table to help you understand the Common Core State Standards that are taught in this unit. Refer to the lessons listed after each standard for exploration and practice.

COMMON CORE **Standards for Mathematical Content**	**What It Means For You**
CC.8.SP.1 Construct and interpret scatter plots for bivariate measurement data to investigate patterns of association between two quantities. Describe patterns such as clustering, outliers, positive or negative association, linear association, and nonlinear association. Lesson 6-1	You will make and interpret scatter plots. You will describe patterns in two-variable data including trends, clusters, outliers, and association.
CC.8.SP.2 Know that straight lines are widely used to model relationships between two quantitative variables. For scatter plots that suggest a linear association, informally fit a straight line, and informally assess the model fit by judging the closeness of the data points to the line. Lesson 6-2	You will draw a trend line to model data displayed in a scatter plot. You will use that line to make predictions.
CC.8.SP.3 Use the equation of a linear model to solve problems in the context of bivariate measurement data, interpreting the slope and intercept. Lesson 6-2	You will write an equation for a trend line that models two-variable data. You will interpret the slope of the line and y-intercept and use the equation for the line to make predictions.
CC.8.SP.4 Understand that patterns of association can also be seen in bivariate categorical data by displaying frequencies and relative frequencies in a two-way table. Construct and interpret a two-way table summarizing data on two categorical variables collected from the same subjects. Use relative frequencies calculated for rows or columns to describe possible association between the two variables. Lesson 6-3	You will use two-way tables to organize data and calculate relative frequencies. You will use relative frequencies to describe possible associations between two variables or events.

Unpacking the Common Core State Standards

This page lists and explains the Standards for Mathematical Content that are addressed in this unit. For information about the Standards for Mathematical Practice, which are integrated throughout the text, see Teacher Edition pages vii–xiii.

Notes

_____

_____

_____

_____

_____

_____

_____

_____

_____

_____

_____

Scatter Plots and Association

Essential question: How can you construct and interpret scatter plots?

COMMON CORE **Standards for Mathematical Content**

CC.8.SP1 Construct and interpret scatter plots for bivariate measurement data to investigate patterns of association between two quantities. Describe patterns such as clustering, outliers, positive or negative association, linear association, and nonlinear association.

Vocabulary

bivariate data

scatter plot

cluster

outlier

association

Prerequisites

Graphing in the coordinate plane

Math Background

Bivariate data records the relationship between two variables. This relationship can be displayed as a scatter plot which consists of points in the coordinate plane. When the values of each variable increase together, the relationship between the variables is positive. When the values of one variable increase while the other decreases, the relationship is negative. The scatter plot may also show clusters of data points or outliers.

INTRODUCE

Have students answer two questions, such as "How many people live in your home?" and "How many pets do you have?" on one index card. Collect the cards and make a scatter plot on the board. As you plot each point, read the answers aloud so the students can see how the data is reflected in the graph. Tell students they will be investigating graphs of two-variable data.

TEACH

1 EXPLORE

Questioning Strategies

- What does a *trend in the data* mean? **a pattern or a relationship between data points**

- How can you explain why the pattern in the scatter plot is upward from left to right? **It makes sense that test grades will increase as time studying increases. A downward trend would indicate that grades decrease as students study more, which is very unlikely.**

Differentiated Instruction

You can have students use centimeter cubes on a large coordinate plane to make a scatter plot. Students can plot the points and check one another's graphs before plotting the points on paper.

2 EXAMPLE

Questioning Strategies

- What are some reasons that there might be clusters in the data? **When the variability of data is small, it tends to cluster.**

- How can you identify an outlier in a scatter plot? **An outlier can be identified in a scatter plot as a point that greatly diverges from the trend shown by the majority of data points.**

Teaching Strategies

As students work through examples and exercises, have them circle clusters that they see in the data and highlight any outliers.

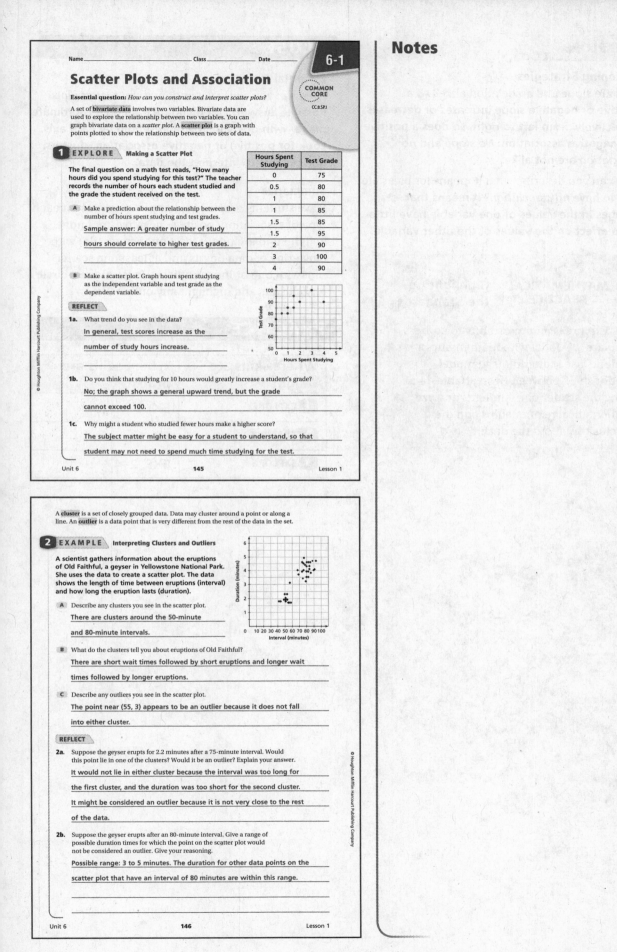

6-1

COMMON CORE
CC.8.SP.1

Scatter Plots and Association

Essential question: *How can you construct and interpret scatter plots?*

A set of **bivariate data** involves two variables. Bivariate data are used to explore the relationship between two variables. You can graph bivariate data on a *scatter plot*. A **scatter plot** is a graph with points plotted to show the relationship between two sets of data.

1 EXPLORE Making a Scatter Plot

The final question on a math test reads, "How many hours did you spend studying for this test?" The teacher records the number of hours each student studied and the grade the student received on the test.

Hours Spent Studying	Test Grade
0	75
0.5	80
1	80
1	85
1.5	85
1.5	95
2	90
3	100
4	90

A Make a prediction about the relationship between the number of hours spent studying and test grades.

Sample answer: A greater number of study

hours should correlate to higher test grades.

_____

B Make a scatter plot. Graph hours spent studying as the independent variable and test grade as the dependent variable.

REFLECT

1a. What trend do you see in the data?

In general, test scores increase as the

number of study hours increase.

_____

1b. Do you think that studying for 10 hours would greatly increase a student's grade?

No; the graph shows a general upward trend, but the grade

cannot exceed 100.

1c. Why might a student who studied fewer hours make a higher score?

The subject matter might be easy for a student to understand, so that

student may not need to spend much time studying for the test.

A **cluster** is a set of closely grouped data. Data may cluster around a point or along a line. An **outlier** is a data point that is very different from the rest of the data in the set.

2 EXAMPLE Interpreting Clusters and Outliers

A scientist gathers information about the eruptions of Old Faithful, a geyser in Yellowstone National Park. She uses the data to create a scatter plot. The data shows the length of time between eruptions (interval) and how long the eruption lasts (duration).

A Describe any clusters you see in the scatter plot.

There are clusters around the 50-minute

and 80-minute intervals.

B What do the clusters tell you about eruptions of Old Faithful?

There are short wait times followed by short eruptions and longer wait

times followed by longer eruptions.

C Describe any outliers you see in the scatter plot.

The point near (55, 3) appears to be an outlier because it does not fall

into either cluster.

REFLECT

2a. Suppose the geyser erupts for 2.2 minutes after a 75-minute interval. Would this point lie in one of the clusters? Would it be an outlier? Explain your answer.

It would not lie in either cluster because the interval was too long for

the first cluster, and the duration was too short for the second cluster.

It might be considered an outlier because it is not very close to the rest

of the data.

2b. Suppose the geyser erupts after an 80-minute interval. Give a range of possible duration times for which the point on the scatter plot would not be considered an outlier. Give your reasoning.

Possible range: 3 to 5 minutes. The duration for other data points on the

scatter plot that have an interval of 80 minutes are within this range.

_____

_____

Questioning Strategies

- **How are slope and association alike?** As a positive or negative slope increases or decreases, respectively, from left to right, so does a positive and negative association. *No slope* and *no association* are not alike.

- **How can you describe what it means for bivariate data to have *no association*?** It means that changes in the values of one variable have little or no effect on the values of the other variable.

MATHEMATICAL PRACTICE **Highlighting the Standards**

This Explore is an opportunity to address Standard 4 (Model with mathematics). Students use scatter plots to model relationships between two-variable data. Using the scatter plot, students analyze mathematical relationships and draw conclusions about the data.

CLOSE

Essential Question

How can you construct and interpret scatter plots?
Possible answer: Plot bivariate data on a coordinate plane, with one variable represented by each axis. Look for positive or negative association, clusters, and outliers to interpret the data.

Summarize

Have students graph a scatter plot to represent each type of association: positive, negative, and none. Tell them to include at least one scatter plot with clustering of data points and at least one scatter plot with one or more outliers. Have students circle any clusters and highlight any outliers.

PRACTICE

Where skills are taught	Where skills are practiced
1 EXPLORE	EX. 1
2 EXAMPLE	EX. 5
3 EXPLORE	EXS. 2–4

Association tells you how sets of data are related. A positive association means that both data sets increase together. A negative association means that as one data set increases, the other decreases. No association means that changes in one data set do not affect the other data set.

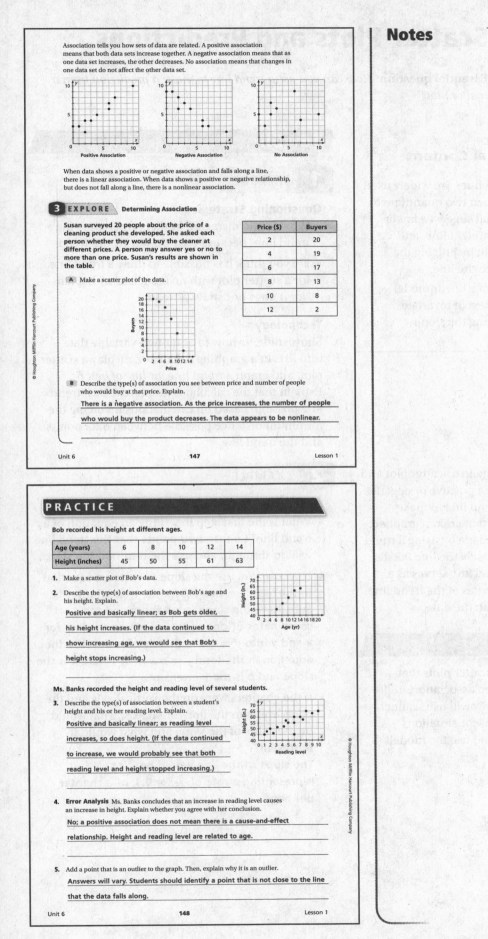

Positive Association

Negative Association

No Association

When data shows a positive or negative association and falls along a line, there is a linear association. When data shows a positive or negative relationship, but does not fall along a line, there is a nonlinear association.

3 EXPLORE Determining Association

Susan surveyed 20 people about the price of a cleaning product she developed. She asked each person whether they would buy the cleaner at different prices. A person may answer yes or no to more than one price. Susan's results are shown in the table.

Price ($)	Buyers
2	20
4	19
6	17
8	13
10	8
12	2

A Make a scatter plot of the data.

B Describe the type(s) of association you see between price and number of people who would buy at that price. Explain.

There is a negative association. As the price increases, the number of people who would buy the product decreases. The data appears to be nonlinear.

PRACTICE

Bob recorded his height at different ages.

Age (years)	6	8	10	12	14
Height (inches)	45	50	55	61	63

1. Make a scatter plot of Bob's data.

2. Describe the type(s) of association between Bob's age and his height. Explain.

   Positive and basically linear; as Bob gets older, his height increases. (If the data continued to show increasing age, we would see that Bob's height stops increasing.)

Ms. Banks recorded the height and reading level of several students.

3. Describe the type(s) of association between a student's height and his or her reading level. Explain.

   Positive and basically linear; as reading level increases, so does height. (If the data continued to increase, we would probably see that both reading level and height stopped increasing.)

4. **Error Analysis** Ms. Banks concludes that an increase in reading level causes an increase in height. Explain whether you agree with her conclusion.

   No; a positive association does not mean there is a cause-and-effect relationship. Height and reading level are related to age.

5. Add a point that is an outlier to the graph. Then, explain why it is an outlier.

   Answers will vary. Students should identify a point that is not close to the line that the data falls along.

Scatter Plots and Predictions

Essential question: *How can you use a trend line to make a prediction from a scatter plot?*

COMMON CORE **Standards for Mathematical Content**

CC.8.SP2 Know that straight lines are widely used to model relationships between two quantitative variables. For scatter plots that suggest a linear association, informally fit a straight line, and informally assess the model fit by judging the closeness of the data points to the line.

CC.8.SP3 Use the equation of a linear model to solve problems in the context of bivariate measurement data, interpreting the slope and intercept.

Vocabulary

trend line

Prerequisites

Scatter plots and association

Math Background

When you graph bivariate data in a scatter plot and you notice that the data have a positive or negative association, you can use a trend line to make predictions about the values that are not graphed. The accuracy of predictions made by using a trend line can be judged by how closely the line fits the data. The equation of the trend line serves as a model of the data, and properties of the trend line have meanings associated with the data.

INTRODUCE

Briefly review with students scatter plots that have positive, negative, and no association. Tell students that in this lesson they will use scatter plots to write equation models for situations involving two-variable data and use the models to make predictions.

TEACH

1 EXPLORE

Questioning Strategies

- Why do you disregard outliers when drawing a trend line? because they do not fit the trend

- Do you think it is possible to draw a trend line for a scatter plot with no association? Explain. No; it does not show a trend.

Technology

Show students how to enter two-variable data into lists in a graphing calculator, display a scatter plot, and graph a trend line, or *line of best fit*. Explain that the calculator graphs the best trend line possible based on calculations involving the minimum distance possible between data points and the trend line.

2 EXAMPLE

Questioning Strategies

- What is the first step in writing an equation of a trend line? Choose two points that the trend line will go through, and use them to find the slope.

- How can you use the slope to write an equation in the form $y = mx + b$ for the trend line? Substitute the slope value for m and the coordinates of one of the points on the line for x and y into $y = mx + b$. Solve for b. Write the equation in the form $y = mx + b$, where x is the slope and b is the y-intercept.

- If the chapters were on the vertical axis and the pages were on the horizontal axis, what would be the value of the slope and what would it represent? The slope of the line would be $\frac{1}{10}$, representing a rate of $\frac{1}{10}$, or 0.1, of a chapter per page.

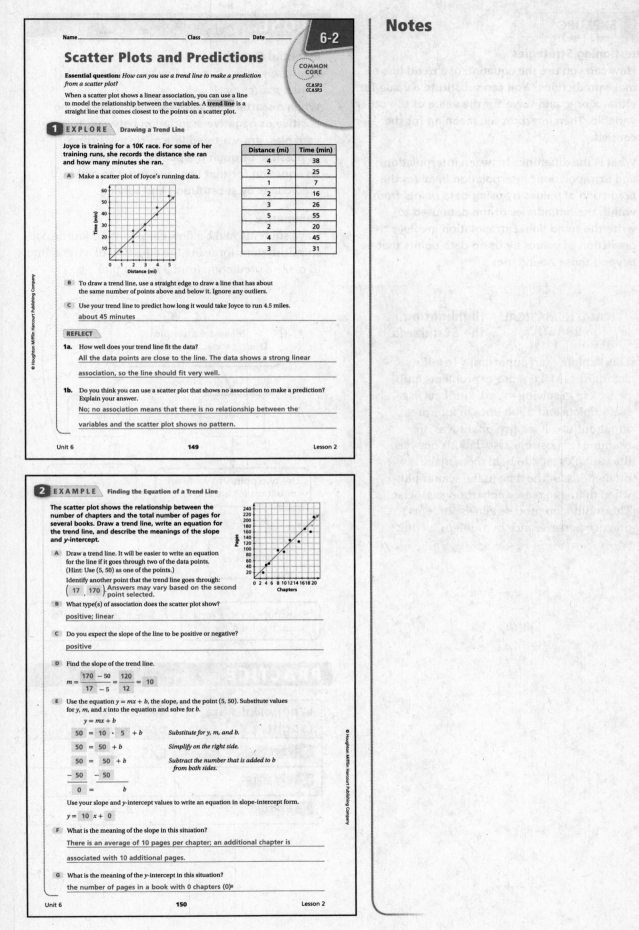

Scatter Plots and Predictions

6-2

COMMON CORE

CC.8.SP.2
CC.8.SP.3

Essential question: *How can you use a trend line to make a prediction from a scatter plot?*

When a scatter plot shows a linear association, you can use a line to model the relationship between the variables. A **trend line** is a straight line that comes closest to the points on a scatter plot.

1 EXPLORE   Drawing a Trend Line

Joyce is training for a 10K race. For some of her training runs, she records the distance she ran and how many minutes she ran.

A Make a scatter plot of Joyce's running data.

Distance (mi)	Time (min)
4	38
2	25
1	7
2	16
3	26
5	55
2	20
4	45
3	31

B To draw a trend line, use a straight edge to draw a line that has about the same number of points above and below it. Ignore any outliers.

C Use your trend line to predict how long it would take Joyce to run 4.5 miles.

about 45 minutes

REFLECT

1a. How well does your trend line fit the data?

All the data points are close to the line. The data shows a strong linear

association, so the line should fit very well.

1b. Do you think you can use a scatter plot that shows no association to make a prediction? Explain your answer.

No; no association means that there is no relationship between the

variables and the scatter plot shows no pattern.

Unit 6   149   Lesson 2

2 EXAMPLE   Finding the Equation of a Trend Line

The scatter plot shows the relationship between the number of chapters and the total number of pages for several books. Draw a trend line, write an equation for the trend line, and describe the meanings of the slope and *y*-intercept.

A Draw a trend line. It will be easier to write an equation for the line if it goes through two of the data points. (Hint: Use (5, 50) as one of the points.)

Identify another point that the trend line goes through:
(17 , 170). Answers may vary based on the second point selected.

B What type(s) of association does the scatter plot show?

positive; linear

C Do you expect the slope of the line to be positive or negative?

positive

D Find the slope of the trend line.

$$m = \frac{170 - 50}{17 - 5} = \frac{120}{12} = 10$$

E Use the equation $y = mx + b$, the slope, and the point (5, 50). Substitute values for *y*, *m*, and *x* into the equation and solve for *b*.

$y = mx + b$

$50 = 10 \cdot 5 + b$ *Substitute for y, m, and b.*

$50 = 50 + b$ *Simplify on the right side.*

$50 = 50 + b$ *Subtract the number that is added to b from both sides.*

$-50 \quad -50$

$0 = b$

Use your slope and *y*-intercept values to write an equation in slope-intercept form.

$y = 10 x + 0$

F What is the meaning of the slope in this situation?

There is an average of 10 pages per chapter; an additional chapter is

associated with 10 additional pages.

G What is the meaning of the *y*-intercept in this situation?

the number of pages in a book with 0 chapters (0)

Unit 6   150   Lesson 2

Questioning Strategies

- How can you use the equation of a trend line to make predictions? **You can substitute a value for either *x* or *y*, and solve for the value of the other variable. Then interpret the meaning for the context.**

- What is the difference between interpolation and extrapolation? **Interpolation involves the prediction of values by using data points from within the boundaries of the data used to write the trend line. Extrapolation involves the prediction of values by using data points that lie beyond those boundaries.**

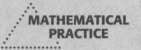

MATHEMATICAL PRACTICE   **Highlighting the Standards**

This Explore is an opportunity to address Standard 1 (Make sense of problems and persevere in solving them). Students use scatter plots and trend lines to interpret situations involving two unknowns, to examine for possible associations between the variables, and to help them make predictions for the data in the scatter plot when there is a reasonably strong association. This multi-step process allows students to practice perseverance in problem solving.

CLOSE

Essential Question

How can you use a trend line to make a prediction from a scatter plot?

When a scatter plot shows a reasonably strong positive or negative association between two variables, draw a trend line as closely fitting as possible through the points. Then write an equation for that line, and use it to make predictions by substituting and solving.

Summarize

Have students make a flow chart in their journals to show the steps for using the equation of a trend line to make a prediction from a scatter plot.

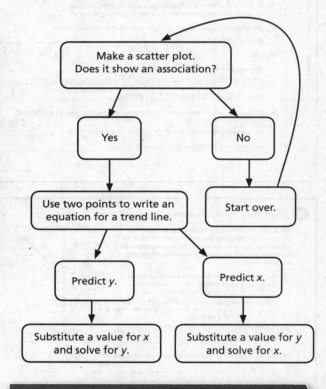

PRACTICE

Where skills are taught	Where skills are practiced
1 EXPLORE	EXS. 1–2, 7
2 EXAMPLE	EX. 3
3 EXPLORE	EXS. 4–6

When you use a trend line or its equation to predict a value between data points that you already know, you *interpolate* the predicted value. When you make a prediction that is outside the data that you know, you *extrapolate* the predicted value.

3 EXPLORE Making Predictions
Answers may vary depending on the equation found in the previous Example.

Refer to the scatter plot and trend line in **2**.

A Use the equation of the trend line to predict how many pages would be in a book with 26 chapters.

Is this prediction an example of interpolation or extrapolation?

extrapolation

$y =$	10x	*Write the equation for your trend line.*
$y =$	10(26)	*Substitute the number of chapters for x.*
$y =$	260	*Simplify.*

I predict that a book with 26 chapters would have ___260___ pages.

B Use the equation of the trend line to predict how many pages would be in a book with 14 chapters.

Is this prediction an example of interpolation or extrapolation?

interpolation

$y =$	10x	*Write the equation for your trend line.*
$y =$	10(14)	*Substitute the number of chapters for x.*
$y =$	140	*Simplify.*

I predict that a book with 14 chapters would have ___140___ pages.

REFLECT

3a. How well do your new points fit the original data?

They fall close to the original data, so they fit well.

3b. Do you think that extrapolation or interpolation is more accurate? Explain.

Possible answer: Interpolation is more accurate because the predicted value

fits between known points where the trend is known. There is no guarantee

that a trend will continue beyond the known data points.

PRACTICE

Angela recorded the price of different number of ounces of bulk grains. She made a scatter plot of her data. Use the scatter plot for 1–5.

1. Draw a trend line for the scatter plot.
Answers for 1-5 may vary slightly.

2. How do you know whether your trend line is a good fit for the data?

Most of the data points are close to the trend

line and there is about the same number of

points above and below the line.

3. Write an equation for your trend line. $y = 2x + 1$

4. Use the equation for your trend line to interpolate the price of 7 ounces.

15¢

5. Use the equation for your trend line to extrapolate the price of 50 ounces.

101¢; $1.01

6. A scatter plot shows the relationship between a baby's length and age. Why might an extrapolated data point not be very accurate?

Sample answer: Babies grow very quickly at first, but as they age, their growth

rate decreases. Eventually, a person's length (height) stops increasing.

7. **Error Analysis** Carl graphed the data shown in the scatter plot and then drew a trend line. Why is a trend line not a good fit for this data?

The data does not show a linear association,

so a linear model is not a good fit.

Notes

Two-Way Tables

Essential question: *How can you construct and interpret two-way tables?*

COMMON CORE Standards for Mathematical Content

CC.8.SP4 Understand that patterns of association can also be seen in bivariate categorical data by displaying frequencies and relative frequencies in a two-way table. Construct and interpret a two-way table summarizing data on two categorical variables collected from the same subjects. Use relative frequencies calculated for rows or columns to describe possible association between the two variables.

Vocabulary

frequency

two-way table

relative frequency

Prerequisites

Percents

Math Background

Two-way tables are used to show frequencies of data that is categorized two ways. The columns represent one categorization for the population and the rows represent a different categorization for the population. You can use relative frequencies in two-way tables to draw conclusions about whether or not there is an association between the two categories.

INTRODUCE

Present to students the following scenario: A car dealership has four categories of automobiles (SUV, car, truck, or minivan) and five color categories (black, white, brown, red, and other). Have students think of ways to visually organize this data. Explain that in this lesson they will learn how to organize this type of data.

TEACH

1 EXPLORE

Questioning Strategies

- If 40% of the people own a bike, what percent of the people do not own a bike? **60% of the people do not own a bike.**

- How do you find the numbers to put in the table? **Use the percents to calculate numbers that belong in each cell of the table.**

- What does the vertical *Total* column represent? The horizontal *Total* row? **The *Total* column represents the total numbers of people who own a bike, people who do not own a bike, and people polled. The *Total* row represents the total numbers of people who shop at the farmer's market, people who do not shop at the farmer's market, and people polled.**

Teaching Strategies

Review operations with percents if necessary. Remind students that the entire population is 100%. Point out that the last row and the last column should have the same total in the shared cell.

2 EXAMPLE

Questioning Strategies

- How are frequency and relative frequency alike and how are they different? **Frequency is the number of times an event occurs. Relative frequency is the ratio of the frequency of an event to the total number of frequencies.**

- How can you determine from a two-way table whether there is an association between the two variables? **If the relative frequency of an event to the whole population is different than the relative frequency within a sub-population, then there is an association.**

Two-Way Tables

Essential question: *How can you construct and interpret two-way tables?*

The **frequency** is the number of times an event occurs. A **two-way table** shows the frequencies of data that is categorized two ways. The rows indicate one categorization and the columns indicate another.

COMMON
CORE

CC.8.SP.4

1 EXPLORE Making a Two-Way Table

A poll of 120 town residents found that 40% own a bike. Of those who own a bike, 75% shop at the town's farmer's market. Of those who do not own a bike, 25% shop at the town's farmer's market.

	Farmer's Market	No Farmer's Market	TOTAL
Bike	36	12	48
No Bike	18	54	72
TOTAL	54	66	120

A Start in the bottom right cell of the table. Enter the total number of people polled.

B **Fill in the right column.** 40% of those polled own a bike.

40% of 120 is ___48___

The remaining people polled do not own a bike. The number who do not own a bike is 120 − ___48___ = ___72___

C **Fill in the top row.** 75% of those who own a bike also shop at the market.

75% of ___48___ is ___36___.

The remaining bike owners do not shop at the market. The number of bike owners who do not shop at the market is ___12___

D **Fill in the second row.** 25% of those who do not own a bike shop at the market.

25% of ___72___ is ___18___

The remaining people without bikes do not shop at the market. The number without a bike who do not shop at the market is ___54___

E **Fill in the last row.** In each column, add the numbers in the first two rows to find the total number of people who shop at the farmer's market and who do not shop at the farmer's market.

© Houghton Mifflin Harcourt Publishing Company

F What percent of all the residents polled shop at the farmer's market?

$\frac{54}{120} = 0.45$

___45___% of people polled shop at the farmer's market.

REFLECT

1. How can you check that your table is completed correctly?

The last number in each row or column should be the sum of the other numbers in that row or column.

Relative frequency is the ratio of the number of times an event occurs to the total number of events. In **1**, the relative frequency of bike owners who shop at the market is $\frac{36}{120} = 0.30 = 30\%$. You can use relative frequencies to decide if there is an association between two variables or events.

2 EXAMPLE Deciding Whether There Is an Association

Determine whether there is an association between the events.

A One hundred teens were polled about whether they are required to do chores and whether they have a curfew. Is there an association between having a curfew and having to do chores?

	Curfew	No Curfew	TOTAL
Chores	16	4	20
No Chores	16	64	80
TOTAL	32	68	100

Find the relative frequency of having to do chores.

Total who have to do chores → $\frac{20}{100} = 0.20 = $ ___20___ %
Total number of teens polled →

Find the relative frequency of having to do chores among those who have a curfew.

Number with a curfew who have to do chores → $\frac{16}{32} = 0.50 = $ ___50___ %
Total number with a curfew →

Compare the relative frequencies. Students who have a curfew are less likely/**more likely** to have to do chores than the general population.

Is there an association between having a curfew and having to do chores? Explain.

Yes; the relative frequencies show that having a curfew makes it more likely that a student will have to do chores.

© Houghton Mifflin Harcourt Publishing Company

- How can you find the relative frequency for international flights being late? Find the total number of all international flights: 50. Find the number of international flights that are late: 10. The relative frequency is 10 out of 50, or 20%.

Teaching Strategies

Have students highlight the cells with which they are working. Choose different colored highlighters to represent the whole population and the sub-population relative frequencies. This may help students focus on the correct numbers in the table.

| MATHEMATICAL PRACTICE | Highlighting the Standards |

This Example is an opportunity to address Standard 6 (Attend to precision). When constructing two-way tables, students need to be accurate with their computations and precise in their recording of the data. The row elements and column elements must be correctly placed in order for the totals to be calculated correctly.

CLOSE

Essential Question

How can you construct and interpret two-way tables?
Possible answer: Make a two-way table in which columns represent one set of categories for the population and the rows represent a different set of categories for the population. You can analyze data in two-way tables to see if there is an association between categories by comparing their relative frequencies.

Summarize

Have students collect data and make their own categories for a two-way table in their journals. Tell them to compare the relative frequencies and to draw any possible conclusions about associations between two categories.

PRACTICE

Where skills are taught	Where skills are practiced
1 EXPLORE	EX. 1
2 EXAMPLE	EXS. 2–7

B Data from 200 flights was collected. The flights were categorized as domestic or international and late or not late. Is there an association between international flights and a flight being late?

	Late	Not Late	TOTAL
Domestic	30	120	150
International	10	40	50
TOTAL	40	160	200

Find the relative frequency of a flight being late.

Total flights that are late → $\dfrac{40}{200}$ = 0.20 = 20 %
Total number of flights →

Find the relative frequency of a flight being late among international flights.

Number of international flights that are late → $\dfrac{10}{50}$ = 0.20 = 20 %
Total number of international flights →

Compare the relative frequencies. International flights are less likely / equally likely / more likely to be late than flights in general.

Is there an association between international flights and a flight being late? Explain.

No; the relative frequencies show that international flights are just as likely

to be late as any other flight.

REFLECT

3a. Compare the relative frequency of having a curfew and having chores to the relative frequency of not having a curfew and having chores. Does this comparison help you draw a conclusion about whether there is an association between having a curfew and having chores? Explain.

The relative frequency of having a curfew and having chores $\left(\dfrac{16}{32} = 50\%\right)$ is

greater than the relative frequency of not having a curfew and having chores

$\left(\dfrac{4}{68} \approx 6\%\right)$, so there seems to be an association between the two events.

3b. Compare the relative frequency of domestic flights being late to the relative frequency of international flights being late. Does this comparison help you draw a conclusion about whether there is an association between international flights and being late? Explain.

The relative frequency of late domestic flights $\left(\dfrac{30}{150} = 20\%\right)$ is equal to the

relative frequency of late international flights $\left(\dfrac{10}{50} = 20\%\right)$, so there seems

to be no association between the two events.

PRACTICE

Karen asked 150 students at her school if they played sports. She also recorded whether the student was a boy or girl. Of the 150 students, 20% did not play sports, 60% of the total were girls, and 70% of the girls played sports.

	Sports	No Sports	TOTAL
Boys	57	3	60
Girls	63	27	90
TOTAL	120	30	150

1. Complete the two-way table.

2. What is the relative frequency of a student playing sports? _____ 80%

3. What is the relative frequency of a boy playing sports? _____ 95%

4. Is there an association between being a boy and playing sports at Karen's school? Explain.

Yes; the relative frequency of being a boy and playing sports is greater

than the relative frequency of total students who play sports, so there is

an association between being a boy and playing sports.

Aiden collected data from 80 students about whether they have siblings and whether they have pets.

	Siblings	No Siblings	TOTAL
Pets	49	21	70
No Pets	7	3	10
TOTAL	56	24	80

5. What is the relative frequency of a student having pets? _____ 87.5%

6. What is the relative frequency of a student with siblings having pets? _____ 87.5%

7. Is there an association between having siblings and having pets? Explain.

No; the relative frequency of having pets is the same for students with

siblings as for the general student, so there is no association between

having siblings and having pets.

Problem Solving Connections 🌐

Give me a T!

COMMON **Standards for**
CORE **Mathematical Content**

CC.8.SP.1 Construct and interpret scatter plots for bivariate measurement data to investigate patterns of association between two quantities. Describe patterns such as clustering, outliers, positive or negative association, linear association, and nonlinear association.

CC.8.SP.2 Know that straight lines are widely used to model relationships between two quantitative variables. For scatter plots that suggest a linear association, informally fit a straight line, and informally assess the model fit by judging the closeness of the data points to the line.

CC.8.SP.3 Use the equation of a linear model to solve problems in the context of bivariate measurement data, interpreting the slope and intercept.

CC.8.SP.4 Understand that patterns of association can also be seen in bivariate categorical data by displaying frequencies and relative frequencies in a two-way table. Construct and interpret a two-way table summarizing data on two categorical variables collected from the same subjects. Use relative frequencies calculated for rows or columns to describe possible association between the two variables.

INTRODUCE

Discuss with students some common variables that you might assume have either a positive or negative association. Some examples may be:

Positive

- Amount of sleep vs. Amount of energy
- Amount of sunshine vs. Amount of plant growth

Negative

- Amount of sleep vs. Amount of fatigue
- Amount of sunshine vs. Amount of rain

Tell students they will use given data to determine the association between and make predictions about the variables *height* and *arm span*.

TEACH

1 Making Scatter Plots

Questioning Strategies

- Do you see an association? If so, what kind? Explain. **Yes, the arm spans and heights seem to increase together or decrease together. It has a positive association.**
- Do you see any clusters? Do you see any outliers? Explain. **There may be slight clustering between 60 and 65 inches, which is likely due to the ages of Annika's classmates. There is an outlier at about (50, 62), which is possibly due to error in measurement.**

Avoid Common Errors

Students may confuse which variable goes on which axis. Although it does not matter in this example which variable is graphed on which axis, students must make sure they label the axes and graph each point according to the same labels.

2 Finding a Trend Line

Questioning Strategies

- What points can you choose to sketch a trend line? **Possible answer: (55, 55) and (65, 65)**
- About what arm span would you predict for a 72-in. tall person? Is this interpolation or extrapolation? Explain. **72 in.; extrapolation; 72 in. is greater than the maximum in the data.**
- About what arm span would you predict for a 57-in. tall person? Is this interpolation or extrapolation? Explain. **57 in.; interpolation; 57 in. is between the minimum and maximum in the data.**

Technology

Have students use their calculators to display and compare the scatter plot and trend line for this data in two different ways: (1) with height on the x-axis and arm span on the y-axis, and (2) with arm span on the x-axis and height on the y-axis. Lead students to the conclusion that the results are the same both ways.

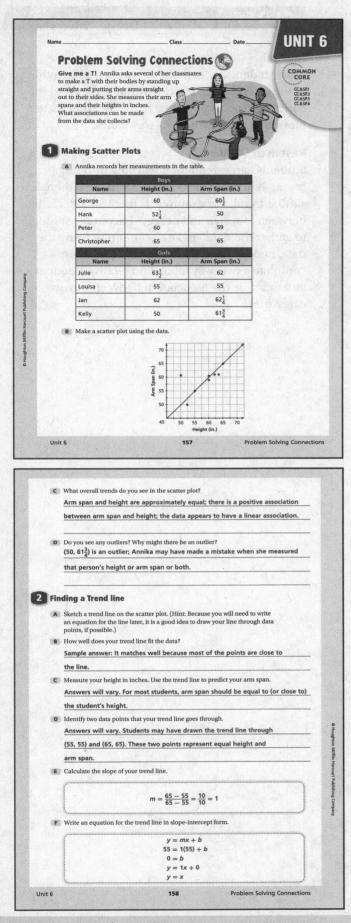

Name_____ Class_____ Date_____

UNIT 6

Problem Solving Connections

Give me a T! Annika asks several of her classmates to make a T with their bodies by standing up straight and putting their arms straight out to their sides. She measures their arm spans and their heights in inches. What associations can be made from the data she collects?

COMMON CORE
CC.8.SP.1
CC.8.SP.2
CC.8.SP.3
CC.8.SP.4

1 Making Scatter Plots

A Annika records her measurements in the table.

Boys		
Name	Height (in.)	Arm Span (in.)
George	60	$60\frac{1}{2}$
Hank	$52\frac{1}{4}$	50
Peter	60	59
Christopher	65	65

Girls		
Name	Height (in.)	Arm Span (in.)
Julie	$63\frac{1}{2}$	62
Louisa	55	55
Jan	62	$62\frac{1}{4}$
Kelly	50	$61\frac{3}{4}$

B Make a scatter plot using the data.

Unit 6   **157**   Problem Solving Connections

C What overall trends do you see in the scatter plot?

Arm span and height are approximately equal; there is a positive association

between arm span and height; the data appears to have a linear association.

D Do you see any outliers? Why might there be an outlier?

$(50, 61\frac{3}{4})$ is an outlier; Annika may have made a mistake when she measured

that person's height or arm span or both.

2 Finding a Trend line

A Sketch a trend line on the scatter plot. (Hint: Because you will need to write an equation for the line later, it is a good idea to draw your line through data points, if possible.)

B How well does your trend line fit the data?

Sample answer: It matches well because most of the points are close to

the line.

C Measure your height in inches. Use the trend line to predict your arm span.

Answers will vary. For most students, arm span should be equal to (or close to)

the student's height.

D Identify two data points that your trend line goes through.

Answers will vary. Students may have drawn the trend line through

(55, 55) and (65, 65). These two points represent equal height and

arm span.

E Calculate the slope of your trend line.

$$m = \frac{65 - 55}{65 - 55} = \frac{10}{10} = 1$$

F Write an equation for the trend line in slope-intercept form.

$$y = mx + b$$
$$55 = 1(55) + b$$
$$0 = b$$
$$y = 1x + 0$$
$$y = x$$

Unit 6   **158**   Problem Solving Connections

3 Making a Two-Way Table

Questioning Strategies

- With the given row and column heads, what should be the row totals and column totals? **Row totals top to bottom should be 4, 4, 8. Column totals left to right should be 2, 6, 8.**

- What are some conclusions you can make from the data displayed in the two-way table? **Possible answer: More people in the study have arm spans and heights that are not equal; there were an equal number of boys and girls surveyed.**

Teaching Strategies

Discuss with students what Annika could have done differently that would have changed the data and the resulting conclusions. For example, she could have taken multiple measures of the same person and recorded the average in order to achieve greater accuracy in measurements. She could have included more people in her sample in order to achieve a more representative sample.

4 Answer the Question

Questioning Strategies

- What conclusion can be drawn from the data? **A person's arm span and height are approximately equal in length.**

- Are the results the same for both boys and girls? **Yes, both boys and girls appear to have equal height and arm span.**

.·**MATHEMATICAL** **Highlighting**
·   **PRACTICE**   **the Standards**
·........·

This problem-solving activity addresses Standard 4 (Model with mathematics). Students model a sample of data of arm span and height in a scatter plot, with a trend line, and in a two-way table. Then students use each of these models to analyze the data and make conclusions or predictions about the general population.

CLOSE

Journal

Have students write in their journal a description of the categories in the two-variable data and the conclusions or predictions made by using scatter plots, trend lines, and two-way tables.

Research Options

Students can extend their learning by doing research of other measurements to see if there is a similar trend. For example, is there an association between foot size and height? Encourage students to gather the data, make a scatter plot using the data, and find a trend line. Then, have them complete a two-way table, find relative frequencies, and describe the association between the two categories.

G   Use your trend line to interpolate how wide someone's arm span is if the
individual is 58 inches tall.

$$y = x$$
$$y = 58$$

H   Choose a height for which you would have to extrapolate, and use your
trend line to predict what the arm span would be.

Check students' answers. Height should a reasonable height for a person
and be greater than 65 inches or less than 50 inches. Arm span should
equal height.

I   Under what circumstances might this trend line not be a good predictor
of arm span?

Babies and children do not have the same ratio of height to arm span.

When a person is having a growth spurt, their proportions may be

different.

3 Making a Two-Way Table

A   Complete the two-way table using Annika's data.

	Arm Span Equal to Height	Arm Span Not Equal to Height	TOTAL
Boys	1	3	4
Girls	1	3	4
TOTAL	2	6	8

B   How can you check that you completed the table correctly?

The values in each total column or row should be the sum of the other

numbers in that column or row.

C   What is the relative frequency of boys?

$$\frac{\text{Number of boys} \rightarrow 4}{\text{Total number of students} \rightarrow 8} = 0.50 = 50\%$$

D   What is the relative frequency of equal height and arm span for all students?

$$\frac{\text{Total number with equal height and arm span} \rightarrow 2}{\text{Total number of students} \rightarrow 8} = 0.25 = 25\%$$

E   What is the relative frequency of equal height and arm span among boys?

$$\frac{\text{Boys with equal height and arm span} \rightarrow 1}{\text{Total number of boys} \rightarrow 4} = 0.25 = 25\%$$

4 Answer the Question

A   Does there appear to be an association between being a boy and having
equal height and arm span? Explain.

No; the relative frequency of boys with equal height and arm span is equal to

the relative frequency of all students with equal height and arm span, so there

is no association between being a boy and having equal height and arm span.

B   Why might this data set be misleading?

Sample answers: The sample is small (only 8 students). The students may all be

the same age, so the conclusions may only be true for people at that age.

C   What conclusions can Annika draw from her data?

Annika can conclude that, in general, a person's height and arm span are

approximately equal. She can also conclude that this relationship is true for

girls and boys.

COMMON CORE CORRELATION

Standard	Items
CC.8.SP.1	1, 8, 9
CC.8.SP.2	2, 4, 10
CC.8.SP.3	3, 5, 11
CC.8.SP.4	6, 7

TEST PREP DOCTOR ⊕

Multiple Choice: Item 1
- Students who answered **A** or **D** may not recognize that if both variables increase together, it represents a positive association.
- Students who answered **C** may not realize that no association is different than negative association.

Multiple Choice: Item 4
- Students who answered **F** may have miscounted the scale for each axis.
- Students who answered **G** calculated the slope correctly, but did not use the correct y-intercept.
- Students who answered **J** used the wrong sign for the y-intercept.

Multiple Choice: Item 6
- Students who answered **F** may have used the percents as the totals.
- Students who answered **H** may have divided the total in half for each category.
- Students who answered **J** may have estimated the totals for each row, using values that sum to 50.

Free Response: Item 9
- Students who answered that there is a **positive association** may not understand that in a positive association, data points should increase from left to right.
- Students who answered **no association** may not understand that *no association* is not the same as *negative association*.

Notes

Name _____ Class _____ Date _____

MULTIPLE CHOICE

1. Which graph shows a negative association?

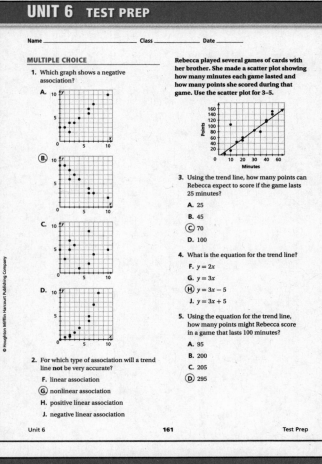

   A.

   B.

   C.

   D.

2. For which type of association will a trend line **not** be very accurate?

   F. linear association

   G. nonlinear association

   H. positive linear association

   J. negative linear association

Rebecca played several games of cards with her brother. She made a scatter plot showing how many minutes each game lasted and how many points she scored during that game. Use the scatter plot for 3–5.

3. Using the trend line, how many points can Rebecca expect to score if the game lasts 25 minutes?

   A. 25

   B. 45

   C. 70

   D. 100

4. What is the equation for the trend line?

   F. $y = 2x$

   G. $y = 3x$

   H. $y = 3x - 5$

   J. $y = 3x + 5$

5. Using the equation for the trend line, how many points might Rebecca score in a game that lasts 100 minutes?

   A. 95

   B. 200

   C. 205

   D. 295

A survey of 50 adults asked whether the person had children and whether they had a cat. Use the table for 6–7.

	Cat	No cat	TOTAL
Children	5	27	
No children	16	2	
TOTAL	21	29	50

6. Of those surveyed, 64% said they do have children. Which values complete the last column of the table?

   F. Children: 64; No children: 36

   G. Children: 32; No children: 18

   H. Children: 25; No children: 25

   J. Children: 30; No children: 20

7. Which conclusion can be drawn?

   A. There appears to be an association between having no children and having a cat.

   B. The total number of people with cats is 32.

   C. There is no association between having children and having a cat.

   D. The relative frequency of people with no children is 18%.

FREE RESPONSE

Noah researched the weekly high temperature in his city. He chose several weeks between July and December to put in a table. (The first week of July was numbered Week 1 in Noah's source material.) Use this data for Questions 8–11.

Week	High Temp (°F)
16	78
25	55
3	100
17	65
13	75
5	90

Week	High Temp (°F)
12	78
7	95
10	84
9	90
15	74
21	62

8. Use Noah's data to make a scatter plot.

9. What type of association is shown on the scatterplot? Explain.

   negative linear association; as weeks
   increase, temperature decreases.

10. Draw a trend line on the scatter plot.

11. Remember that Week 1 represents the first week of July so Week 25 represents a week in December. Would your trend line lend to good predictions of high temperatures in May of the next year? Explain.

   No; temperatures will not continue
   to decrease as time passes into the
   next year.

Correlation of *On Core Mathematics Grade 8* to the Common Core State Standards

The Number System	Citations
CC.8.NS.1 Understand informally that every number has a decimal expansion; the rational numbers are those with decimal expansions that terminate in 0s or eventually repeat. Know that other numbers are called irrational.	pp. 19–22
CC.8.NS.2 Use rational approximations of irrational numbers to compare the size of irrational numbers, locate them approximately on a number line diagram, and estimate the value of expressions (e.g., π^2).	pp. 23–26

Expressions and Equations	Citations
CC.8.EE.1 Know and apply the properties of integer exponents to generate equivalent numerical expressions.	pp. 3–6, 27–30
CC.8.EE.2 Use square root and cube root symbols to represent solutions to equations of the form $x^2 = p$ and $x^3 = p$, where p is a positive rational number. Evaluate square roots of small perfect squares and cube roots of small perfect cubes. Know that $\sqrt{2}$ is irrational.	pp. 15–18, 23–26
CC.8.EE.3 Use numbers expressed in the form of a single digit times an integer power of 10 to estimate very large or very small quantities, and to express how many times as much one is than the other.	pp. 7–10, 27–30
CC.8.EE.4 Perform operations with numbers expressed in scientific notation, including problems where both decimal and scientific notation are used. Use scientific notation and choose units of appropriate size for measurements of very large or very small quantities (e.g., use millimeters per year for seafloor spreading). Interpret scientific notation that has been generated by technology.	pp. 11–14, 27–30
CC.8.EE.5 Graph proportional relationships, interpreting the unit rate as the slope of the graph. Compare two different proportional relationships represented in different ways.	pp. 39–42, 43–46, 53–56, 61–64
CC.8.EE.6 Use similar triangles to explain why the slope m is the same between any two distinct points on a non-vertical line in the coordinate plane; derive the equation $y = mx$ for a line through the origin and the equation $y = mx + b$ for a line intercepting the vertical axis at b.	pp. 47–48, 61–64, 137–140
CC.8.EE.7 Solve linear equations in one variable. a. Give examples of linear equations in one variable with one solution, infinitely many solutions, or no solutions. Show which of these possibilities is the case by successively transforming the given equation into simpler forms, until an equivalent equation of the form $x = a$, $a = a$, or $a = b$ results (where a and b are different numbers). b. Solve linear equations with rational number coefficients, including equations whose solutions require expanding expressions using the distributive property and collecting like terms.	pp. 69–72, 73–74, 83–86

CC.8.EE.8 Analyze and solve pairs of simultaneous linear equations. a. Understand that solutions to a system of two linear equations in two variables correspond to points of intersection of their graphs, because points of intersection satisfy both equations simultaneously. b. Solve systems of two linear equations in two variables algebraically, and estimate solutions by graphing the equations. Solve simple cases by inspection. c. Solve real-world and mathematical problems leading to two linear equations in two variables.	**pp. 75–78, 79–82, 83–86**

Functions	**Citations**
CC.8.F.1 Understand that a function is a rule that assigns to each input exactly one output. The graph of a function is the set of ordered pairs consisting of an input and the corresponding output.	**pp. 35–38, 61–64**
CC.8.F.2 Compare properties of two functions each represented in a different way (algebraically, graphically, numerically in tables, or by verbal descriptions).	**pp. 53–56**
CC.8.F.3 Interpret the equation $y = mx + b$ as defining a linear function, whose graph is a straight line; give examples of functions that are not linear.	**pp. 39–42, 47–48, 49–52, 61–64**
CC.8.F.4 Construct a function to model a linear relationship between two quantities. Determine the rate of change and initial value of the function from a description of a relationship or from two (x, y) values, including reading these from a table or from a graph. Interpret the rate of change and initial value of a linear function in terms of the situation it models, and in terms of its graph or a table of values.	**pp. 49–52, 53–56, 61–64**
CC.8.F.5 Describe qualitatively the functional relationship between two quantities by analyzing a graph (e.g., where the function is increasing or decreasing, linear or nonlinear). Sketch a graph that exhibits the qualitative features of a function that has been described verbally.	**pp. 57–60, 61–64**

Geometry	**Citations**
CC.8.G.1 Verify experimentally the properties of rotations, reflections, and translations: a. Lines are taken to lines, and line segments to line segments of the same length. b. Angles are taken to angles of the same measure. c. Parallel lines are taken to parallel lines.	**pp. 95–96, 105–108**
CC.8.G.2 Understand that a two-dimensional figure is congruent to another if the second can be obtained from the first by a sequence of rotations, reflections, and translations; given two congruent figures, describe a sequence that exhibits the congruence between them.	**pp. 97–98, 105–108**
CC.8.G.3 Describe the effect of dilations, translations, rotations, and reflections on two-dimensional figures using coordinates.	**pp. 91–94, 99–102, 105–108**
CC.8.G.4 Understand that a two-dimensional figure is similar to another if the second can be obtained from the first by a sequence of rotations, reflections, translations, and dilations; given two similar two-dimensional figures, describe a sequence that exhibits the similarity between them.	**pp. 103–104, 105–108**
CC.8.G.5 Use informal arguments to establish facts about the angle sum and exterior angle of triangles, about the angles created when parallel lines are cut by a transversal, and the angle-angle criterion for similarity of triangles.	**pp. 113–116, 117–120, 121–124, 137–140**
CC.8.G.6 Explain a proof of the Pythagorean Theorem and its converse.	**pp. 125–126, 131–132, 137–140**

CC.8.G.7 Apply the Pythagorean Theorem to determine unknown side lengths in right triangles in real-world and mathematical problems in two and three dimensions.	**pp. 127–130, 137–140**
CC.8.G.8 Apply the Pythagorean Theorem to find the distance between two points in a coordinate system.	**pp. 127–130, 137–140**
CC.8.G.9 Know the formulas for the volumes of cones, cylinders, and spheres and use them to solve real-world and mathematical problems.	**pp. 133–136, 137–140**
Statistics and Probability	**Citations**
CC.8.SP.1 Construct and interpret scatter plots for bivariate measurement data to investigate patterns of association between two quantities. Describe patterns such as clustering, outliers, positive or negative association, linear association, and nonlinear association.	**pp. 145–148, 157–160**
CC.8.SP.2 Know that straight lines are widely used to model relationships between two quantitative variables. For scatter plots that suggest a linear association, informally fit a straight line, and informally assess the model fit by judging the closeness of the data points to the line.	**pp. 149–152, 157–160**
CC.8.SP.3 Use the equation of a linear model to solve problems in the context of bivariate measurement data, interpreting the slope and intercept.	**pp. 149–152, 157–160**
CC.8.SP.4 Understand that patterns of association can also be seen in bivariate categorical data by displaying frequencies and relative frequencies in a two-way table. Construct and interpret a two-way table summarizing data on two categorical variables collected from the same subjects. Use relative frequencies calculated for rows or columns to describe possible association between the two variables.	**pp. 153–156, 157–160**